Linux

Bill Ball

A Division of Macmillan Computer Publishing, USA
201 W. 103rd Street
Indianapolis, Indiana 46290

SAMS

Visually in **Full Color**

How To Use Linux

International Standard Book Number: 0-672-31545-9

Library of Congress Catalog Card Number: 98-89192

Printed in the United States of America

First Printing: February 1999

This book was produced digitally by Macmillan Computer Publishing and manufactured using computer-to-plate technology (a film-less process) by GAC, Indianapolis, Indiana.

02   01   00   99   4   3   2   1

Trademarks

Warning and Disclaimer

Executive Editor
Christopher A. Will

Acquisitions Editor
Tracy Williams

Development Editor
Kate Shoup Welsh

Managing Editor
Brice P. Gosnell

Project Editor
Sara Bosin

Copy Editor
Michael Dietsch

Indexer
Kevin Kent

Proofreader
Andrew Beaster

Technical Editor
Eric Richardson

Software Development Specialist
Michael Hunter

Design
Nathan Clement

Layout Technicians
Ayanna Lacey
Heather Hiatt Miller
Trina Wurst

Contents at a Glance

Contents

About the Author

Bill Ball is the author of the best-selling *Sams Teach Yourself Linux in 24 Hours*. A technical writer, editor, and magazine journalist for 20 years, he has published articles in magazines such as *Computer Shopper* and *MacTech Magazine*. He first started editing books for Que in 1986. His latest works include Que's *Using Linux* and the third edition of Sams' *Red Hat Linux Unleashed*. He lives in the Shirlington area of Arlington County, Virginia. A fond fan of classic British MGB sports cars, he also is an avid fly fisherman, builds bamboo fly rods, and fishes on the nearby Potomac River.

Acknowledgments

To the kind folks at Macmillan: Theresa Ball,
Lynette Quinn, Kate Welsh, and Tracy Williams (all
authors should be so lucky to work with such
great people), and Chris Will (for believing in this
project). To Richard M. Stallman; Linus Torvalds;
The XFree86 Project, Inc.; Larry Wall; and the
thousands of programmers around the world who
have contributed to the success and magic of
Linux. And finally, to Cathy Taulbee, for putting up
with me before I've had my coffee in the morning.

Dedication

*To Ray and Lil—I hope you can put up with your
crazy new son-in-law.*

Tell Us What You Think!

As the reader of this book, *you* are our most important critic and commentator. We value your opinion and want to know what we're doing right, what we could do better, what areas you'd like to see us publish in, and any other words of wisdom you're willing to pass our way.

As an executive editor for the Operating Systems team at Macmillan Computer Publishing, I welcome your comments. You can fax, email, or write me directly to let me know what you did or didn't like about this book—as well as what we can do to make our books stronger.

Please note that I cannot help you with technical problems related to the topic of this book, and that due to the high volume of mail I receive, I might not be able to reply to every message.

When you write, please be sure to include this book's title and author, as well as your name and phone or fax number. I will carefully review your comments and share them with the author and editors who worked on the book.

Fax: 317-581-4663

Email: lowop@mcp.com

Mail: Executive Editor
           Operating Systems
           Macmillan Computer Publishing
           201 West 103rd Street
           Indianapolis, IN 46290 USA

How To Use This Book

The Complete Visual Reference

Each chapter of this book is made up of a series of short, instructional tasks, designed to help you understand all the information that you need to get the most out of your computer hardware and software.

 Click: Click the left mouse button once.

 Double-click: Click the left mouse button twice in rapid succession.

 Right-click: Click the right mouse button once.

 Pointer Arrow: Highlights an item on the screen you need to point to or focus on in the step or task.

 Selection: Highlights the area onscreen discussed in the step or task.

 Click and Type: Click once where indicated and begin typing to enter your text or data.

Click & Drag

Release

How to Drag: Point to the starting place or object. Hold down the mouse button (right or left per instructions), move the mouse to the new location, and then release the button.

 Key icons: Clearly indicate which key combinations to use.

Each task includes a series of easy-to-understand steps designed to guide you through the procedure.

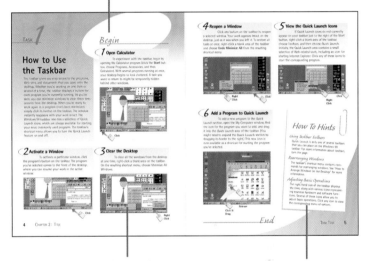

Each step is fully illustrated to show you how it looks onscreen.

Extra hints that tell you how to accomplish a goal are provided in most tasks.

Menus and items you click are shown in **bold**. Words in *italic* are defined in more detail in the glossary. Information you type is in a `special font`.

Continues

If you see this symbol, it means the task you're in continues on the next page.

Introduction to OpenLinux

*W*elcome to Linux! This book contains all the software and directions you need to install, configure, and run Caldera's OpenLinux distribution. You'll find the Linux operating system, X Window System graphical interface software, more than 1,200 pages of documentation, 200 help files or HOWTO documents, and nearly 3,000 programs included on this book's CD-ROM.

Linux is the *kernel* or core operating system. OpenLinux is a distribution of Linux, specially configured by Caldera to be easy to install, configure, use, and maintain. Linux has become widely popular around the world in the last few years since its initial release in 1991 by its author, Linus Torvalds, then a graduate student at the University of Helsinki, Finland.

Linux is not a toy operating system. Although it is relatively new, Linux draws on more than one-quarter century of heritage and experience inherited from the UNIX operating system. But this operating system is not just for techno-geeks and computer nerds. Linux can be kind and gentle, yet robust and industrial-strength—it won't let you down. If you have healthy computer hardware, it will not crash.

Want to play some awesome games? You'll find more than 200 included with OpenLinux. Need a word processor? There are nearly a dozen on this book's CD-ROM. How about using a spreadsheet? You'll need to choose among several. In fact, you'll also get the complete integrated office suite, Star Division's StarOffice, which includes word processing, spreadsheet, and graphics applications.

Want to learn how to run a Web site? All the software you need is included. Want to learn programming? You'll find compilers and interpreters for C, C++, FORTRAN, Perl, Java, Lisp, Python, Tcl/Tk, BASIC, Pascal, and more. Want to set up a computer network at home or in the office? All the software you need is on this book's CD-ROM.

Graphics artists will appreciate the GNU Image Manipulation Program, or GIMP, which has features rivaling those of commercial graphics programs. Math and science students will like the math, modeling, simulation, and plotting software. If you're busy and on-the-go, OpenLinux includes database and personal information programs to help keep you organized. And if you have a 3Com Palm computer, you'll find support with the included pilot-xfer suite of programs.

Start by following the instructions in Appendix A, "Installing Caldera OpenLinux." After you install Linux, this book will help you learn how to configure and use Linux. Step-by-step instructions will show you

- ✓ How to start and shut down Linux
- ✓ How to start the X Window System
- ✓ How to use the K Desktop Environment
- ✓ How to configure your computer's desktop
- ✓ How to read manual pages and program documentation
- ✓ How to manage windows and programs
- ✓ How to back up and install or remove software
- ✓ How to connect to the Internet
- ✓ How to create text and graphics documents
- ✓ How to set up a printer and print text and graphics
- ✓ How to use the StarOffice office suite of programs
- ✓ How to play games and music CDs

Use this book to save time and effort in getting started with Linux. Each chapter contains several tasks designed to help you build your Linux knowledge. Each task will visually guide you along with way with step-by-step instructions and pictures. This book also includes nearly 200 useful How-to Hints of tips, tricks, and traps you can use to avoid or overcome problems.

How to Use Linux is the first four-color Linux book and includes more than 500 screenshots of Linux in action. You'll quickly see that Linux **is** ready for prime time. Welcome to the world of Linux!

Task

Getting Started with Caldera OpenLinux

*T*his chapter shows you how to get started with Caldera System's OpenLinux distribution of Linux, including several ways you can start and then log in to Linux (directions and tips for installing Linux are in Appendix A, "Installing Caldera OpenLinux"). You also learn how to make the Linux command line a little safer. In addition, you see how to log directly into the graphical interface for Linux, the X Window System. Make sure you've correctly configured X to work with your computer's graphic card and monitor before you begin. Make sure to follow the directions in Appendix A!

When you first log in to Linux, you're in your home directory. This directory has a location, or pathname, such as **/home/yourusername** where **yourusername** is the name you selected when you first installed Linux. ●

How to Start Linux

This task shows you a number of ways to start Linux using the Linux loader, or LILO, prompt. This task assumes you've installed OpenLinux and LILO on your computer's hard drive (see Appendix A), but each step will work if you're booting from a floppy disk.

Begin

1 Start Linux

Turn on your computer. When the Caldera OpenLinux screen appears, you see the boot prompt at the bottom of your screen. If you don't type anything, your computer will boot to Linux in 20 seconds. To see a list of boot images to use, press Tab. You should then see the words *linux* and *dos*. To boot to DOS, type **dos** and press **Enter**. To boot to Linux, type **linux** and press **Enter**.

```
Caldera OpenLinux(TM)
Version 1.3
Copyright 1996-1998 Caldera Systems, Inc.

login:
```

2 Enter Your Username and Password

Type your username and press **Enter**; then type your password and press **Enter** again. You end up in your home directory at the command line of your shell (you did choose bash for your default shell, right?). If you've logged in before, Linux will tell you when and what console, or terminal, you used.

3 Configure Your Environment

Some of the most basic commands—such as **cp** for copying files, **mv** for moving or renaming files, or **rm** for deleting files—can be dangerous. At the command line of your console, use the pico text editor (part of the pine email program) to open the bash shell's resource file **.bashrc** by typing **pico -w .bashrc** and pressing **Enter**.

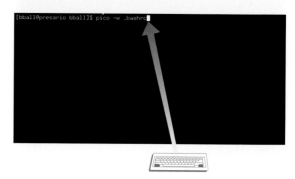

4 Edit the .bashrc File

Press the down-arrow key to scroll to end of the **.bashrc** file. Enter an alias definition for the **cp** (copy) command by typing **alias cp='cp -i'** and pressing **Enter**. Follow this with an alias for the **rm** (delete); type **alias rm='rm-i'** and press **Enter**. Next, enter a definition for the **mv** (rename) command by typing **alias mv='mv -i'** and pressing **Enter**. When finished, press **Ctrl+X**. The pico editor will ask whether you want to save your changes; press **Y** and then **Enter** to save the file. These changes will ensure that from now on, after you reboot and log back in, each command will ask for permission before deleting or overwriting a file.

5 Reboot Linux

If you are the root operator, simply enter the **shutdown** command and its **-r** option to reboot Linux. If you are not root, you must use the **su** (substitute user) command to reboot Linux. Type the command line **su -c "/sbin/shutdown -r now"** and press **Enter**. You're asked for the root operator's password; type it in and press **Enter** to reboot Linux.

End

How-To Hints

How Do I Learn to Use the Command Line?

There are many ways to use the command line, better known as the *shell*. One of the best ways to learn about Linux is to read Matt Welsh's *Linux Installation and Getting Started Guide*. You can use the Lynx browser to read a copy that was installed on your hard drive when you installed OpenLinux; type **lynx /usr/doc/LDP/install-guide/install-guide-3.2.html/index.html**, press **Enter**, and navigate to Chapter 3.

How Do I Change My Password?

At the shell prompt, type **passwd** and press **Enter**. OpenLinux will respond with the prompt **Enter New UNIX Password**. Type a new password and press **Enter**; verify the new password by retyping it and pressing **Enter**. Don't forget your password, especially your root operator password!

What Are Some Basic Commands I Should Know?

See the document "Common OpenLinux Commands," included on this book's CD-ROM, for a list of common commands you should know when learning how to use Linux.

How to Boot Linux to the X Window System

This task shows you how to boot directly to the X Window System using LILO. You must have correctly configured the X Window System in order to boot directly to X (see Appendix A for information on configuring X). Chapter 2, "Getting Started with the X Window System," shows you what to do after you start an X session.

Begin

1 Boot Directly to X with LILO

Start your computer. At the LILO boot prompt, type **linux 5** and press **Enter**. When Linux finishes booting, your display clears and you see a login window. Type your username and press **Enter**. Then, type your password and press **Enter** to start an X session using the AfterStep window manager.

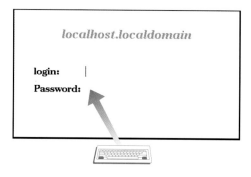

2 Open /etc/inittab

Log in as the root operator. At the command line, use the pico text editor to open the file **inittab** under the **/etc** directory. Be careful! You should first make a copy of this file with the **cp** command; type **cp /etc/inittab /etc/inittab.org** and press **Enter**. To open the file for editing, type **pico -w /etc/inittab** and press **Enter**.

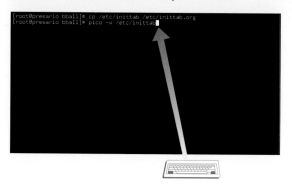

3 Set Default Boot Level

Scroll through the file until you see the **Default runlevel** entry. This entry normally contains the command **id:3:initdefault:**, which starts Linux in the multiuser mode with a console command-line prompt. Cursor to the number **3** and change the **3** to **5**. Press **Ctrl+X** to save the file and then press **Y** to confirm the save. The next time you boot Linux, you'll be presented with a login screen, as shown in step 1.

4 Set Default Boot to KDE

To configure OpenLinux to be able to boot directly to KDE, repeat step 3, changing the runlevel to a **5**. Don't save the file **inittab** yet; instead, scroll to the end of the file until you come to the **Run xdm in runlevel 5** entry. Insert a pound sign (**#**) in front of this line and then retype the line to tell OpenLinux to start the kdm login manager instead of XDM, by typing **x:5:respawn:/opt/kde/bin/kdm -nodaemon** and pressing **Enter**. Press **Ctrl+X** and then press **Y** to save the file.

5 Boot to the kdm Login

Reboot Linux. When Linux reboots, the K Desktop Environment login screen appears. Click your username and then type your password. To boot to KDE, click the **Go** button.

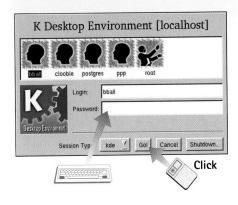

End

How-To Hints

The KDE Login Won't Let Me Log In!

KDE's configuration for using the kdm daemon to log in might not be correct (this is not Caldera Systems' fault). To get out of the login screen press **Ctrl+Alt+F1** and log in as the root operator. You can then edit the **/etc/inittab** file to have OpenLinux boot normally. Then, browse to **http://www.calderasystems.com** and look in the **Support** section for help on logging in with KDE's kdm.

What Is KDE?

KDE is a collection of programs, including an X11 program, or *client*, called kwm. The kwm client is a window manager, and is used to control and manage your desktop during your X session. See Chapter 3, "Getting Started with the K Desktop Environment," for more information.

What Is X11?

The X Window System, also known as *X11* or *X*, is a collection of software that includes programs, fonts, documentation, and critical programs called *servers*. This graphical interface system can be used on a standalone desktop or laptop or set up to provide graphics drawing across a network. Getting X to run on your computer is critical to enjoying software such as KDE, but you should realize that OpenLinux can also be used productively without X. See Chapter 2 for more information about X.

Task

2

Getting Started with the X Window System

*T*his chapter shows you how to use the X Window System included with OpenLinux. The X Window System, known as *X11* or *X*, is the graphical interface to Linux. For information about configuring X to work with your computer's graphic card, see Appendix A, "Installing Caldera OpenLinux." Although configuring X requires a little effort, that effort is well rewarded—a new world of graphical applications are available to you during your Linux sessions.

In this chapter, you learn how to start different X11 clients, or programs, and control how the programs appear on your display. You discover how you can set the background color of your desktop, view fonts, and use the clipboard to copy and paste text. You also see how to start your X11 sessions using different window managers, such as the K Desktop Environment (KDE), AfterStep, and **twm**. Window managers are X11 programs that control how X handles your desktop, client windows, and other aspects of your X session. The KDE is used as the default window manager throughout this book, but the techniques discussed in this chapter work with any window manager. ●

How to Start an X11 Session

This task shows you how to start an X11 session using different window managers. You learn how to start both of the default window managers, and then learn to configure OpenLinux to start your own window manager.

1 Start X11 Using AfterStep

At the command line of your console, type **startx** and press **Enter**. If you've installed and configured X11 properly (according to directions in Appendix A), the screen clears and you start your X session with the AfterStep window manager running the Looking Glass desktop.

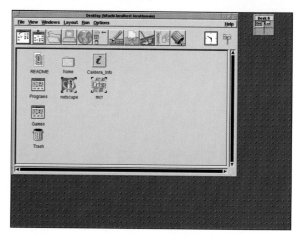

2 Stop X11 Using AfterStep

To stop your X11 session, click a blank area of the desktop, click **Exit Desktop**, and then choose **Quit Desktop**. You end up back at your console.

Click

3 Start X11 Using KDE

To start an X11 session with the K Desktop Environment, use the **kde** command. At the command line of your console, type **kde** and press **Enter**. If you've installed KDE, the screen clears and your X session starts at the KDE desktop.

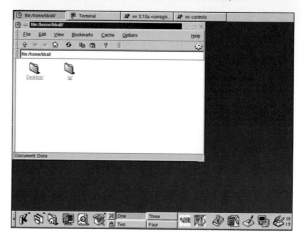

4 Stop X11 Using KDE

Click the **Application Starter** button on your desktop's panel, and then click **Logout**. A logout dialog appears.

Click

5 Configure Your .xinitrc File

To start an X11 session using the **twm** window manager, use your favorite Linux text editor (such as the pico editor included with the pine email program) to create a file called **.xinitrc**. At the command line of your console, type **pico .xinitrc**. In the pico window, enter three lines of text like this:

```
xsetroot -solid lightblue
exec xterm &
twm
```

Press **Ctrl+X** to save the file. Then type **startx** at the command line and press **Enter**.

6 Stop X11 Using twm

To stop your X11 session, click a blank area of the desktop and choose **Exit**.

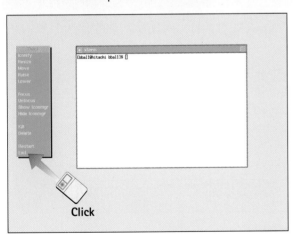

Click

End

How-To Hints

What startx Starts

When you start an X session with **startx**, OpenLinux uses the AfterStep window manager and runs the Looking Glass graphical desktop. Looking Glass is an X11 client that you can use to launch programs and organize your files. For more information about using Looking Glass, start the Netscape Navigator browser from the command line of a terminal window by typing **netscape/usr/doc/html/Caldera_Info**. You can then read the Looking Glass Desktop Interface Users Guide.

How Many Window Managers?

You're not limited to the window managers included with OpenLinux. Browse to **http://www.PLiG.org/xwinman** and you can find links to more than 60 different window managers. One of the great reasons to run OpenLinux and X is that you can make your computer look like other computers or anything you want!

How to Start X11 Terminal Windows

This task shows you how to use different command-line options when starting X11 terminals. You see how to control the size, placement, and background and foreground colors of X11 terminal windows. A terminal window is an important tool during an X11 session because it gives you access to the OpenLinux command line. Before you begin, start an X11 session using the **startx** command.

Begin

1 Start a Terminal

Click the **Terminal** icon. An **xterm** terminal appears. Click the title bar and drag to move the window to a different part of your desktop. To resize the window, click the edge or corner of a window and drag.

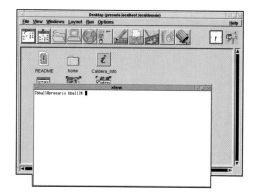

2 Minimize the Terminal

Click the terminal's control button, and then choose **Iconify**. The terminal becomes an icon in the lower-left corner of your desktop. To restore the terminal, click its icon.

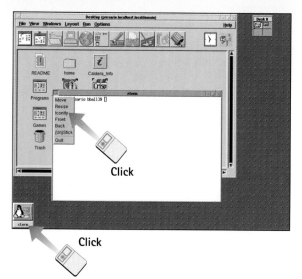

3 Use Specific Colors

Use the **fg** and **bg** options to start a new terminal with specific colors. At the command line of a terminal, type **xterm -fg black -bg lightgreen** and press **Enter**. A new terminal appears with black text on a light-green background. Click the original terminal window and press **Ctrl+C** to close the new terminal.

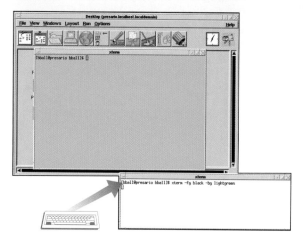

4 Choose a Font and Background

Use the **-fn** option to start a new terminal with a different font. At the command line of a terminal, type **xterm -fg black -bg lightblue -fn 9x15 &** and press **Enter**. A new terminal appears using the specified color and font. The ampersand (**&**) runs the window independently of the original terminal (this is known as starting a program in the *background*). Click the **Close** button to quit the new terminal.

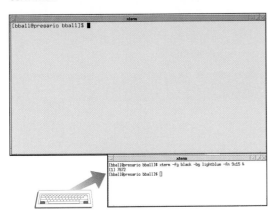

6 Run a Program in a Terminal

Use the **-e** option to run a program in a terminal window. At the command line, type **xterm -fg black -bg PapayaWhip -fn 9x15 -geometry 60x15+200+150 -cr red -e /usr/bin/pico**. A new terminal window appears, using a red cursor with the pico text editor.

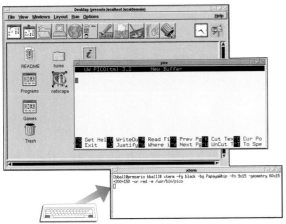

End

5 Use a Specific Size and Location

Use the **-geometry** option to start a terminal with a specific size and location. *Geometry* settings represent width, height, x-offset, and y-offset. The offset values can be positive or negative. An x-offset of **+0** and a y-offset of **+0** represent the upper-left corner of your display. A geometry offset of **-0, -0** is the lower-right corner of your display. At the command line, type **xterm -fg black -bg PeachPuff -fn 9x15 -geometry 50x15+200+150**. A new terminal appears with a 50-character wide, 15-line window, with the window's left edge 200 pixels from the left edge of the desktop, and it's top edge 150 pixels below the top edge of the desktop.

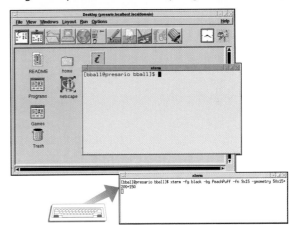

How-To Hints

What Colors Are Available?

Read the file **rgb.txt** under the **/usr/X11R6/lib/X11** directory for a list of color names you can use during your X sessions. Use the **less** pager at the command line like so: **less /usr/X11R6/lib/X11/rgb.txt**. Press **Q** when you've finished reading the file. Also see the next task, "How to See Fonts and Colors."

What Fonts Are Available?

OpenLinux comes with nearly 600 fonts that can be used during your X sessions. Many of these fonts are international, so everyone can enjoy using a graphical interface to Linux. See the next task, "How to See Fonts and Colors," for more information.

How to See Fonts and Colors

This task introduces you to several X clients that help you with colors and fonts. You also learn how to quickly set the font of an xterm terminal window.

Begin

1 Start a Terminal and xfontsel Client

Click a blank area of the desktop, and then click **Applications | Miscellaneous | Terminals | Xterm** to open an **xterm** window. Again, click a blank area of the desktop, and then click **Applications | Miscellaneous | XFontsel**. The **xfontsel** window appears.

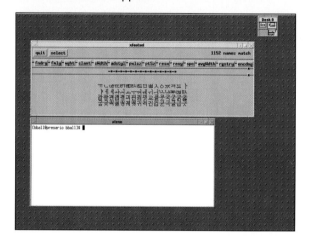

2 Select a Font

In the **xfontsel** window, click **fmly** and select **courier**. Click the **slant** button and choose **r** (for Roman). Click the **pxlsz** button and select **12**. Next, click the **select** button. Then, move your mouse to the **xterm** window, hold down the **Ctrl** key, right-click in the window, and choose **Selection**. The **xterm** window now uses the font you've selected.

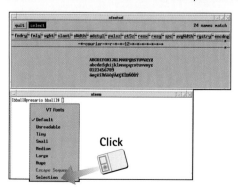

Click

3 View a Font Character Set

Use the **xfd** (X font display) client to see a font's character set. Use **xfd**'s **–fn** option, followed by the name of a font, to view the **xfd** window with the font's characters: **xfd -fn -adobe-courier-medium-r-normal — 14-140-75-75-m-90-iso8859-1**.

4 View a Colormap

Use the **cmap** X11 client to see a grid of currently available colors on your display. Click a blank area of the desktop and choose **Applications | Graphics | Xcolormap**. Your desktop's colors appear in a window. If you click a color in the grid, its Red/Green/Blue (RGB) values appear in hexadecimal (base 16) format.

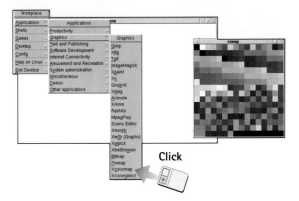

Click

5 Select Colors with xcolorsel

Click a blank area of the desktop, and choose **Applications | Graphics | Xcolorselect**. A window appears, listing available colors, along with RGB values in decimal (base 10) format. To see the RGB value of a color, click **Grab Color** then click the color itself. **xcolorsel** then displays the color's name and RGB value.

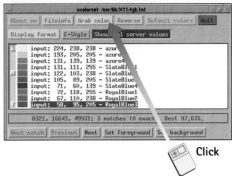

Click

End

How-To Hints

Listing Your System's Fonts

X11 fonts reside under several directories in the **/usr/X11R6/lib/X11/fonts** directory. To view a list of your system's fonts, pipe the output of the **xlsfonts** client through a text pager, such as **less** (use this command line: **xlsfonts ¦ less**). Press the **Q** key when you've finished viewing the list.

Using Colors—Try This!

You can use the RGB values or color names to build interesting backgrounds for your root display. Send the output of the **bggen** command through the X11 graphics program **xv** (which is introduced in Chapter 15, "Capturing and Creating Graphics") like this: **bggen red green blue ¦ xv -root -quit -**. Read the **bggen** man page for more examples.

How to Copy and Paste Text

This task shows you how to copy and paste text between X11 windows. You see how to use the **xcutsel** and **xclipboard** clients. Copy-and-paste is a handy way to transfer long file names or chunks of text between editors or other programs.

Begin

1 Open Two Terminals

Start two **xterm** terminals. Open a text file, **mytextfile.txt** for example, in one window with your favorite text editor, such as pico, by typing `pico mytextfile.txt` and pressing **Enter**. Open another text file (with a different name, such as **newfile.txt**) in the other window.

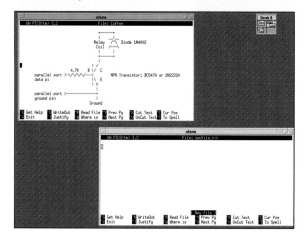

2 Start the xclipboard Client

Click a blank area of the desktop and choose **Applications | Miscellaneous | Clipboard**.

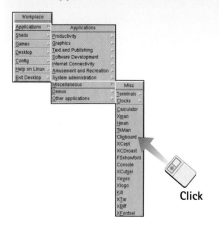

Click

3 Highlight and Copy Text

Click and drag to highlight desired text in the first terminal window. Then, move your cursor to the **xclipboard** window and press the middle mouse button (or simultaneously press both the left and right buttons if you have a two-button mouse). The highlighted text appears in **xclipboard**'s display.

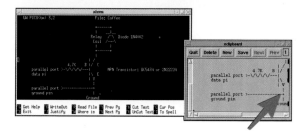

4 Save Clipboard Text

In the **xclipboard** window, click **Save**. A small dialog appears. Click **Accept** to save the text in a file called **clipboard**.

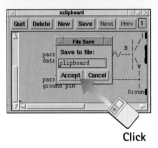

Click

5 Paste the Text

Move your mouse to the other window, and press the middle mouse button (alternatively, you can press **Shift+Ins**). The copied text appears in the new window.

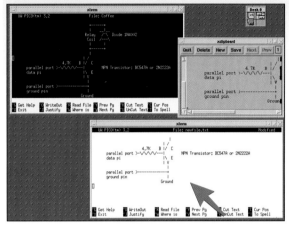

End

How-To Hints

Clipboard Versus Pasting Directly

You can copy text by first highlighting part of one window and then pressing the middle mouse button in another. But with **xclipboard**, you can save your copied text. This program comes in handy because not all X11 programs accept pasted text.

Easy Highlighting

An alternative to using click and drag to highlight text is to click an insertion point with your mouse, then hold down the **Shift** key, and click in a different area of the display. All text between the insertion point and where you click is highlighted.

What About Graphics?

See the next task, "How to Copy and Paste Graphics," to learn how to copy images between windows.

How to Copy and Paste Graphics

This task shows you how to copy and paste graphics between X11 graphic clients. You learn how to use the **xmag** program. Copying and pasting images is very easy!

Begin

1 View a Graphic

Use the **xv** client to display a favorite graphic. From the command line of a terminal, type a command such as **xv nat.jpg &** (where **nat.jpg** is the name of the file you want to display) and press **Enter**. The graphic is displayed on your desktop.

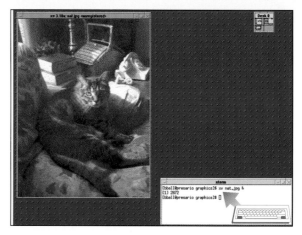

2 Start the xmag Client

At the command line of the terminal, use the **xmag** client to capture a 200-by-200 pixel area of your graphic at a 1:1 ratio (the default is 1:5). Type a command such as **xmag -mag 1 - source 200x200 &**, and then press **Enter**.

3 Copy Graphic

Your X11 cursor changes to a backward 7. Move your mouse to the area of the graphic you'd like to capture and click. The copied graphic appears in **xmag**'s window.

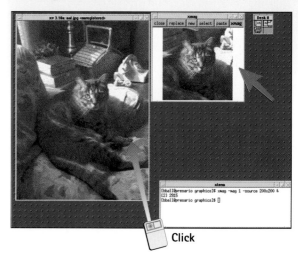

Click

4 Start the xpaint Client

At the command line of your terminal, start the **xpaint** client by typing **xpaint &**. Open the **File** menu, and then click **New with Size**.

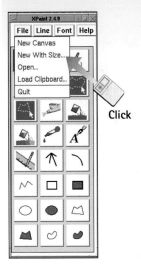

Click

5 Specify Size

Erase the entry in the **Width** field and type **100**. Next, erase the entry in the Height field and type **100** again (this creates a 100-by-100 pixel image, but you can create a larger one if you like). Then click **OK**.

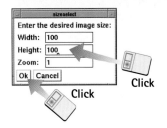

Click

Click

6 Paste the Image into xpaint

Click **Select** in **xmag**'s window, open the **File** menu in the new **xpaint** window, and click **Paste**. The selected graphic appears in **xpaint**'s drawing window; edit it as needed.

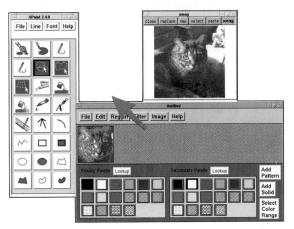

End

How-To Hints

Using Other Graphics Programs

See Chapter 15 for information about how to use other X11 graphics programs. You can also use the **xmag** program to paste graphics into a GNU Image Manipulation Program (GIMP) document.

StarOffice Copy and Paste

See Chapters 11–14 to learn how to copy and paste text, graphics, and data between StarOffice programs and documents. Copy and paste operations are a lot easier when performed between programs—such as StarWriter and StarCalc—that are designed to work together.

How to Change Your Desktop and Mouse

This task shows you how to change the appearance of your desktop and mouse cursor. You see how to use several programs to create special effects or dress up your X11 desktop.

Begin

1 Set a Background Color

Click a blank area of your desktop and choose **Desktop | Background**. You see a list of background colors, such as **Mesh Steelblue** and **Mesh Slategray** (the default is **Blue Points**). Click one to change the background, or root, display.

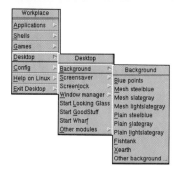

2 Screensave the Background

Use the **hopalong** command to create a livelier display. Start a terminal, and then type **hopalong -root**. Press **Enter**, and your desktop comes alive with a fractal display. To quit, press **Ctrl+C**.

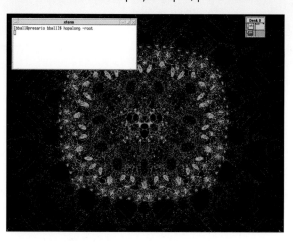

3 Go Fish!

To make your desktop really come alive, click a blank area of your desktop and choose **Desktop | Background | Fishtank**. This starts the **xfishtank** client. Within seconds, your display is swarming with marine vertebrates (and a few odd-looking creatures).

4 Show Available Cursors

Use the **xfd** client to show the available cursors. At the command line of a terminal, type **xfd -fn cursor** and press **Enter**. You see a grid of available cursors. Alternatively, you can read the list of cursor names by typing **less /usr/X11R6/include/X11/cursorfont.h**. To change your cursor to a spider, use the xsetroot command by typing **xsetroot -cursor_name spider** and pressing **Enter**. Use the cursor name **X_cursor** to reset your cursor back to the default.

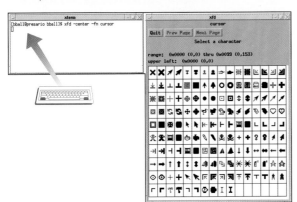

5 Configure Mouse

At the command line of a terminal window, type **xmseconfig** and press **Enter**. A dialog appears, showing your current mouse settings. Test your button by pressing the left, middle, or right mouse buttons while your cursor is over **xmseconfig**'s window. Click **Emulate3Buttons** to turn off three-button emulation. Click **High**, **Medium**, or **Low** to change the mouse's resolution. Do not change the type of mouse unless you are sure the protocol you click (such as **GlidePointPS/2**) works with your mouse—your mouse might become inactive. When finished, click the **Apply** button. Click **Exit** to quit.

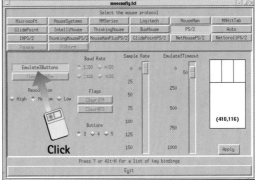

End

How-To Hints

Okay, How Do I Stop the Fish?

The **xfishtank** program is started in the background. If you select **Fishtank** again, you run two **xfishtank**s, and your desktop goes crazy! One way to stop **xfishtank** is to log out of X or stop your X server with **Ctrl+Alt+Backspace**.

Keyboard Mousing

You can also use your keyboard to move your mouse. Press and hold down **Ctrl+Alt**, and then press a desired cursor key.

Using Desktops

When you use **startx** to start an X session, you have four different desktops. Click one of the four squares in your desktop pager's window to move to a different desktop. The pager is a small square window in the upper-right corner of your display and shows little rectangles to represent running programs. You can use one window for word processing, another for graphics, and others for other programs. You can also press **Ctrl** and tap a cursor key to move to a different desktop.

Task

Getting Started with the K Desktop Environment

he K Desktop Environment, or KDE, is the newest and most popular collection of graphical-interface programs for Linux and the X Window System. Although some people consider KDE a window manager for X11, it is much, much more. KDE is one of the first freely available graphic environments for Linux, includes more than 70 programs (or clients), and provides some important features that can help you be more productive. Some of these features include

- ✓ Built-in help with nearly every client
- ✓ A drag-and-drop interface for handling files
- ✓ Double-click launching of programs
- ✓ Easy-to-use graphic tools
- ✓ Point-and-click configuration of the desktop

Some of these features are covered next in Chapter 4, "Managing Your Linux System." In this chapter, you'll learn how to configure KDE so that it looks and works the way you want it to!

First things first: In order to use KDE, you must first log into Linux (see Chapter 1, "Getting Started with Caldera OpenLinux"). To use KDE, type the word **kde** on the command line, and press **Enter**. When the graphical desktop appears, you can go to work! ●

How to Configure Your Desktop

When you use KDE, you'll see different elements on your computer screen, such as the KDE panel (along the bottom), a taskbar (along the top), several icons (such as Trash), and perhaps a window displaying files or folders in your home directory. Notice that your root display color (or desktop background) is blue by default. You can customize this background by choosing a new color, showing a picture, changing how your windows look, and choosing your fonts!

Begin

1 Open the Display Properties Menu

Right-click a blank area of your desktop, and choose the **Display Properties** item from the pop-up menu that appears.

Click

2 Change Desktop Fonts

To change the type of font used for filenames or programs in KDE's taskbar, click the **Typeface** drop-down list and select a different menu. You'll see a preview of the font in the **Sample Text** area. To have all windows, buttons, or menus look like those of that "other" operating system, check the **Draw Widgets in the Style of Windows 95** box at the top of the dialog. To use your new setting right away, click the **Apply** button.

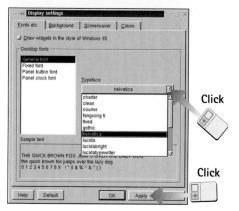

Click

Click

3 Click the Background Tab

Click the **Background** tab. To change the background to a picture, click the drop-down menu in the **Wallpaper** section. You'll see a list of different background patterns and pictures. Scroll through the list, and select the wallpaper you want to use by clicking its name. A preview of the selected wallpaper appears near the top of the dialog. Click the **Apply** button to change your display's background.

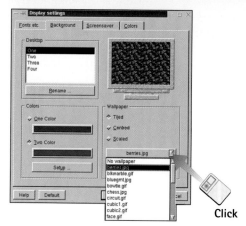

Click

4 Select a Screensaver

Click the **Screensaver** tab, and then scroll through the list of screensavers; a preview of the selected screensaver appears in the dialog. Click **Setup** to enter various parameters for the selected screensaver. Click **Test** to see the screensaver in action. To set how long your system is idle before the screensaver appears, enter a number in the **Wait for** field. Click the **Require Password** checkbox, and your password will be required for you to return to work after the screensaver kicks in. To use the selected screensaver, click the **Apply** button.

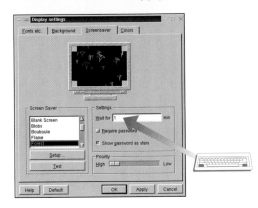

5 Change How Windows Look

Click the **Colors** tab, and scroll through the list of color schemes to change how your windows' title bars, frames, menus, or selected text looks. Note that the scheme will be shown in preview as you click each different color scheme.

6 Change Window Element Colors

KDE comes with 14 color schemes, but you can create your own by selecting specific items and assigning colors in the **Widget color** area of the **Colors** tab on the **Display Settings** dialog. Select a window element from the pop-down menu, and then click the rectangle below the menu to display the **Select Color** dialog. Select a color by choosing one from the **System Colors** palette, or create your own by holding down your left mouse button and moving over the color box in the upper-right quadrant of the dialog. When you're satisfied with the color, click the **OK** button. To use the new color for the desired window item, click the **Apply** button in the **Display Settings** dialog.

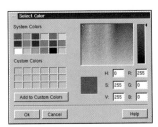

How-To Hints

Setting Desktop Options Directly

You can change the desktop's background, colors, screensaver, or fonts directly by clicking the **Application Starter** button (the large K) in KDE's panel, scrolling up to the **Settings** menu item, and then selecting the **Desktop** submenu item. A third submenu will appear, and you can then choose the item to change. This is handy if you can't find a blank area of your root display, but want to change how your desktop looks.

Custom Controls for Screen Saving

A hidden feature in the **Screensaver** tab of the **Display Settings** dialog lets you set KDE to ignore, screen save, or lock (password protect) your display. Click the **Screensaver** tab in the **Display Settings** dialog, and then click in one corner of the preview dialog. A small pop-up menu will appear, from which you can select an action for that corner. For example, to immediately run a screensaver when you move your mouse cursor to the bottom left of your display, move your mouse cursor to the bottom left of the preview box, click, and select **Save Screen**.

End

How to Configure Your Keyboard and Mouse

If you are left-handed, or you want to hear your keyboard click as you type, use KDE's control client, or KDE Control Center. This program is used to perform keyboard and mouse (and other) settings during KDE sessions.

1 Select the KDE Control Center

Move your mouse cursor to KDE's panel at the bottom of your screen, and click the **Application Starter** button (the big K) to display its menu. Move your mouse up to the **KDE Control Center** menu item, and then click it.

Click

2 Select Input Devices

When the KDE Control Center appears, click the small plus (+) sign to the left of the **Input Devices** icon. A menu tree, showing **Keyboard** and **Mouse** icons, will appear.

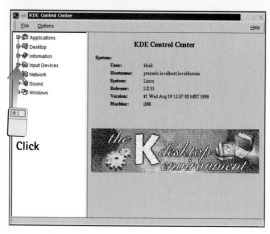

Click

3 Click the Keyboard Icon

Click the **Keyboard** icon; the **Keyboard** control panel will appear in the KDE Control Center. Click the **On** or **Off** radio buttons to enable or disable keyboard repeat (*keyboard repeat* refers to whether a character repeats itself onscreen when you hold down its key on your keyboard). Adjust the slider to increase or decrease the **Key Click Volume**. (A setting of **0%** will turn off key clicks.) To use your settings immediately, click the **Apply** button.

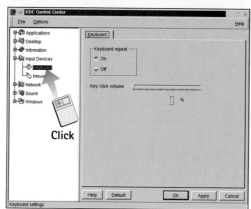

Click

4 Click the Mouse Icon

Click the **Mouse** icon in the left-hand panel to open the **Mouse** control panel in the KDE Control Center. Adjust the **Acceleration** or **Threshold** controls by dragging the slider. The **Acceleration** slider controls how quickly your mouse moves across your display, whereas the **Threshold** slider controls how far your mouse cursor moves before acceleration kicks in. Normal values are **2** for **Acceleration**, and **4** for **Threshold**. To use your settings immediately, click the **Apply** button.

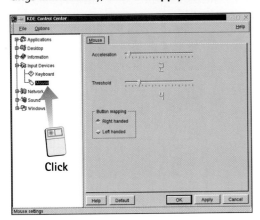

Click

5 Set the Mouse for Use by Lefties

If you're left handed, click the **Left Handed** radio button under the **Button Mapping** section. This reverses the left and right mouse buttons. To use your settings immediately, click the **Apply** button.

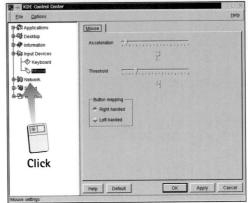

Click

End

How-To Hints

Setting Your Cursor

Although you won't find a cursor-appearance control program with KDE (yet!), you can use the **xsetroot** command from the command-line of a kvt terminal window to change how your cursor looks. For example, to change your X11 cursor to a sailboat, use the **xsetroot** command, followed by its **–cursor_name** option, and the word **sailboat**, like this: **xsetroot -cursor_name sailboat** (the default cursor name is **X_cursor**).

X Settings with the xset Client

Using a mouse and KDE's graphical dialogs to control your keyboard and mouse is easy. More experienced and intrepid Linux users will use the xset program from the command line of a terminal window to control numerous settings for the mouse, keyboard, screensaver, and even the keyboard's LEDs (light-emitting diodes indicating Caps or Num Lock states). For example, to turn off keyboard repeat, use xset's **r** option like this: **xset r off**. To turn repeat back on, **use: xset r on**.

Manual Mouse Mapping

If you find it faster or more convenient, you can also use the **xmodmap** command from the command line of a kvt terminal to quickly remap your mouse's buttons. For example, left-handed users can use **xmodmap** with its **–e** (execute) option to reverse the left and right mouse buttons, like this: **xmodmap -e "pointer 3 2 1"**. Use **xmodmap** with its **–pp** option to show the current mouse button map.

How to Configure the KDE Panel and Taskbar

The KDE panel, or KPanel, is used to launch applications, control and configure your KDE sessions, navigate to different "virtual" desktops or program windows, and log out of KDE. The panel has a number of controls: the **Application Starter** button; a pop-up window list; pop-up program menus; **Logout**, **Screenlock**, and **Virtual Desktop** buttons; program-launching icons; and a **Panel Hide** button. This task will show you how to add and delete panel programs, and how to hide, resize, or reorient the panel.

1 Hide the KPanel

Hiding the panel is a handy way to create more screen real estate. Move your mouse cursor to the far left of the panel. Note the small rectangle next to the **Application Starter** (the big K) button. To hide the panel, click the rectangle. The panel will disappear and shrink to a vertical button. To make the panel reappear, click the button again.

2 Start the KPanel Configuration

If you don't want the panel at the bottom of your display, you can put it at the top or left side of your screen; you specify this from the **KPanel Configuration** dialog. You can click the **Application Starter** button, scroll up to the **Panel** menu item, and then select **Configure**.

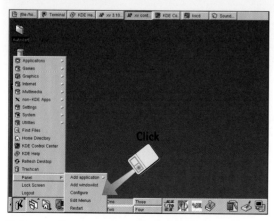

3 Reorient the KPanel and Taskbar

To reorient the panel to the left side of your display, click the **Left** button in the **Location** section of the **KPanel Configuration** dialog, and then click the **Apply** button. To reorient or hide the taskbar, click the appropriate button in the **Taskbar** section of the dialog. The buttons in the **Style** section control the size of the icons in the panel. Select the size you want for your display, and then click the **Apply** button.

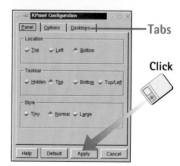

Tabs

Click

4 Change KPanel and Taskbar Options

Click the **Options** tab of the **KPanel Configuration** dialog to set other options, such as pop-up help, autohiding, and the panel clock. Click **Show Menu Tooltips** to toggle pop-up help over panel controls. Drag the **Delay** slider control to set the amount of time before help appears (1000 ms equals one second, obviously). To have the panel or taskbar hide automatically, click the appropriate button in the **Others** section. When you auto hide the panel or taskbar, it will appear only when your mouse cursor lingers in the panel or taskbar's normal location. Don't forget to click the **Apply** button.

5 Change Desktop Buttons

Click the **Desktops** tab to configure the **Desktop** buttons in the panel. These buttons are used to navigate to different "virtual" desktops—it's like having four different displays at the same time! If you need more than four desktops, drag the **Visible** sliding control to the right, and two new desktops will appear (you can use as many as eight). To control the size of the desktop buttons in the panel, drag the **Width** slider to the left or right. Note that the default desktop buttons' labels are **One**, **Two**, **Three**, and **Four**. To change the name of a desktop, click in the text field of the desktop whose name you want to change and enter your own label.

End

How-To Hints

Can't See the KPanel Clock?

The default KPanel configuration uses normal-sized icons. This means that if your X sessions use an 800×600-pixel display, you might not see the clock (it's at the far-right end of the panel). To see the clock, select the **Tiny Style** setting in the panel's configuration dialog, delete unwanted icons from the panel, or try using the panel vertically.

Make a Mistake?

Be careful! Although in many cases you can revert back to KDE's original settings by clicking the **Default** button in configuration dialogs, this doesn't always work (KDE is a "work in progress"). Note your original settings before making major changes to your desktop.

Using and Labeling Desktops

Using desktops and desktop labels is a handy way to organize your work. For example, if you run Netscape in one desktop and StarOffice in another, labeling Netscape's desktop as **Internet**, and StarOffice's as **Office** not only serves as a reminder, but can also keep related activities in single screens.

How to Change the KPanel

The panel, besides hosting the **Application Starter** menu and other controls, is a handy tool that you can use to quickly launch your favorite programs. This section will show you how to install, move, configure, or remove program buttons from the KPanel.

1 Add a Panel Application

To add an application to the panel, open the **Application Starter** menu, select the **Panel** menu item, and then choose the **Add Application** menu item. A menu of applications and applications groups will appear. To add a graphic application, such as the KPaint program, select its icon from the **Graphics** menu. The program's button will appear in your panel immediately to the right of the panel's desktop buttons. Existing buttons will be pushed to the right.

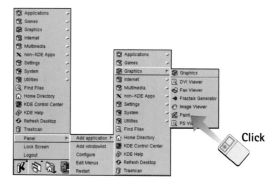

Click

2 Add a Panel Menu

To add a menu to the panel, again open the **Application Starter** menu, select the **Panel** menu item, and then choose the **Add Application** menu item. Select a menu of applications (in this example, **Graphics**), and then select an application group from the menu (again, **Graphics**). The icon of the application group will appear on the panel.

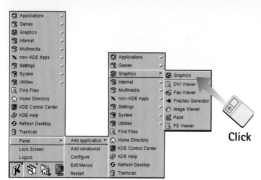

Click

3 Remove a Panel Application or Menu

To remove an application or menu from your panel, right-click the application's or menu's icon and select **Remove** from the small pop-up menu that appears.

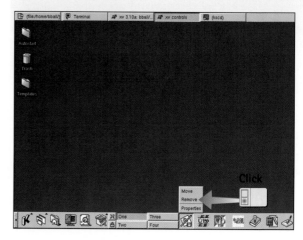

Click

4 Move a Panel Application

To move an application or menu on your panel, right-click the application's or menu's icon and select **Move** from the small pop-up menu that appears. Then, holding down your left mouse button, drag the icon to the left or right, and release when the icon is where you want it to be. Note that any panel icons to the right of the moved icon will shift to the right to make room.

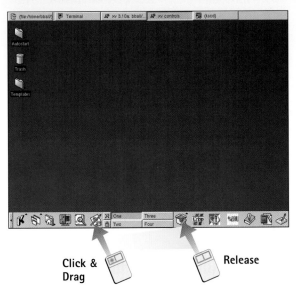

Click & Drag   Release

5 Change Tooltips

To change the pop-up text, or tooltip, displayed by a panel application, right-click the program's icon, and click **Properties**. In the **kfm** dialog, click the **Application** tab. Click and enter new text in the **Comment** field, and then click **OK**.

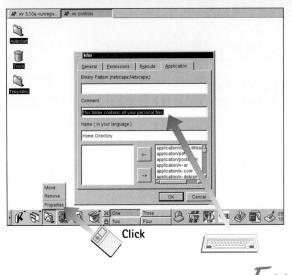

Click

End

How-To Hints

The KPanel: a Moving Experience

All items on your panel can be moved, including the desktop group of buttons. Simply right-click the desktop buttons and drag them where you want. Unfortunately, the **Logout** and **Screenlock** buttons will go along for the ride!

Orientation Can Organize Your Panel

The default horizontal panel puts the **Application Starter** and other system utilities on the left, with important programs on the right. This might not be what you want, especially if you use your panel vertically. Think carefully before arranging your panel applications and menus.

Manual Configuration

If you're an experienced user, you can configure the panel by editing a file called **kpanelrc**, found in your home directory under **.kde/share/config**.

How to Edit Panel Menus

You've learned how to customize your desktop panel, but what if you want to add or remove programs from the panel's menus? This section will show you how.

Begin

1 Select the Panel Menu Editor

Click the **Application Starter** button, choose **Panel**, and then select **Edit Menus** to launch the Menu Editor.

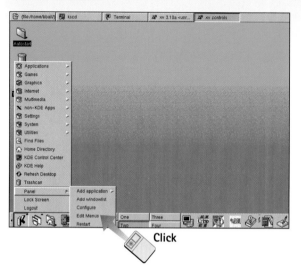

Click

2 Create a Custom Menu

The Menu Editor will appear (you might first get a dialog asking for a directory location—press the **Enter** key and continue). Note that your initial menu appears to be called **EMPTY**. This is not its name, but rather a placeholder that appears until you add items. To give your menu a name, open the **Options** menu. Click **Change Menunames**.

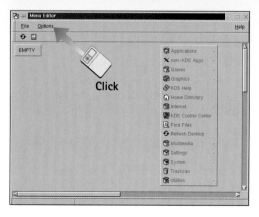

Click

3 Name Your Menu

In the **Change Menunames** dialog, click in the **Personal** text field, and type the name you'd like for your menu. Click the **OK** button when you're finished.

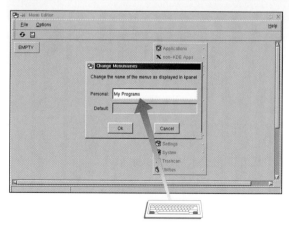

4 Add Programs to Your Menu

The easiest way to build your own menu quickly is to pick your favorite programs from the existing menu. To add a whole group of programs and submenus, select a menu list from the default menu (such as **Applications**), press your left mouse button, and then drag and release the menu item onto your **EMPTY** menu. You can also use copy and paste to add programs to your menu. Simply right-click a desired program in the default menu, and then select the **Copy** menu item. Next, move your mouse to your new menu, right click, and select **Paste** to paste the program into your menu.

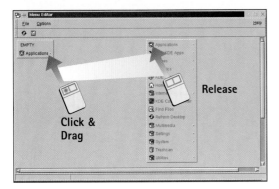

6 Save and Use Your New Menu

To save your new menu, click the **File** menu and select **Save**. Then quit by clicking **File**, **Quit**. Your new menu will appear above the **Panel** menu with the name you chose in the **Change Menunames** dialog. This menu works exactly like any other. Note that when you copied the **Applications** menu to your personal menu, all programs under it were also copied!

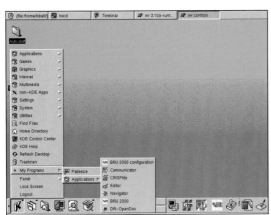

5 Delete Undesired Menu Items

When you're finished building your new menu, edit out any unwanted items, such as the initial **EMPTY** menu item. Right-click the unwanted item, and select **Cut** or **Delete** to remove it.

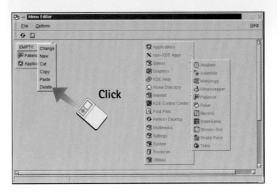

How-To Hints

Menu Shortcuts

If you don't want to "mouse around," use handy keyboard shortcuts when starting programs. For example, the **Alt+F1** key combination will bring up the **Application Starter** menu. You can then use the cursor keys to scroll up, down, left, and right through the menus. When a desired program is highlighted, press the **Enter** key to launch it. Pressing the **Esc** key will close each open menu.

Hidden Programs

More than 2,000 programs are installed on your hard drive during a full OpenLinux installation—that's a lot of programs! (Okay, there might be a duplicate or two, and only the root operator can use a number of them.) Are all these programs installed in your KDE menus? Nope. For details about installing other programs, use the **Help** menu in the **kmenuedit** (Menu Editor) client, and read about entry types. You should also read the **kfm** help pages.

End

How to Manage Desktop Windows

As you have seen, you can have several virtual desktops running at the same time, each containing a number of running programs. Although you can navigate to each desktop, or name and organize your desktops by function (such as **Browsing**, **Editing**, and so on), you'll now learn how to navigate directly to a program running in a different desktop. You'll also learn how to manage your desktop's windows.

1 Select the KPanel's Windowlist Icon

Click the **Windowlist** icon on the panel. You'll see a menu containing the names of your desktops, along with any running applications. This is a handy index to the number of currently running programs. To jump right to a running application in another desktop, scroll up through the list, and click the desired program.

Click

2 Arrange the Windows

To manage or arrange the windows in the current desktop, right-click a blank area of your screen. The desktop's root menu will appear. To rearrange your windows, select **Unclutter Windows** or **Cascade Windows**.

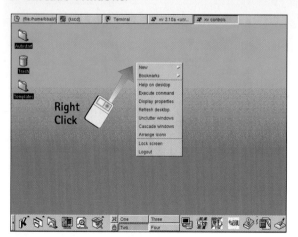

Right Click

3 Configure KDE Windows

To configure how KDE draws and handles your windows, start the KDE Control Center from the **Application Starter** menu, and then expand the **Windows** list item in the **KDE Control Center** dialog.

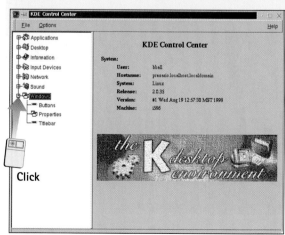

Click

4 Configure Window Buttons

Select **Buttons** under the **Windows** list item. When you use KDE, you can configure any application's window buttons. Select those buttons you'd like to move or turn off, and then click the **Apply** button to immediately see your changes.

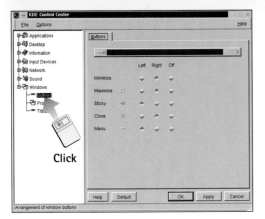

5 Configure Window Properties

Select **Properties** under the **Windows** list item. Select the **Opaque** option to make your windows be solid when you drag them around the screen. Drag the **Animation** slider to control how quickly windows appear or disappear when you use various window buttons. Select **Maximize Vertically** to have a window enlarge only vertically when maximized. **Placement Policy** tells KDE how to place new windows on your desktop. Choose **Focus Follows Mouse** in the **Focus Policy** drop-down menu so that when you move your mouse cursor across the desktop, any window underneath it will become active.

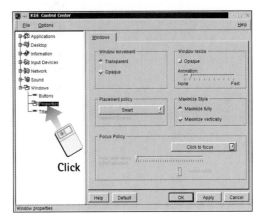

6 Configure Window Title Bars

Select the **Titlebar** menu item under the **Windows** list item to configure how you want your program's title bars to look during your KDE session. The title bars can appear in many different hues, can look plain, or can even have pictures. The **Mouse Action** section enables you to select a type of action, such as resize, close, or iconify, when you double-click your left mouse button on the title bar. Drag the **Title Animation** slider to the left to speed up scrolling window titles, and to the right (to increase the delay) to slow down title scrolling.

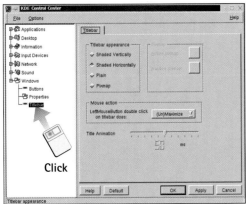

How-To Hints

Who's Got the Buttons?

If you turn off the **Close**, **Menu**, **Maximize**, and **Minimize** buttons, you might think there's no way to quit or hide a program's window. Don't worry—you can always get a pop-up window control menu by right clicking in the window's title bar.

Window Jumping Made Easy

There are several handy keyboard shortcuts you can use during your KDE sessions. For example, to switch between windows on your desktop, press the **Alt+Tab** key combination. To close a window, press **Alt+F4**. To access a window's menu, press **Alt+F3**, and click the **up**, **down**, **left**, or **right arrow** keys to scroll through the menu.

End

Task

4

Managing Your Linux System

*T*his chapter shows you how to take care of your OpenLinux system. You'll learn how to manage files, software, other users, and software services. You'll also see how to back up your system, an important task all computer users should take seriously—losing any data means losing time, effort, and money!

Before you begin, start an X session using the K Desktop Environment, or KDE. See Chapter 2, "Getting Started with the X Window System," for details on starting X11, and Chapter 3, "Getting Started with the K Desktop Environment," for information about KDE. You can start an X session using KDE from the command line of your console by typing **kde**. ●

How to Manage Your Files

There are several ways to manage files using OpenLinux. This task uses KDE's desktop for its examples. See the How-To Hints section for information about other ways to manipulate files.

Begin

1 Click a File or Folder

Right click a file or folder on the desktop, and choose **Properties** from the pop-up menu.

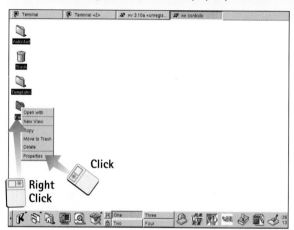

2 Rename a File or Folder

Click in the **Name** field, enter a new filename, and click **OK**.

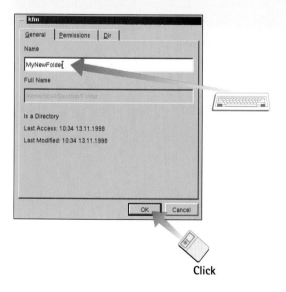

3 Delete a File or Folder

You can delete a file or folder in two ways. You can put the file in the desktop's trash can, or you can delete the file entirely. To put the file in the trash can, right-click it, and choose **Move to Trash** from the pop-up menu. The file disappears from the desktop and the **Trash** icon changes to show that its lid is ajar. To delete a file, right-click it and choose **Delete** from the pop-up menu. KDE asks you to confirm the deletion; click **Yes**.

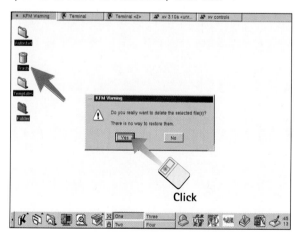

4 Copy a File to the Desktop

KDE's desktop supports moveable icons and drag-and-drop action. This means that you can open a folder and drag files into and out of it. You can copy or move files into a folder by dragging the file's icon and dropping it either onto a folder's icon or into an open folder's window. To copy a file, click it, and then, holding down the mouse button, drag it to the desktop. When you release your mouse button, a small menu appears. Click **Copy**.

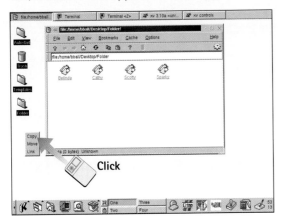

5 Move a File to the Desktop

Note that the file is still in the folder, but a copy is also on the desktop. To move a file, repeat the previous step, but click **Move** instead. Note that the file is no longer in the folder.

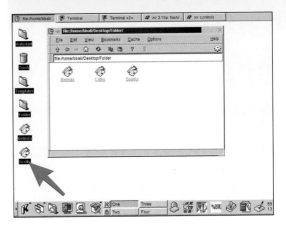

6 Create a Link

Repeat the previous drag and drop, but this time click **Link** in the pop-up menu. KDE creates a new file with the same name as the original, but with a slightly different icon. A *link* is a pointer to a corresponding original file. If the original file is a text document, clicking its link loads the original document. If you delete the link, you are not deleting the original file; however, if you delete the original document, the link is useless.

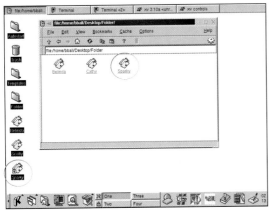

How-To Hints

Renaming Files and Folders with mv

Use the **mv** command to rename files on the command line. For example, the command **mv Scotty Belinda** renames the file **Scotty** to **Belinda**. You can also use **mv** to move files. For example, **mv /home/bball/Whoopie /home/bball/Desktop** moves the file **Whoopie** to your KDE desktop. If you give the original file a new name in the destination path, such as **/home/bball/Desktop/Freaky**, the file **Whoopie** is moved and renamed at the same time. For safety's sake, always use **mv**'s **–i** (interactive) option. This way, **mv** first asks whether it's okay before writing over an existing file.

End

How to Manage Your Users

When you install OpenLinux, you're in charge of the system. It's your job to protect Linux from people sitting at your computer's console, calling in on a phone line, or logging in through a network. This task shows you how to add users and change passwords to your system.

Begin

1 Start the usercfg Client

Log in as the root operator and start the **usercfg** command by typing **usercfg&**. The main dialog appears. Click **Add**.

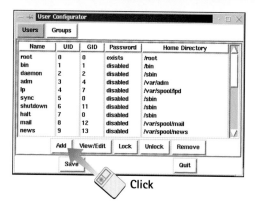

Click

2 Add a User

In the **Edit User Definition** dialog, enter the new user's username (the name typed at the OpenLinux **login:** prompt), full name, office location (or other information), office phone, home phone (or other information), and pathname of the user's directory. Open the **Shell** drop-down list to select the shell to be used when the user logs in. When finished, click **Shadow Management**.

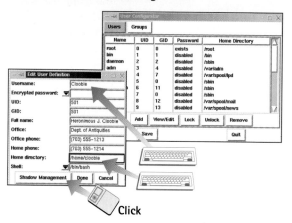

Click

3 Configure Password Management

In the **Edit Account Management** dialog, enter a number (in days) to control how the user's passwords are handled. When finished, click **Done** in the Edit Account Management dialog, and again in the End User Definition Dialog. In the **User Configurator** dialog, click **Save**.

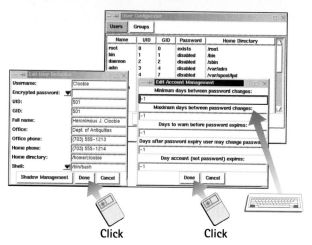

Click   Click

4 Start User Delete

Start **usercfg**. In the **User Configurator** dialog, scroll through the user list, highlight the desired user, and click **Remove**.

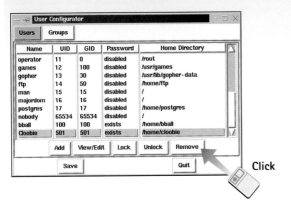

Click

5 Select Delete Options

Click the desired delete options for the user in the **Delete User** dialog; click **Done** when you're finished.

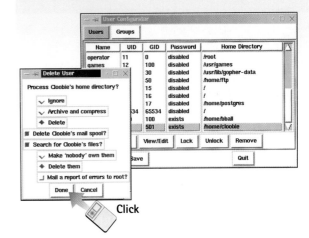

Click

6 Confirm the Deletion

You'll be asked whether you're sure you want to delete the user; click **Really Delete**.

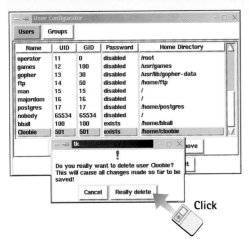

Click

End

How-To Hints

Adding Users Without X11

Use the **adduser** command to create a new user on the command line. For example, the command **adduser Freddie** creates a new user named **Freddie**. Next, type **passwd Freddie** to assign user **Freddie** a password.

User Administration with lisa

You do not have to use X in order to run **lisa**. Use the **lisa** command's **—useradm** option to jump right into user administration for your system by typing **lisa —useradm**. You'll see a menu of options to view, add, or change users.

Secure Your System!

Although it's okay to allow anyone to use your computer, be smart and protect yourself and your files. Make sure to perform frequent backups, ensure that important files and directories have correct access permissions (see the **chmod** command's man page), and keep your password protected.

How to Manage Your Software with kpackage

Fortunately for OpenLinux users, nearly all software installation and removal is handled by the Red Hat Package Manager, or the **rpm** command. The **rpm** command also maintains a database of installed software for your system under the **/var/lib/rpm** directory.

This section shows you how to use the **kpackage** graphical interface program to run rpm. You must be logged in as the root operator in order to install and remove software. If you're not logged in as the root operator, start **kpackage** from the command line of an X11 terminal window by typing **su -c "kpackage"**.

Begin

1 Start kpackage

Click the **Application Starter** button on your desktop's panel, choose **Utilities**, and click **kpackage**.

Click

2 View Package Folders

The **kpackage** window appears, listing the groups of packages installed on your system. Click the plus sign in front of the **Archiving** folder to view a list of packages in the **Archiving** group. Click the **taper** entry.

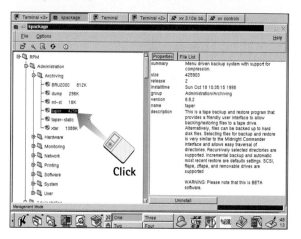

Click

3 Get Package File List

Click the **File List** tab; a listing of each file in the taper package and the file's location in your Linux file system appears.

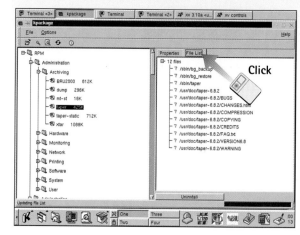

Click

4 Uninstall a Package

To uninstall a package, click the **Uninstall** button (near the bottom of the pane on the right side of the screen). In the dialog that appears, click **Uninstall**. If you'd like to test the uninstall to see whether removing this package can cause other programs not to work, click **Test** and then click **Uninstall**.

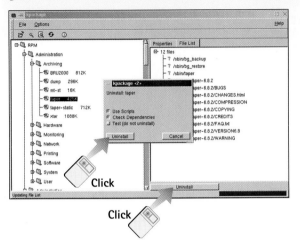

5 Start Package Install

Open your computer's CD-ROM bay, and insert your OpenLinux CD-ROM. Type **su -c "mount /mnt/cdrom"** to mount the CD-ROM, and then choose **Open** from the **File** menu. The **kpackage Open** dialog appears. Erase the **Location** entry, type **/mnt/cdrom/Packages/RPMS**, and press **Enter**. Scroll through the list of packages and click the **taper rpm** file, and then click **OK**.

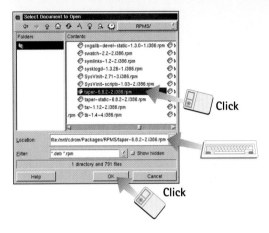

6 Finish Package Install

The **Install Package** window appears; click the **Install** button.

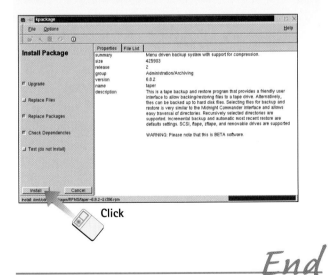

End

How-To Hints

Using rpm

The **rpm** command can be used from the command line without the X Window System. This flexible and powerful command can also be used to generate reports about your installed software. See the **rpm** man pages, and read about **rpm**'s query options.

The Definitive rpm Guide

The best book about **rpm** is Sams's *Maximum RPM*, by Ed Bailey. This 440-page book shows you how to use all of **rpm**'s features. For details about this book, browse to **http://www.mcp.com**. For online information about **rpm**, browse to **http://www.rpm.org**.

How to Manage Your Software with glint

The **glint** client is a graphical interface program to the **rpm** command. You must be logged in as the root operator in order to install and remove software when using **glint**. Start **glint** from the command line of an X11 terminal window by typing **su -c "glint"**.

Begin

1 Open glint Folders

The **glint** client reads your OpenLinux **rpm** database and displays a window of folders. Click the **Administration** folder, and then click the **Archiving** folder.

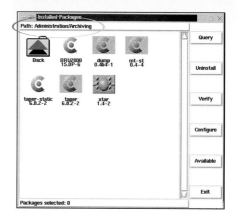

2 View Package Information

Highlight the **taper** icon and click the **Query** button. A query window with information about the package appears. After you finish reading, click **Close**.

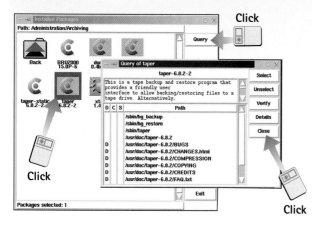

3 Delete Package

Click **Uninstall**. A confirm dialog appears; click **Yes** to uninstall the package.

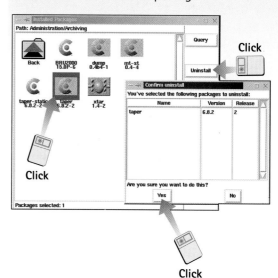

4 Start Package Install

Make sure your CD-ROM is mounted and then click **Available**. **glint** searches the **/mnt/cdrom/Packages** directory on your CD-ROM for **rpm** files. A small **Scanning** dialog appears while **glint** searches your CD-ROM, and then the **Available Packages** window appears.

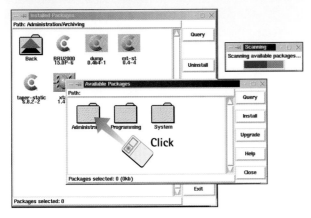

5 Select, Install Package

Click the **Administration** folder, and then the **Archiving** folder. To install the package, click the package icon, and click **Install**.

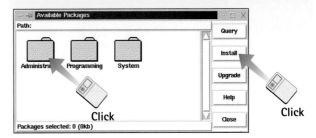

6 Finish Package Install

The **Install Package** window appears. Click **Install**.

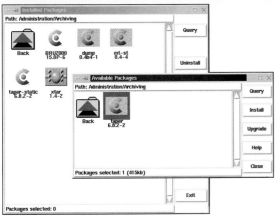

End

How-To Hints

Using Other CD-ROMs with glint

If you'd like to install **rpm** packages from other CD-ROMs or a floppy drive, start **glint**, and then click **Configure**. In the **Package** path field, type the path, such as **/mnt/floppy**, and click **OK**. When you click the **Available** button, **glint** search your floppy diskette.

How to Mount a Floppy

In order to install **rpm** files from a floppy, you should first mount the floppy. For example, to support long filenames on your floppy and to mount it at the **/mnt/floppy** directory, type **mount -t vfat /dev/fd0 /mnt/floppy**.

OpenLinux Says vfat Is not Supported!

Don't worry. Use the **insmod** command to load the **vfat** kernel module supporting long filenames by typing **su -c "/sbin/insmod vfat"**. Then try mounting your floppy again.

Manage Your Software with lisa

The **lisa** command is a graphical interface program to the **rpm** command that does not require the X Window System. You must be logged in as the root operator in order to install and remove software using **lisa**. Start **lisa** from the command line of your console by typing **su -c "lisa — pkg"**.

Begin

1 Select Package Removal

The **lisa** command proceeds right to the **Software Package Administration** dialog; scroll down to item 4, **Remove Software Packages that Have Already Been Installed**, and press **Enter**.

2 Select Package

Next, **lisa** queries your system's **rpm** database and presents a list of installed packages in the **Un-install Software Packages** dialog. Scroll through the package list and press the **Spacebar** to select a package. An **X** appears in the left column. You can select or deselect multiple packages using the **Spacebar**. When finished, press **Enter** to delete the package.

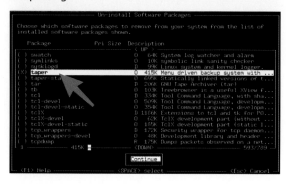

3 Start Package Install

In the **Software Package Administration** dialog, choose **Select Installation Source** and press **Enter**.

4 Select Source

Make sure your CD-ROM is mounted. Select **CD-ROM** in the **Installation Source Selection** dialog and press **Enter**.

5 Select Source Type

Next, **lisa** determines the type of CD-ROM you have installed; press **Enter** to continue. A small info dialog appears. Press **Enter** again.

6 Select, Install Package

Scroll through the list of packages. Press the **Spacebar** to select a package, and then press **Enter**. A small install info dialog appears. Press **Enter** to install the package.

End

How-To Hints

Getting Package Info

The **lisa** command displays information about a package. In the **Software Package Administration** dialog, select item 4, **Information About the Available Software Packages**. Press **Enter**, and then scroll through the list of package names. To get information about the currently highlighted package, press **Enter**.

Use Netscape to Search for Packages

You can use Netscape Navigator to search for installed packages. See the How-To Hint "Using Netscape and Apache to Search for Packages" in the "How to Manage Your Services" task.

How to Back Up Files with BRU 2000

If you use a stable Linux kernel (such as the one provided on your OpenLinux CD-ROM), you'll enjoy the benefits of using a nearly crash-free operating system. But this doesn't mean that all the software included with OpenLinux is immune to a software glitch or two. If a program barfs, you can easily kill the offending process using the shell's **kill** command and start anew—this means no Blue Screen of Death with Linux! However, in order to avoid any problems with lost files, always back up and save important documents.

This section shows you how to use the **BRU 2000** client to back up files to floppy disks. You must be logged in as the root operator in order to use **BRU 2000**. Start this program from your desktop's panel menu or the command line of an X11 terminal window by typing **su -c xbru**.

Begin

1 Configure BRU 2000

Click the **File** menu, and then click **Configure BRU**.

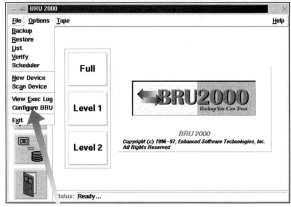

  Click

2 Start Device Configuration

The **BRU Configuration** dialog appears; click **Devices**. A **/etc/brutab** window appears. Click **New**.

Click

3 Select a Device

Open the **Device Type** drop-down menu in the **New Device** window, and choose **1.44Mb Floppy**. Then click the **Device node** field, type **/dev/fd0**, and click **Create**.

Click

4 Name the Device

Click the **Device Name** field and type **Floppy Backup**, and then choose **Save** from the **File** menu. Finally, click **File | Exit**.

Click

6 Select Files

Click the **Backup Data to Archive** button in the main **BRU 2000** window. Scroll through your home directory, click a desired file or directory to back up, and then click **Add**. When finished, insert a floppy disk into your computer and click **Start Backup**. **BRU 2000** asks for an archive label, gives you an estimate of how many disks are needed, and begins the backup.

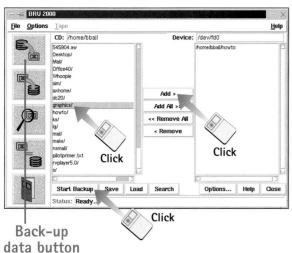

Back-up data button

Click

Click

Click

5 Select New Device

Choose **New Device** from **BRU 2000**'s **File** menu. In the **Select Device** dialog, open the Device drop-down menu, choose **/dev/fd0**, and click **OK**.

Click

How-To Hints

Other Devices You Can Use with BRU 2000

Nearly 40 different backup devices are listed in **BRU 2000**'s configuration files, but you can also define your own. All you really need to know is the name of the device under the **/dev** directory—such as **/dev/sda4** for a parallel-port Iomega Zip drive—and the capacity of the device (100MB per disk).

Another Backup Program You Can Use

Use the **taper** command's **-T** option, followed by the name of a backup device, to start a backup. The **taper** command does not require the X Window System and can be started from the command line of your console. Make sure to read the taper FAQ under the **/usr/doc/taper** directory. However, this program is so simple and easy to use, you don't need a manual! For example, to start a backup session and use your floppy drive as the backup medium, type **taper -T r**.

Using the tar Command

You can also use the **tar** command to back up files to your floppy drive. For example, use a command such as **tar cvf /dev/fd0 -M myfiles** to back up the contents of the **myfiles** directory. The **-M** option tells **tar** that the backup is a multivolume archive. When the first disk fills up, **tar** prompt you to insert the next disk.

End

How to Manage Your Services

The **lisa** command helps you administer nearly any aspect of your system. This section shows you how to configure different software services on your system. The **lisa** program does not require X, so you can use it at the command line of your console. You must be logged in as the root operator.

Begin

1 Select System Configuration

Scroll down to the **System Configuration** entry in the **LISA Main Menu** window, and press **Enter**.

2 Select System Configuration

The **System Configuration** menu appears. Scroll down to **System Configuration** and press **Enter**.

3 Select Software Services

Scroll down to the **Configure Daemon/Server Autostart** entry, and press **Enter**. *Daemons* are programs that are often started when you boot Linux. They run in the background, coming alive only when needed and, if so designed, spawning copies of themselves and new processes (daemons or processes that have died but still show up in the process table shown by the **ps** command are known as *zombies*).

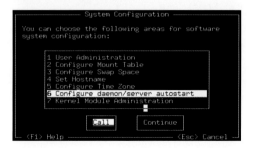

4 Review Current Services

The **lisa** command lists nearly 30 different software services (depending on the software you've installed on your system). You should have at least four services start when you boot Linux: Cron for scheduling events; Print Server for printing; Mail Transfer Agent so you can send electronic mail; and System Loggers for creating your system's logs under the **/var/log** directory.

5 Select Web Server

For example, to have the Apache Web server start the next time you boot Linux, scroll down to the **WEB Server (Apache)** item, press the **Spacebar**, and then press **Enter**.

End

How-To Hints

What Are These Different Services?

OpenLinux can be used as a desktop computer operating system or a platform to support large-capacity and high-demand Internet services. This book's CD-ROM contains nearly all the software needed to use Linux on a personal computer, a high-end graphics workstation, or a network server. To learn more about how to administer Linux, use your favorite Web browser to read the System Administrator's Guide (**/usr/doc/html/sag/sag.html**). To learn about using different network services, read the Network Administrator's Guide (**/usr/doc/html/nag/nag.html**).

Using Netscape and Apache to Search for Packages

If you start the Apache Web server, you can use Netscape Navigator to search for installed packages and get detailed information about found packages. This is a convenient HTML interface to your system's **rpm** database. Start Apache, and then start Netscape. Browse to **file:/usr/doc/html/Caldera_Info** and click the **What's Installed on This Computer?** link. A search page appears, and you can then enter queries about different programs. For example, using a search term such as **X11** returns links to every package containing **X11** in its **rpm** database description entry.

Task

5

Getting Help

Y ou can find lots of help when using OpenLinux. Some programs have helpful pop-up tips, whereas other applications have built-in help menus—and nearly every command has a corresponding manual page. Help files for programs and procedures are literally scattered all over your OpenLinux file system. You can find help files, manual pages, and documentation under the following directories:

- ✓ **/usr/man**   More than 10 directories of manual pages for nearly 3,000 programs, system files, or programming functions
- ✓ **/usr/info**   Nearly 500 hyperlinked GNU info files
- ✓ **/usr/doc**   More than 400 directories of program documentation, with 200 HOWTOs and FAQs.
- ✓ **/usr/X11R6/man**   More than 1,200 files of manual pages

Sometimes the problem is having too information! To compound this overload, you can find information in all sorts of different formats, such as compressed text, HTML, PostScript, or nroff (used to format man pages). This chapter shows you how to find the answers you need, and how to read these different documentation file formats. Note: This chapter assumes you use KDE (discussed in Chapters 2, "Getting Started with the X Window System," and 3, "Getting Started with the KDE Desktop Environment") for your X sessions! ●

How to Use the xman Client

You use the xman client to read Linux program manual pages during your X11 sessions. This program provides an easy way to read documentation for many of the programs that come with OpenLinux. Found under the **/usr/X11R6/bin** directory, **xman** is the X counterpart to the **man** command, which can be used to read man pages from the command line of your console (without running X11), or from the command line inside an X11 terminal window.

Begin

1 Start xman

Start xman from the command line of an X11 terminal window by typing **xman &**. The xman **Manual Browser** window appears on your desktop.

2 Read xman's Manual Page

Click the **Manual Page** button to open the initial manual page, which will be for xman. Scroll through the page by dragging the scrollbar on the left side of the window.

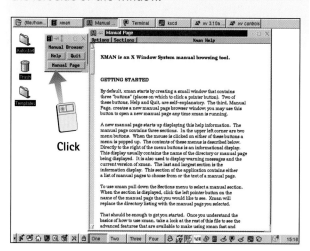

Click

3 Display Manual Page Index

Click the **Sections** button, and select (1) **User Commands** to display an index of manual pages for this section.

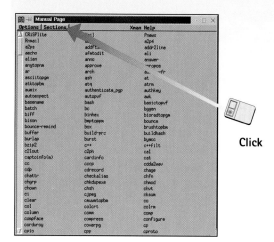

Click

4 Display a Manual Page

Scroll through the index. When you find a desired program's manual page listed in the index (for example, **pilot-xfer**), click the entry. A small window appears, telling you the page is being formatted, and then the man page displayed.

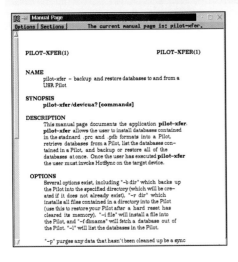

5 Search for a Manual Page

Click the **Options** button in the **Manual Page** window, and then press and hold down the left mouse button. A menu of xman options appears; select **Search**. In the small search window that appears, type a command and click the **Manual Page** button. If found, the command's manual page displays.

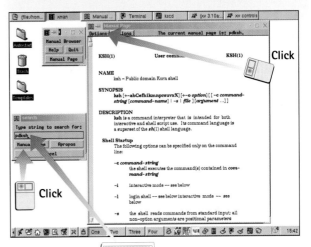

6 Search on a Subject

To find out which programs to use, say, to manipulate your computer's floppy drive, select **Search** from xman's **Options** menu. Type **floppy**, and click the **Apropos** button. Any manual pages with the word *floppy* appear (unfortunately, you can't click in the list of pages to link to a manual page—you have to remember the name of the page and use it in your next search).

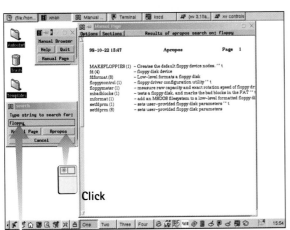

How-To Hints

More About Man Pages

Manual pages for programs in your OpenLinux distribution are grouped by category into sections. These categories and sections are documented in the man page in section 7. To read this man page from your console or the command line of an X11 terminal window, type **man 7 man**.

Just Want a Little Info?

You can use the **whatis** command, followed by the name of a program, to see the program's manual page section and a one-line synopsis.

End

How to Use KDE Help

The K Desktop Environment features a consistent help interface, usually through a **Help** menu in the menu bar of each KDE client's window. One of the most helpful programs in the KDE collection is the kdehelp client. You can use it not only to find out more about KDE and its programs, but also to find out about other commands included with OpenLinux. To open the **KDE Help** window, click the **Application Starter** button on your desktop panel, and then click the **KDE Help** menu item.

Begin

1 Navigate KDE Help Pages

To go to an index of different KDE clients, click **KDE application help index**.

2 Select a Man Page Section

To read the man page for a command, click **System man page contents** in the **KDE Help** window shown in step 1. An index of man page sections appears. Click the appropriate section, and then click a command's name to view its man page. For now, click the **Previous Document** button in the toolbar to return to KDE Help's main page.

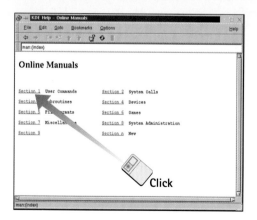

3 Select an Info Document

Many programs included with OpenLinux are from the Free Software Foundation and include documentation in *info* format. To use KDE Help to read info documents, click **System GNU info contents** in KDE Help's main page (refer to step 1). An index of GNU info documents and categories appears. To read an info file, click a name, such as **cp**.

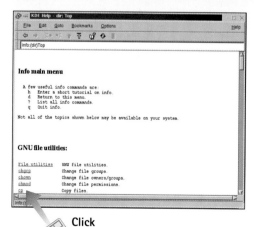

4 Read an Info Document

The **cp** info page appears. Use your **up-arrow** and **down-arrow** keys, or drag the scrollbar to scroll through the document. Note that several of the node buttons on KDE Help's toolbar are now active. Click these buttons to navigate through the GNU info-page structure, or use the **Previous Document** button to return back through your pages.

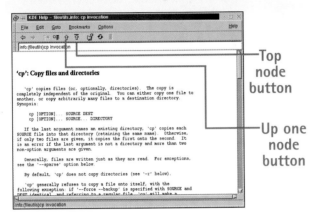

Top node button

Up one node button

5 Set KDE Help Options

Click the **Options** menu to set various KDE options, such as which toolbars or information fields appear in the main window. The **General Preferences** menu item enables you to set the type and size of fonts, and colors used to display help text.

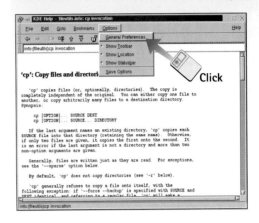

Click

6 Search for Help

One of the most useful KDE Help features is its search function. From the main **KDE Help** window (refer to step 1), click the **Search for Keyword** text item to display the KDE Help form. Enter a term, such as **floppy**, in the **Enter Keywords** field. To search man pages, click the **Online Manuals** button, and then click the **Submit Search** button. In the **KDE Help** window, you see a list of topics and files matching your search. Click a topic or man page to view the documentation.

Click

End

How-To Hints

Browsing with KDE Help

If you have an active Internet connection (see Chapter 7, "Connecting to the Internet") and click a Web site name or link while using KDE Help, you go directly to that site's Web page! This feature, called *Network Transparent Access*, or *NTA*, is built into KDE and supported by many applications, including KDE Help.

Using KDE Help's Toolbar

KDE Help provides a toolbar that operates in much the same way as toolbars on Web browsers. Buttons include **Previous Document**, **Next Document**, **Previous Node**, **Next Node**, **Up One Node**, **Top Node**, **Help Contents**, **Reload Current Document**, and **Stop**. The node buttons are handy tools you can use to navigate through GNU info documents, and they save you the trouble of memorizing GNU info keyboard commands.

How to Read Documents

You run across a lot of different document files when you use OpenLinux. Of course, you've already seen how to read man pages and info files, but there are other file types on your system. These files can be text, compressed text, HTML, device independent, PostScript, or SGML. In the following examples, you see how to open and read different types of documents from your KDE desktop.

Begin

1 Open a Text File

Right-click file's icon a text (**.txt**) on the desktop. In the pop-up menu that appears, KDE suggests an application to use to open the file. Select **Editor**.

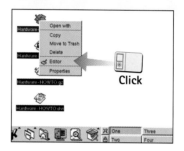

2 Read a Text File

The KEdit editor launches and displays your file. Use your cursor keys or drag the vertical or horizontal scrollbars with your mouse to read the document.

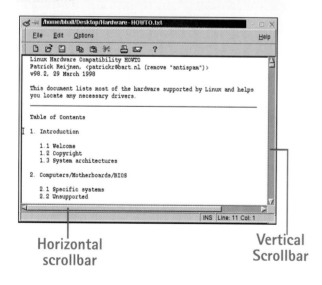

Horizontal scrollbar

Vertical Scrollbar

3 Open and Read a Compressed Text

To open and read a compressed text file (usually a file with **.gz** or **.bz2** at the end of its name), click the file's icon. KDE launches the KZip program to decompress the file, and then loads the file into KEdit to be read.

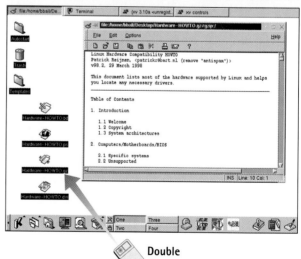

Double Click

4 Open and View a PostScript

To view a PostScript document (a file with **.ps** at the end of its name), click the document's icon. KDE launches the kghostview application to display the file. Click a page number in the left portion of the **kghostview** window to go to different pages.

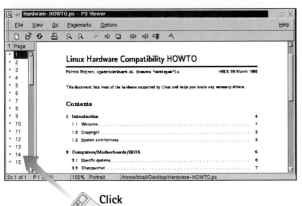

Click

5 Open and View a Device

To open a DVI file (**.dvi**), click the document's icon with your left mouse button. KDE launches the KDVI viewer after processing the file (there might be a delay before the document is displayed on your desktop).

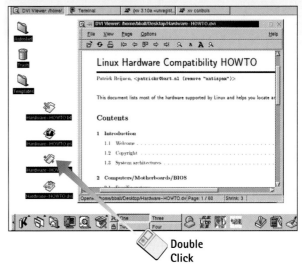

Double Click

End

How-To Hints

Casual Browsing From the Command Line

You can also read text documents from the command line of your console or a terminal window. Without a doubt, the best program to use is the less pager, which provides a way to interactively move forward, backward, and even sideways through a file. This program also has search and bookmark capabilities. To read a file, such as the Hardware-HOWTO, use a command such as **less Hardware-HOWTO**.

Can't Read Compressed Text Files?

If you try to use the **less** command to read a compressed text file, such as **Italian-HOWTO.gz** under the **/usr/doc/HOWTO** directory, you get a message that says **"Italian-HOWTO.gz" may be a binary file. See it anyway?**. Use the **zless** command instead, which decompresses and displays compressed text files on the fly.

What Is TeX?

TeX is a complex and capable text-formatting and typesetting system included with your OpenLinux distribution. More than 65 programs and numerous fonts are included under the **/usr/TeX** directory. Getting into the details about using TeX is beyond the scope of this book, but if you're interested, you can find a large amount of documentation and sample files in the **/usr/TeX/texmf/doc** directory.

How to Read HTML and PostScript Files

If you choose not to use KDE as your desktop environment, or want to try other programs to read HTML and PostScript files, a number of alternative programs are included with OpenLinux. Some of the best programs for reading HTML files are Web browsers, and an excellent PostScript viewer, **gv**, is included on your OpenLinux CD-ROM

Begin

1 Read HTML with Lynx

Open an HTML file by typing **lynx** on the command line, followed by the pathname to the HTML file, like so: **lynx /usr/doc/html/index.html**. You'll see a great HTML interface to the OpenLinux documentation on your system. Navigate through a page by using your **up-arrow** and **down-arrow** keys. To follow a link, press the **Enter** key. Use the **left-arrow** and **right-arrow** keys to go to previous or next pages.

2 Read HTML with Amaya

The Amaya Web browser can also be used to display local HTML files. Open the Caldera OpenLinux documentation page from the command line of an X11 terminal window by typing **amaya /usr/doc/html/index.html**.

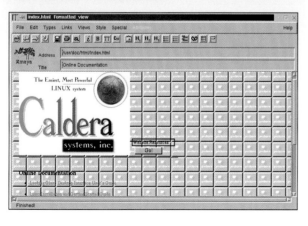

3 Read HTML with KDE Help

You can use the KDE Help browser to read local HTML files. From the command line of an X11 terminal, use the **kdehelp** command like so: **kdehelp /usr/doc/html/index.html**. You navigate through the HTML just like you do with KDE's help files.

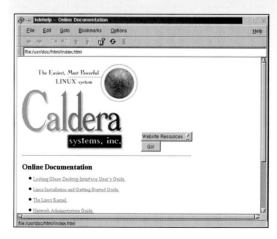

4 Read HTML with Netscape

The Navigator component of Netscape's Communicator suite of Internet tools can be used to open and browse local HTML files. Type **netscape**, followed by the path to a file, like so: **netscape /usr/doc/html/index.html**. Netscape has the most features of any browser included with OpenLinux.

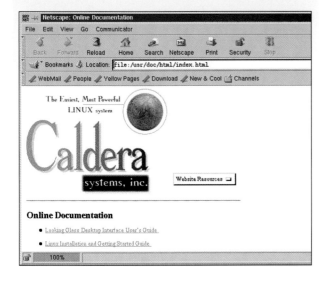

5 Read PostScript with gv

From the command line of a terminal window, type **gv**, followed by the path to a PostScript document like so: **gv /usr/doc/xv-3.10/ xvdocs.ps.gz**. To scroll around a page, move your mouse cursor to the sliding box underneath the **Save Marked** menu item on the main window. Click and drag the box to scroll the currently displayed page. To scroll forward through the document, press the **Spacebar**. To move backward, press the **B** key.

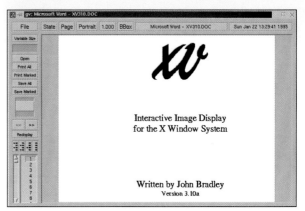

End

How-To Hints

A Foxy Trick Using Lynx

Did you know that the Lynx browser can be used to read Usenet newsgroups? This browser is full of tricks, including one you can use to get the contents of a Web page without even loading the page to your display! Pick a favorite Web site that displays updated information. On the command line, type **lynx**, followed by the page's URL, and the Lynx **-dump** option to retrieve and save the information to a file like so: **lynx http://www.yahoo. com/headlines/news -dump >news.txt**.

Wait a Second! gv Can Read a Compressed Document!

That's right. The gv client decompresses and then displays compressed PostScript documents. It also tries to do a creditable job of handling PDF files! Read the gv manual page for more info.

The Default Navigator Home Page

The Caldera folks must like Netscape as much as many Linux users. When you start Netscape, its home page is pre-configured to **/usr/doc/html/index.html**, a great starting place to learn about OpenLinux!

How to Read Portable Document Format Files

The Portable Document Format is a popular medium for many types of documents. This file format can include links similar to HTML files and supports embedded graphics, video, and sound. The most powerful PDF file viewer is Adobe's Acrobat Reader, which you can download from **http://www.adobe.com/ prodindex/acrobat/readstep.html**. Follow the directions on the Adobe Web pages and download Acrobat for Linux **ar302lin.tar.Z**. If you don't feel like using Adobe's software, you can try the xpdf client, found under the **/usr/X11R6/bin** directory.

Begin

1 Install Adobe Acrobat

Download the file to your home directory and then type **tar xvzf ar302lin.tar.Z**. This decompresses the downloaded Acrobat archive, and then creates a directory called **ILINXR.install**. To navigate to the new **ILINXR.install** directory, type **cd ILINXR.install**.

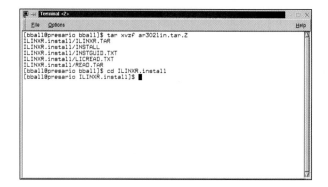

2 Read License Agreement

Type **su -c INSTALL**. After you enter the root password and press the **Enter** key, the installation process presents a license file. Scroll through the license file by pressing the **Spacebar**.

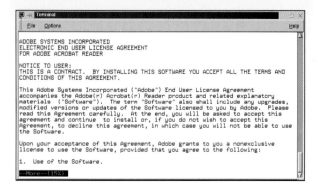

3 Finish Installation

Type the word **accept** and press **Enter**. The install process asks for an installation directory (**/usr/local/Acrobat3**). Press **Enter**. If the directory does not exist, you're asked whether it's okay to create it. Press **Enter** and the installation finishes.

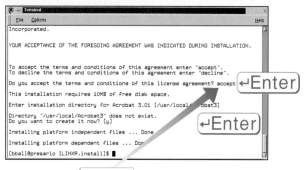

4 Start Adobe Acrobat

From the command line of a terminal window, type the complete path to Adobe acrobat: **/usr/local/Acrobat3/bin/acroread &.** Acrobat's main window appears in your display. Open the **File** menu, and select the **reader.pdf** menu item to display Acrobat's Online Guide. To exit Acrobat, open the **File** menu and select **Exit**.

Change view buttons

Previous, next page buttons

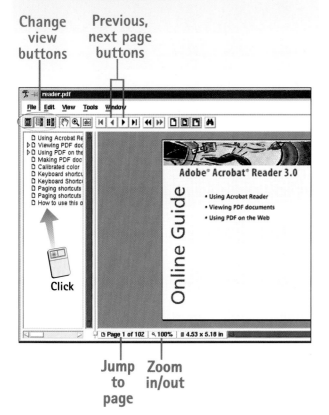

Click

Jump to page

Zoom in/out

5 Read a Portable Document File

Use the xpdf client to read PDF files. From the command line of your terminal window, type **xpdf**, followed by the name of a PDF file, like so: **xpdf /usr/local/Acrobat3/Reader/help /reader.pdf &.** The main **xpdf** window appears. To navigate through a PDF document, click the **Previous Page** or **Next Page** button in the lower-left corner of the display, or follow the document links on a page's display.

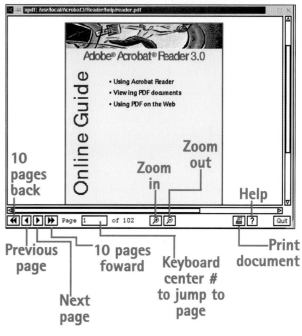

10 pages back

Zoom in

Zoom out

Help

Previous page

Next page

10 pages foward

Keyboard center # to jump to page

Print document

End

How-To Hints

PDF Readers Can Be Handy

Linux users in the United States can appreciate PDF document readers especially during mid-April. The Internal Revenue Service distributes new tax publications and forms in PDF format every year.

Task

6

Finding Files and Text

*T*here will be more than 67,000 files on your hard drive if you do a full installation of OpenLinux. These files include more than 2,000 programs; 11,000 compressed text files; 300 uncompressed text files; 1,100 device files; and 6,000 graphics files. That's a lot of files! At some point you might need to know whether a certain file is installed, where it's located, or what it contains.

This chapter shows you how to find files and how search inside files using the kfind client to find what you need. With a little practice, you should be able to find anything in your OpenLinux system.

How to Use the kfind Client

The kfind program is included with the K Desktop Environment and is a handy tool that you can use to search your OpenLinux directories. You must start an X11 session before using kfind. From the command line of your console, start X and KDE by typing **kde**.

Begin

1 Start kfind

Click the **Find Utility** button on your desktop's panel.

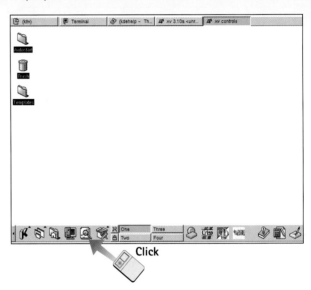

Click

2 Enter a Search File Name

The **kfind** window appears. To start a search, click the **Named** field and type all or part of the name of a file. You can also use wildcards to search for a matching file name. For example, to find any files containing the letters **PPP**, enter **PPP*** in the field.

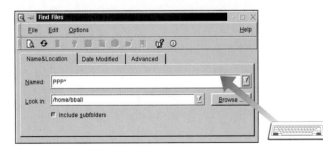

3 Set a Search Location

To tell kfind where to look on your hard drive, click the **Browse** button on the **kfind** window. A small dialog appears. Click the pop-up menu at the top of the dialog, select the **/** character, and then click the **OK** button. The forward slash (**/**), or root directory, is the base of your OpenLinux system. Selecting this directory means that kfind searches your entire hard drive.

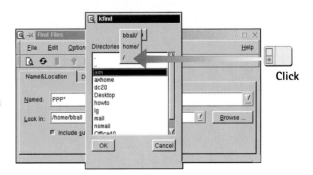

Click

4 Start the Search

To start the search, click the **Start Search** button on kfind's toolbar. Alternatively, you can press **Ctrl+F** or select the **Start Search** menu item from the **File** menu.

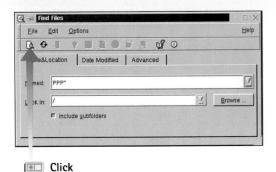

 Click

5 Open a File

The **kfind** window expands and presents a scrolling list of found files and directories. Note that a number of toolbar buttons are now active. These buttons enable you to open a file, select the file for archiving, delete a file, get information about a file (such as ownership or permissions), open the file's folder, or save the search results. To open a file, such as the PostScript version of the PPP FAQ, double-click its filename in the list.

Double Click

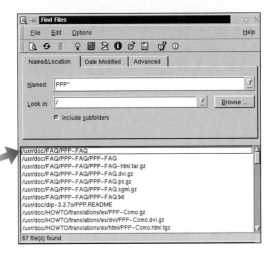

6 Open a File

After you double-click the file, kfind launches the appropriate program to display the file (in this case, kghostview, to read PostScript).

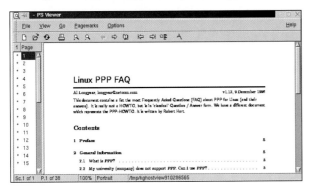

End

How-To Hints

I Only Want to Find New Files

Don't worry. You can use kfind to perform a number of advanced types of searches. See the next task, "How to Do Advanced Searches," for details on searching for files by date.

Is kfind the Only Way to Search?

Certainly not! In fact, you can use nearly a dozen other programs to find files. One of the easiest to use is **whereis**. For details about using **whereis** (which works from the command line of your console or an X11 terminal window), read the **whereis** man page (type **man whereis** at the command prompt).

How to Do Advanced Searches

You can also use the kfind client to perform advanced searches of your OpenLinux system. For example, you can search your system for the largest programs, see a list of all files created in the last 24 hours, or get a list of all the sound files included with OpenLinux.

Begin

1 Start kfind

Start kfind (the easiest way is to click the **Find Utility** button on your desktop's panel). When the **kfind** window appears, click the **Advanced** tab.

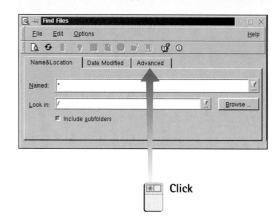

Click

2 Specify a File Type

Click the drop-down menu for the **Of Type** field, and then scroll down and select the type of file you want to find, such as **Pdf Document**. (Portable document files, which usually have the extension **.pdf**, are used by Adobe Acrobat and the xpdf document reader.)

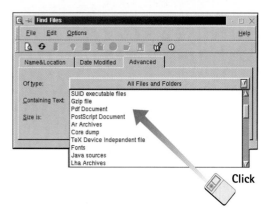

Click

3 Specify a Name and Location

Click the **Name&Location** tab. To find all PDF files, place an asterisk (*) in the **Named** field. To search your entire OpenLinux system, specify the root (/) directory. To start your search, click the **Start Search** button. Any found files appear in the **kfind** window.

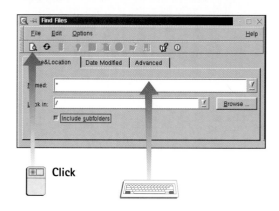

Click

4 Search by Date

Another handy kfind feature is its capability to search your system's files or directories by date. In the main **kfind** window, click the **New Search** button on the far left of kfind's toolbar to clear any previous settings, and then click the **Date Modified** tab. To find files created on your system in the last 24 hours, click the **Find All Files Created or Modified:** button, and then click the **During the Previous** button. The default number of days is **1**, but you can change your search to use any number of days by clicking in the text field and entering a number. When finished, click the **Name&Location** tab, set the location, and then start the search.

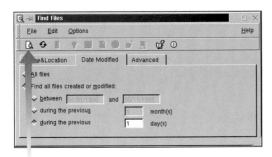

 Click

6 Get File Information

To find out more about a file or directory, select its name in the found file list, and then click the **Properties** button on kfind's toolbar. A dialog appears, showing general information about the file. Click on the other tabs to see who owns the file (its *ownership*) and what you can do with it (its *permissions*).

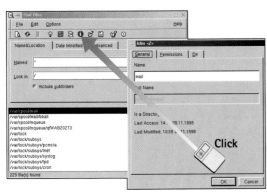

Click

5 Delete a Found File

You'd be surprised how many files are created or modified in a 24-hour period on your OpenLinux computer, especially if you leave the computer on all the time! To delete a found file or directory, select its name in the found files list, and then click the **Delete** button on the kfind toolbar. Fortunately, kfind first asks whether you want to delete the found item.

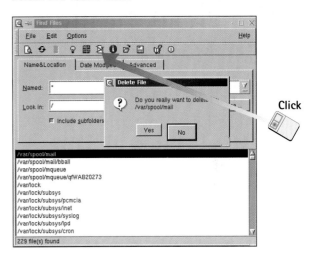

Click

How-To Hints

kfind is Taking Too Long!

If you find that a search is taking too long, click the **Stop Search** button on kfind's toolbar (it looks like a traffic light). Then try entering a more specific search in the **Named** field, or enter a specific directory, such as **/usr**, in the **Look in** field.

Search Expressions

Using wildcards in search expressions is an art form in Linux. As you become more proficient in finding files, you learn how to use pattern-matching characters. Strings of these characters, such as *?*[a-z1-9\)].**, are called regular and extended expressions. To learn more about creating regular and extended expressions, see the **grep** and **ed** man pages.

End

How to Search Documents

By now, you should see how helpful kfind can be when you need to find the name of a file. But what if you want to find a certain word or phrase inside a file, and you're not sure of the file's location or name? Relax. You can use kfind to quickly pinpoint the file you need. This task shows you how to use kfind to find words or phrases inside files—even compressed files!

Begin

1 Browse for the Search Location

Suppose you're looking for help about how to undelete a file. (This is usually a hopeless task, but reading about undeleting now might help you in the future.) First, click kfind's **New Search** button. Next, click the **Browse** button to specify the directory you want to search in the **Look in** field.

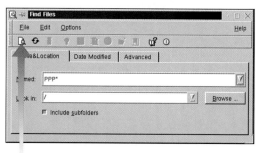

Click

2 Set the Search Location

Navigate to the **/usr/doc/HOWTO** directory, and click the **OK** button.

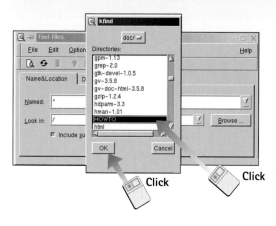

Click Click

3 Set Advanced Search

Click the Advanced tab in kfind's window. In the **Containing Text** field, type **undelete**. Then click the **Start Search** button.

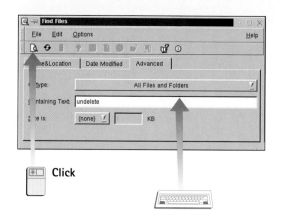

Click

4 Review Found Files

You see a list of found files. Note that the phrase *undelete* is not in any of the files' names! Select a file, such as **Ext2fs-Undeletion.html**, by clicking it.

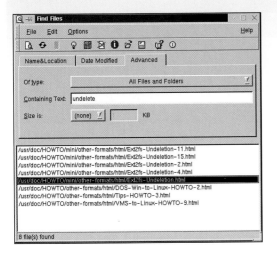

5 Open a Document's Folder

To open a document's folder, or directory, click the **Open Containing Folder** button. The file's directory displays on your desktop.

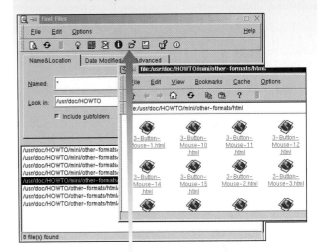

 Click

6 Read the Document

To read the file, double-click its name in kfind's list, or select the file, and then click kfind's **Open** button in the toolbar. The file (in this case, an HTML document) is opened and displayed by the appropriate reader.

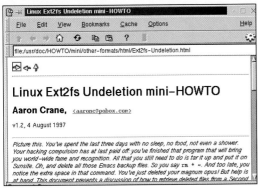

End

How-To Hints

Search and Destroy

You can search and delete found files all at once. It's not recommended that you do so however, until you've honed your searching skills. When you do, you might be ready to tackle the **find** command! This program has a plethora of command-line options and can run other commands that act on found files. Make sure to read the **find** man page before using **find** to delete files!

Other Ways to Search Inside Files

Some of the most capable searching commands included with OpenLinux are in the **grep** family: **grep**, **egrep**, and **fgrep**. Although these commands are easy to use, you can build very arcane and complex search criteria by using regular and extended expressions. Read the **grep** man page for information.

Task

7

Connecting to the Internet

*G*etting connected is an essential part of the computing experience. When you connect your computer to the Internet, you can send and receive electronic mail, browse the World Wide Web, download new software, read Usenet news, even watch TV from other countries! This chapter will show how to connect to your Internet service provider (or *ISP*) using the kppp client included with KDE (KDE is discussed in Chapter 3, "Getting Started with the K Desktop Environment").

I'll assume you're using an ISP that supports the Point-to-Point Protocol, or PPP. Although there are a number of ways to connect to the Internet, PPP is the most commonly supported protocol. And as Linux grows in popularity, more and more ISPs are supporting Linux and with good reason: Linux is a great way to connect and use the Internet!

You need to have a modem connected to your computer, and you need to know the following:

- ✓ Which serial port is connected to your modem
- ✓ Your account name and password for your ISP
- ✓ Your ISP's domain name (such as **erols.com**)
- ✓ Your ISP's domain name server addresses in numerical form (such as **205.198.114.9**)
- ✓ How your Internet address is assigned—that is, whether it is the same all the time (static), or different each time you log on (dynamic)

The methods outlined in this chapter work for many ISPs. You should know that there are a number of different ways to set up and connect to the Internet with Linux. See the How-To Hints for pointers on more information and troubleshooting. ●

How to Set Up Your Modem Connection

Make sure that your modem works and that you can dial out by using the Linux Support Team's Installation and System Administration Utility, or *LISA*. You should know what COM port your modem uses; LISA will create a file called **modem** under the **/dev** directory that points to the correct port. COM (serial communications) ports under Linux have the name **ttyS0**, **ttyS1**, **ttyS2**, or **ttyS3**, and are defined as devices under the **/dev** directory. These devices correspond with COM1, COM2, COM3, or COM4. If you're not sure what COM ports you have (or that Linux has recognized), pipe the output of the **dmesg** command through the **fgrep** command like this: **dmesg | fgrep tty**.

Begin

1 Start the LISA Command

From the command line of your console or a terminal window, run the **su** program with its **-c** command-line option to start the LISA utility: **su -c "lisa —hardware"**. Press **Enter**, type the superuser (or root) password, and press **Enter** again. LISA will start by opening its **Hardware Configuration** menu. Press the **down arrow** key on your keyboard to scroll down to the **Configure Modem** entry and press **Enter** to start the modem configuration.

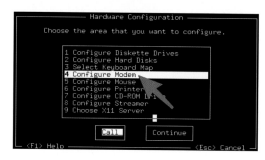

2 Start the Modem Configuration

The **Modem Type Selection** menu will appear. Again, use either the arrow keys or a number key to highlight the type of modem you use with OpenLinux, and then press **Enter**. If you're not sure what type of modem you have, choose either **Unknown modem type** or **Hayes-compatible modem**.

3 Choose the Serial Port for Your

After you select your modem, you'll be asked to select a serial port. Under OpenLinux, the serial device for COM2 is **/dev/ttyS1**. Scroll through the list, pick the port, and press the **Enter** key. For more information about determining which serial port to select, see this task's How-To Hints.

4 Choose Your Modem's Speed

When the **Data Transfer Rate** menu appears, scroll through and pick a rate one menu item higher than advertised for your modem, and then press the **Enter** key. For example, if you have a 56K modem, try selecting **115200 bps**. Unless your ISP limits incoming calls to certain baud rates, it's better to try a connection with a faster rate.

5 Enter Your Fax Number

The next menu asks you to enter a modem fax ID. This is your fax number. Most, but not all, modems support sending and receiving faxes (see Chapter 9, "Sending and Receiving Fax Documents," for details about faxing with OpenLinux). If you want to enter your fax number, simply type it in and then press the **Enter** key (if you don't need to fax, press **Enter** to skip this step). When LISA's main menu reappears, press the **Esc** key, and you're finished!

End

How-To Hints

Sleuthing Serial Ports

For more info about your computer's serial ports and OpenLinux? Run the **zless** text pager from the command line to read the Serial-HOWTO. Type **zless /usr/doc/HOWTO/Serial-Howto.gz**.

Some Modems Will Not Work with Linux!

If you have a so-called *WinModem*, or *controllerless* modem, stop! Go out and buy a "real" modem, which will work with any computer or operating system. Modems that require special drivers or software data pumps in order to work won't work with OpenLinux—period.

Using a PC Card Modem?

Using a laptop with OpenLinux? In order to use a PC card modem, you must first enable PCMCIA service. Log in as the root operator, and then use a text editor to create a file called **pcmcia** under the **/etc/sysconfig** directory. The file should contain (for most users) the following lines:

```
PCMCIA=yes
PCIC=i82365
OPTS="poll_interval=300"
```

For more information about using PC cards with OpenLinux, read the PCMCIA-HOWTO under the **/usr/doc/pcmcia-cs** directory.

How to Set Up Your Internet Connection

This section will show you how to create and configure your Internet connection using the Internet dial-up tool, kppp, included with KDE. After you properly configure your kppp account, you'll be able to log on to the Internet with two mouse clicks.

Begin

1 Start an X Session

Start an X session using KDE from the command line of your console. Type the word **kde** and press the **Enter** key.

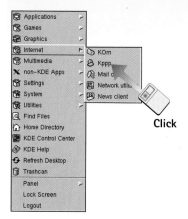

Click

2 Launch the kppp Tool

Click the **Application Starter** button (the large K) on your desktop's panel, select **Internet**, and choose the item **Kppp** to launch kppp. (Alternatively, you can type the command **kppp** on the command line of an X11 terminal window and press the **Enter** key to start kppp.)

```
[bball@presario bball]$ kde
```

3 Create Your Account

In the main kppp dialog, click the **Setup** button. This launches the **kppp Configuration** dialog.

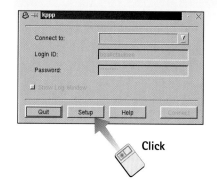

Click

4 Start Configuring Your Account

Note the five tabs in the **kppp Configuration** dialog: **Accounts**, **Device**, **Modem**, **PPP**, and **About**. Click the **Accounts** tab, and then click the **New** button to start the setup.

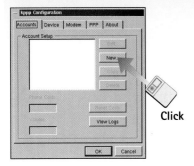

Click

5 Enter Dial Setup Info

In the **New Account** dialog, enter your ISP's name (for example, **Erols**), and the ISP's phone number that your modem will dial. If you don't mind storing your Internet connection's password on your computer (it won't be transmitted when you dial out), check the **Store password** check box. If you'd like to run a program automatically when you connect or disconnect (such as a Web browser), enter its name in the appropriate field.

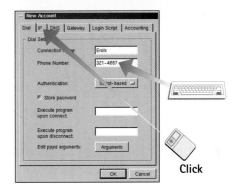

Click

6 Select Your Internet Protocol

Click the **IP** tab. Here, you specify whether your IP address is dynamic or static. If your ISP has provided you with a dynamic address, click the **Dynamic IP Address** button. If you have a static address, click the **Static IP Address** button and enter the address, along with the subnet mask (ask your ISP for details). If you want your computer's hostname to change to one assigned by your ISP, check the **Auto-configure hostname from this IP** button (it's okay to leave this unchecked).

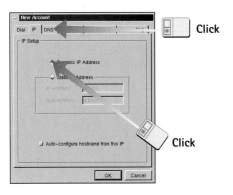

Click

Click

7 Configure Domain Name Service

Click the **DNS** tab, and then enter your ISP's domain name. (This is usually the name you see to the right of the at (@) sign of your email address.) Next, type your ISP's DNS number in the **DNS IP Address** field, and click the **Add** button. If you have a second DNS address, enter it and press the **Add** button again. This information will be temporarily inserted into a file called **resolv.conf** under the **/etc** directory during your PPP session.

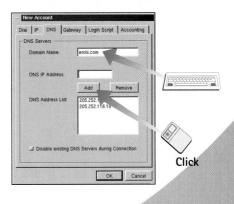

Click

8 Configure Your Login Script

Click the tab. Most ISP's computers will send a prompt such as **login:** after your modem connects, so select **Expect** from the drop-down list next to the text field near the top of the dialog, type the phrase **ogin:** in the text field, and click the **Add** button. Next, select **Send** from the pop-up menu, enter your user name (assigned to you by your ISP), and click **Add**. Next, select **Expect** again, type the phrase **ssword:**, and click **Add**. Finally, select **Send**, type your password, and click **Add**. When finished, click the **OK** button.

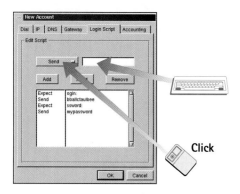

Click

9 Configure the Dial-up Device

The **kppp Configuration** dialog will reappear. Click the **Device** tab to show the serial device you'll use to connect to your ISP. **Modem Device** should be set to **/dev/modem**, **Flow Control** should be set to **CRTSCTS**, and **Line Termination** should be set to **CR/LF**. If you have a 56K (or V.90) modem, select **115200** as the connection speed. Delete any text in the **Modem Lock File**. The **Modem Timeout** value can be set to 60 seconds (this is the amount of time your modem will wait for a connection). The How-To Hints can tell you more about these settings.

10 Set PPP Options

Click the **PPP** tab. In the **kppp Setup** area, enter the number of seconds you'd like the pppd daemon to wait for a PPP connection (60 is a reasonable number). Enable or disable settings such as **Automatic Redial on Disconnect**, **Dock into Panel on Connect**, or **Minimize Window on Connect** by clicking the appropriate buttons. When you're finished, click **OK**.

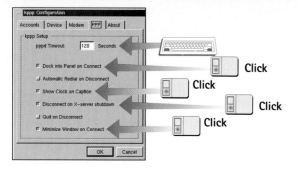

Click
Click
Click
Click

11 Define Additional Accounts

The **kppp** dialog returns, showing your new account and login ID in its dialog. You can define additional accounts by clicking the **Setup** button, and following steps 4–10.

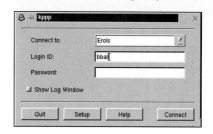

12 Connect

Click **Show Log Window** in the **kppp** dialog to watch the connection and login progress. This is handy to see what information is sent from your ISP's computer. To start your connection, click the **Connect** button in the **kppp** dialog; a **Connecting to** window and a **Login Script Debug Window** will appear. When you're connected, both windows will disappear.

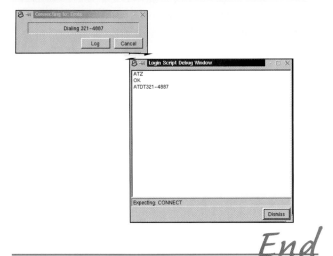

End

How-To Hints

Need More Information About kppp?

The kppp tool comes with a 10-section handbook. To read all about kppp, click the **Help** button in kppp's initial dialog. You'll find loads of tips and tricks, along with detailed information about each of its options and settings.

Make Sure Your OpenLinux Kernel Supports PPP

In order to connect with your ISP, you need not only the pppd software, but also kernel support for PPP. You should be okay with a default OpenLinux installation, but you can quickly check for PPP support from the command line of your console or an X11 terminal window. Pipe the output of the **dmesg** command through the **fgrep** command to search for PPP in your OpenLinux bootup messages like this:

```
dmesg | fgrep PPP
```

You should see something like this:

```
PPP: version 2.2.0 (dynamic
channel allocation)
PPP Dynamic channel allocation
code copyright 1995 Caldera, Inc.
PPP line discipline registered.
```

How to Start, Check, and Stop Your Internet Connection

You'll now see how to start your PPP connection. In addition, you learn about features of the kppp tool that you can also use to check your modem and the progress of your connection for troubleshooting. You'll also learn about other Linux tools that you can use to diagnose your connection.

Begin

1 Start kppp

Start kppp by clicking the **Application Starter** button, selecting **Internet**, and choosing **Kppp**. When the **kppp** dialog appears, select the account you want to connect to from the **Connect to** drop-down list and enter your password (if necessary). To start the connection, click the **Connect** button.

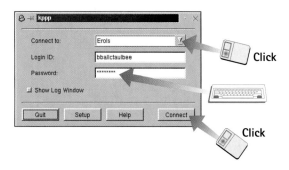

2 Monitor Your Connection

The **kppp Connecting to** dialog will appear. A one-line prompt will tell you the status of the connection. If you selected **Minimize Window on Connect** in the **PPP** tab when you set up your account, the monitor window will disappear into your desktop's taskbar (at the top of your display by default) when the connection is made.

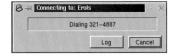

3 Check the Connection

If you'd like to see some information about your connection, click the **kppp Monitor** button in your desktop's taskbar. The connection monitor will appear. Click its **Details** button. The **kppp Statistics** dialog will appear, showing your current IP addresses along with detailed statistics about the type and amount of data flowing into and out of your PPP connection. Note that the connection window shows your connection speed and a running clock of your connection time.

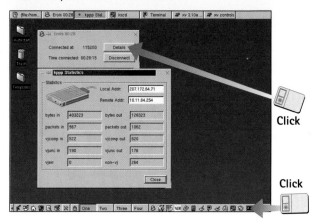

4 Check Your Modem

You can monitor your modem activity during your online sessions if you selected **Dock into Panel on Connect** in the **PPP** tab. A tiny indicator, showing two colored circles, will be embedded in your desktop's panel after a connection is made. Data flowing into and out of your computer through the modem will flash the circles green. This is handy for making sure you'll still connected during long downloads of large files.

5 Stop Your PPP Session

There are at least two ways to stop your PPP session. One is to click the button for kppp's connection dialog in your desktop's taskbar. When the dialog appears, click the **Disconnection** button. Another way is to right-click the kppp modem monitor in your panel and choose **Disconnect** from the pop-up menu.

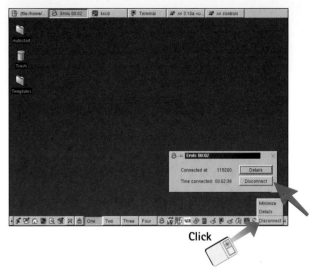

Click

End

How-To Hints

Having Trouble Connecting?

You'll find a number of documents installed on your system concerning setting up and troubleshooting your PPP connection. First, make sure to thoroughly read kppp's handbook (click the **Help** button when you first start kppp). Next, use the **zless** command to read the PPP-HOWTO. From the command line of your console or X11 terminal window, type **zless /usr/doc/HOWTO/PPP-HOWTO.gz**.

Troubleshoot Your Connection Using kppp

Need to see what's going on after you click the **Connect** button? Click the **Show Log Window** button on kppp's main dialog before you click the **Connect** button. A window will appear in the lower-right portion of your display, showing you commands sent to and received by your modem.

Can't See Your kppp Modem Monitor?

Can't see your clock? Chances are you won't see the kppp modem monitor either. You'll need to configure your panel to use smaller icons. Click the **Application Starter**, choose **Panel**, and select **Configure**. A dialog will appear, enabling you to make your panel larger or smaller.

How to Install and Use AOL Instant Messenger

One of the latest and most fun pieces of Internet communications software for Linux is AOL's Instant Messenger, or IM. You don't have to subscribe to AOL to use Instant Messenger, but you can use it to instantly chat with friends who do use AOL or Instant Messenger. The service is free, and you don't have to pay for the software. IM works by constantly checking and instantly notifying you when a friend logs in. You can then send an instant message to chat!

Begin

1 Sign Up for IM

Navigate to **http://www.aol.com/aim/home.html**. Sign up for the service by selecting a screen name and a password and entering your email address. From there, follow the prompts to go to the download section and select the Java version.

2 Open a Terminal Window

Click the **Application Starter** button, choose **Utilities**, and click **Terminal** to start a terminal window.

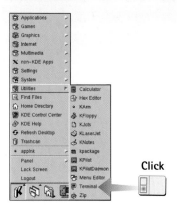

Click

3 Start the Installation

To start the installation, use a command line such as **sh aim_linux.sh**. A license agreement screen will appear. Several screens of information will scroll by. IM will be installed in a directory called **aim** in your home directory.

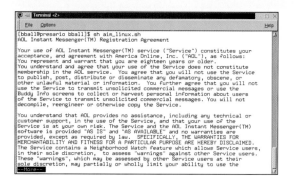

4 Start Instant Messenger

Start your Internet connection, and then start IM by typing **aim/aim&** and pressing the **Enter** key. The IM login dialog will appear. Enter your user name in the **Screen Name** field, press the **Tab** key, and then enter your password and press **Enter** to log into IM.

Click

5 Respond to the Email

The IM main dialog will appear, as will the Login dialog, which informs you that in order to use all IM's features, you must become a registered user by replying to an email message sent by AOL. (See Chapter 8 for details about using email.)

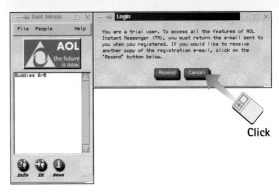

Click

6 Configure AOL Instant

Click IM's **File** menu, and then click **Options** and **Edit Preferences** to configure Instant Messenger.

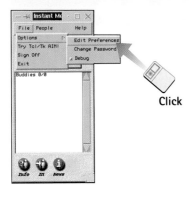

Click

7 Add an IM Buddy

When IM's **Setup** dialog appears, click the **Buddy List** entry on the left-hand side of the window, and then click the **Add Buddy** button. A highlighted ***New Buddy*** entry will appear. Type a friend's AOL screen name, and then click the **Apply** button to add it to your Buddy List. IM notifies you when users named in your Buddy List log in.

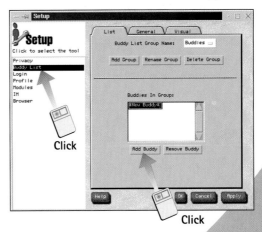

Click

Click

Continues

8 Select Privacy

Click the **Privacy** entry on the left-hand side of the window to configure IM for your privacy preferences. Use the **Permit** tab to specify whom should be notified when you are logged on to IM. Use the **Privacy** tab for other settings, such as email or nickname privacy. When you're finished, click the **OK** button. The dialog will disappear, and IM will wait for your buddies to log in.

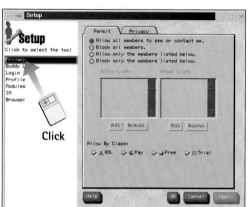

Click

9 Send an Instant Message

When one of your buddies logs in to IM, his or her name will appear in IM's Buddy List. To send an instant message, click your buddy's name, and then click the **IM** button at the bottom of the dialog. A message dialog will appear. Enter your message, and then click the **Send** button.

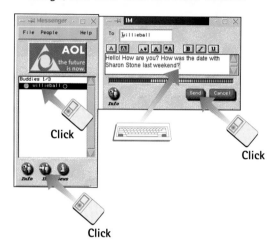

Click

Click

Click

10 Reply to an Instant Message

When your buddy sends or replies to an instant message, you can either ignore the message or click the **Respond** button. The message window will split, with your buddy's message above and a text area for your response below. Enter your response and click the **Send** button to reply. Note that there are formatting buttons, so you can format the text in your reply!

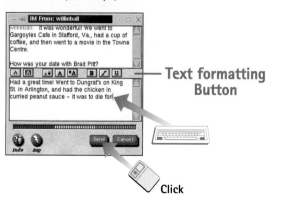

Text formatting Button

Click

11 Quit IM

To quit IM, you can either sign off or quit the program entirely. To quit IM, click the **File** menu and select **Exit**. A dialog will appear and ask you to confirm. Click the **OK** button to exit.

Click

End

How-To Hints

Can't Run AOL's Instant Messenger?

If you install and then try to run IM, but get an error message about not being able to find **Oscar.main**, don't worry! Use the glint client or **rpm** command to uninstall the Java Development Kit. Then, if you're using the bash shell, use the **unset** command to remove the default Java environment variable; simply type **unset JAVA_HOME**. Reinstall IM, and then try starting it again.

Have Too Many Friends?

Well, everyone should be so lucky! But if you have a lot of different friends, acquaintances, students, or even clients, use IM's Buddy List Group feature to categorize and organize your IM buddies. Click **Setup** from IM's initial dialog, or click **File**, then **Options**, and then **Preferences** while logged in. At the top of the **Buddy List** dialog in **Setup**, you'll see buttons to **Add**, **Rename**, or **Delete** buddy groups. This is a handy way to organize your lists.

Configure IM Offline

You don't have to have an active Internet connection or be logged into IM to configure most features of this program. You do have to be online and logged in to change options concerning your nickname or its privacy. You can, however, change which buddies can send instant messages, or which you want blocked. See the **Permit** tab in the **Privacy** dialog (refer to step 8).

Task

8

Using Netscape Communicator

Netscape Communicator is a free suite of Internet tools that you can use with OpenLinux. You can use this software not only to browse the Web, send and receive email, read news, or download files, but also to create your own Web pages. Much of the magic of the Internet comes alive with these easy-to-use software tools for OpenLinux, and these programs are part of the Communicator suite of Internet productivity programs included with OpenLinux on this book's CD-ROM.

Netscape Communicator is installed into the **/opt/netscape** directory during a full OpenLinux installation. You must run X11 in order to use Netscape Communicator (the tasks in this chapter show how to use it with X and KDE; see Chapter 3, "Getting Started with the K Desktop Environment"). You must also have an active Internet connection in order to browse the Web, send and receive email, or read Usenet news (see Chapter 7, "Connecting to the Internet," for details).

In this chapter, you'll see how to set up, configure, and use Netscape Communicator to make the most out of your online sessions. One component not discussed in this chapter is Netscape Composer. But don't despair: For a tutorial on using Composer, select Communicator's **Help** menu, click the **Help Contents** menu item, and then click the **Composing and Editing Web Pages** item in Communicator's **NetHelp** dialog. ●

How to Configure Netscape Communicator

Your first task is to configure Netscape Communicator. By entering several short screens of information, you'll be able to use Communicator to its fullest.

Begin

1 Start Communicator

Click the **Application Starter** button, choose **Applications**, and select **Communicator**.

Click

2 Explore Navigator

After reading the initial **Communicator** license, click the **Accept** button. Communicator will then create a directory called **.netscape** in your home directory and automatically display a Web page from a directory on your hard drive that you can use to read about OpenLinux. Note that Communicator automatically runs Navigator by default when it starts. Navigator has a **File** menu, a toolbar, and numerous drop-down menus and buttons in its window. To start your configuration, click the **Edit** menu, and then choose **Preferences**.

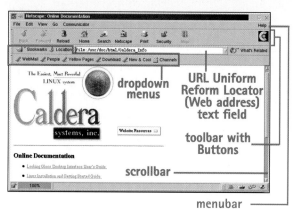

3 Configure Appearance Preferences

The **Appearance** preferences screen opens. In the **On startup, launch** section, select the component you'd like to launch by default. In the **Show Toolbar As** section, select how you want Communicator to display its toolbar. To configure Communicator's default fonts or colors, click the appropriate item under the **Appearance** list in the **Category** window on the left.

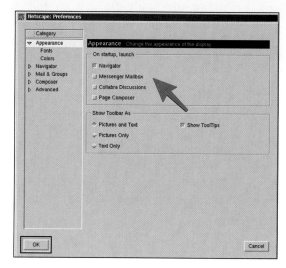

4 Configure Navigator

Click the triangle to the left of the **Navigator** item in the **Category** list to open the **Navigator** preferences screen. Choose how you'd like Navigator to start by clicking the appropriate button in the **Browser starts with** section. If your ISP provides you with a home page, enter its Web address in the **Location** field of the **Home page** section. Tell Navigator how many days it should remember pages you've browsed by entering a number in the **History** section.

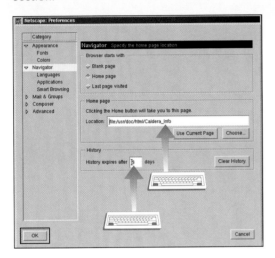

5 Set a New Helper Application

Click **Applications** under **Navigator** in the **Category** list. The **Applications** preferences screen appears. To always save downloaded files to a specific directory, click **Choose** and select a directory. Near the top of the screen, you'll see a list of *helper applications*; these are programs that support specific types of documents on the Web. Click **New** to configure Netscape to handle a new type of program or document (I'll use Adobe Acrobat as an example).

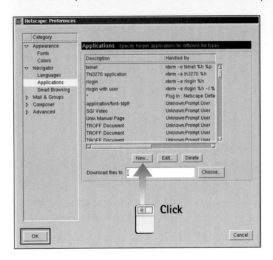

Click

6 Create a New Helper Application

Type **Adobe Acrobat PDF Files** in the **Description** field, enter **application/pdf** in the **MIMEType** field, and type **pdf** in the **Suffixes** field. In the **Handled By** section, click **Application**, and enter the path to Acrobat's executable program. (If you followed along in Chapter 5, this will be **/usr/local/Acrobat3/bin/acroread %s**.) Click **OK** to save the new helper application, and again to exit Communicator's **Preferences** dialog.

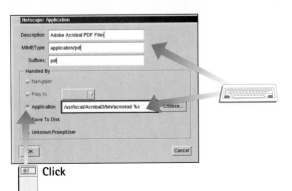

Click

How-To Hints

Using Netscape Command-Line Options

If you start Communicator from the command line of an X11 terminal window, you can use several helpful command-line options. For example, to launch Communicator but only display a small, floating toolbar window with component launch buttons, type **netscape -component-bar &**.

Don't want to use a large Netscape window? Use Communicator's **geometry** option to start with a small window like this: **netscape -geometry 480x320 &**.

Use the **-help** option to see a list of other command-line options.

End

How to Set Up Netscape Messenger for Email

This task will show you how to configure Netscape Messenger to send and receive electronic mail. Note: You'll first need to establish a PPP connection with your ISP. You'll also need to know your email address (such as **bball@staffnet.com**), the name of your ISP's email server (such as **smtp.staffnet.com**), and the type of email protocol your ISP's email server supports (such as POP3).

Begin

1 Select Mail and Groups

Start Netscape Communicator. Select the **Edit** menu, and click **Preferences**. In the **Preferences** dialog, click **Mail & Groups** in the **Category** list.

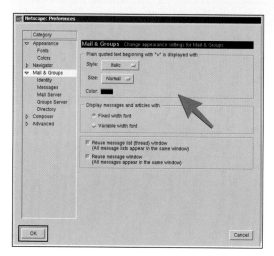

2 Enter Your Identity

Click the **Identity** list item under **Mail & Groups**. Enter your name, and type your full email address *exactly* as provided by your ISP.

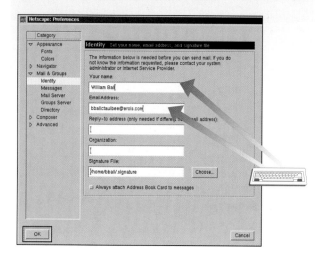

3 Configure Outgoing Messages

Click **Messages** under **Mail & Groups**. In the **Message Properties** section, specify whether you want messages sent as HTML, how you'd like to handle reply messages, and how long you'd like each line of text to be in your messages. Click the **More Options** button to view other message-formatting options.

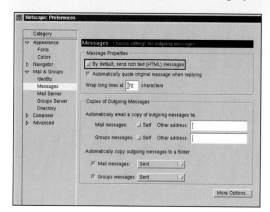

4 Enter Your Mail Server

Click the **Mail Server** list item under **Mail & Groups** in the **Category** list. In the **Mail Server** dialog, enter your mail server user name (such **bballctaulbee**). In the **Outgoing Mail (SMTP) Server** field, enter **localhost**. In the **Incoming Mail Server** field, enter the name of your ISP's mail server (such as **pop.erols.com**). Click the appropriate mail server type (usually POP3, but some ISPs use IMAP4). You can obtain all this information from your ISP.

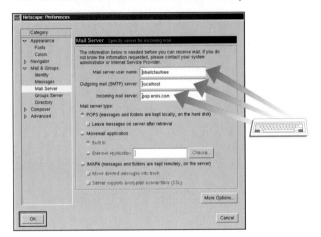

5 Enter Your Groups Server

Click the **Group Server** list item under **Mail & Groups** in the **Category** list. In the **Groups Server** dialog, enter the name of your ISP's news server (such as **news.erols.com**), and then click the **Secure** button. When finished, click the **OK** button. You're now ready to start working with email and Usenet news.

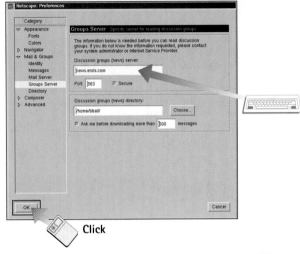

Click

End

How-To Hints

Jump Right to Netscape Mail

An easy way to proceed right into an email session to send or receive mail is to use Netscape's **-mail** option from the command line of the terminal window, like this: `netscape -mail &`. This will start Netscape Communicator's Messenger component right away.

Having Problems with Your ISP Settings for OpenLinux?

When getting ready to configure Netscape or other Internet software, make sure to get as much technical information as you can from your ISP. If you're just starting to search for a service to use, ask your potential ISP about support for Linux. If you have an existing account but are having a hard time getting your system to work right, try attending a local Linux user group, or LUG (browse to **http://www.ssc.com/glue** for more info). Want free support? Try browsing to **http://support.marko.net** and registering as a customer!

How Do I Create A Signature File?

A signature file usually contains your name, email address, organization, and perhaps a witty quote. Traditionally, this four-line text file is named **.signature** and resides in your home directory. Use your favorite text editor to create this file (see Chapter 10, "Word Processing with OpenLinux").

How to Send a Mail Message with Netscape Messenger

You can use Netscape Messenger to compose and send email. In this section, you'll learn how to start Netscape Messenger, compose a message, and then send it.

Begin

1 Select Netscape Messenger

Launch Communicator, open the **Communicator** menu, and click **Messenger Mailbox**.

Click

2 Open the Messenger Mailbox

The main Netscape **Mail & Discussions** window contains a menu bar, a toolbar, a drop-down menu button, and a main display area. The toolbar buttons, labeled **Get Msg**, **New Msg**, **Reply**, **Forward**, and so on, are used to manage your email. To compose an email message, click the **New Msg** button.

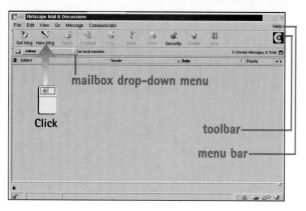

mailbox drop-down menu

Click

toolbar

menu bar

3 Compose an Email Message

In the **Compose** window, type the recipient's email address in the **To** field. In the **Subject** field, type a brief description of the message's subject. Then click the **Text** area and compose your message. Click the **Spell** button on the **Compose** window's toolbar. If an unknown word is found, Netscape will present a **Spell** dialog. Click the appropriate buttons to go through your message; when finished, click the **Stop** button.

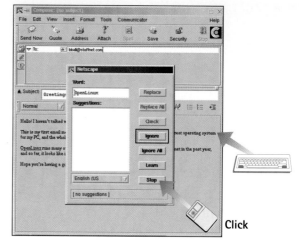

Click

4 Attach a File

To attach a file, such as a graphic image, to your message, click the **Attach** button on the **Compose** window's toolbar. In the menu that appears, click **File**; the **Attach File** dialog will appear. Scroll through your directories, and then double-click a file's name to attach it to your message.

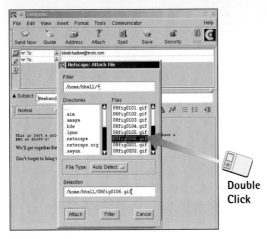

Double Click

5 Save the Message as a Draft

To save the message in draft form, open the **File** menu, and click **Save Draft**. To open a draft file for editing or sending, click the drop-down mailbox menu directly below the toolbar in the main **Messenger** window, and then click **Drafts**. To open the draft message, double click its name in the **Messenger** window, and edit as needed.

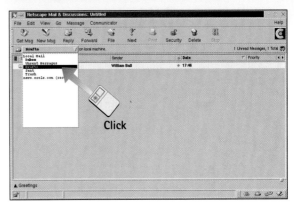

Click

6 Send or Save Your Message

When you're ready to send your message, click the **Send Now** button in the **Compose** window's toolbar. To go back to Messenger, open the **File** menu, and select **Close**.

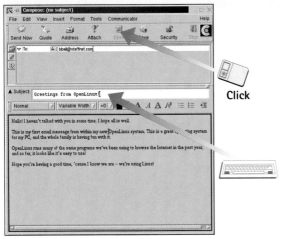

Click

How-To Hints

Formatting and Mail Preferences

If you select HMTL as the default format for your mail messages, you can send formatted messages with different fonts in different sizes with different styles—but if your mail recipient does not use Netscape, your message might look garbled (it can be hard to read HTML in raw form).

How Do I Send Postponed Messages?

If you select **Send Later** from the **File** menu in the **Compose** window, your message will be filed in the **Unsent Messages** mailbox. Access unsent messages such as those in the **Drafts** mailbox; double-click the message in the **Unsent Messages** mailbox. The message will appear in a window. Open the **File** menu, and then click **Edit Message**. You'll then be in the **Compose** window, where you can click the **Send Now** button.

End

How to Receive and Reply to Email

You can use Netscape Messenger to receive, save, and reply to email. To get started, log in to your ISP and start an Internet session.

1 Open the Messenger Mailbox

Launch Communicator, and select **Messenger Mailbox** from the Communicator **File** menu.

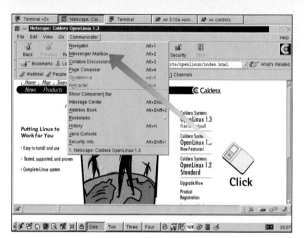

Click

2 Click the Get Msg Button

To get your mail, click the **Get Msg** button on the Messenger window's toolbar. Netscape Messenger will then ask for your password. After you type the password for your Internet account and click **OK**, Messenger will forward a request to your ISP's computer to send any waiting mail.

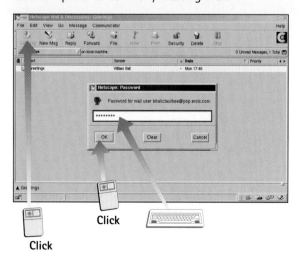

Click

Click

Click

3 Receive Email

If mail is available, a small window will appear to let you know how many messages are available, and a meter will display the progress of the message download. Netscape will store the retrieved messages in the **Inbox Messenger** mailbox, and display the messages by subject in a list. To read a retrieved message, double-click it.

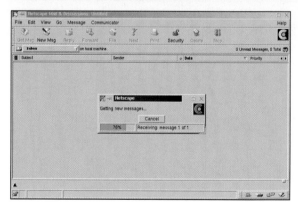

4 Read a Message

Your email will appear in a **Messenger** window. Any file attachments will be listed below the message's text. If you click the small paper-clip icon at the top of the message, a window will appear at the bottom of the message, displaying an icon representing the attachment along with the attachment's filename. If you double-click the file's icon and Netscape recognizes the attachment type, it will launch the appropriate helper application to handle the file. (For example, Adobe Acrobat will open an attached PDF file).

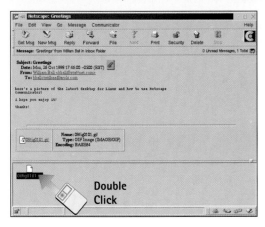

Double Click

5 Reply to a Message

To reply to a message, click the **Reply** button in the message's toolbar. The message will appear in a **Messenger Compose** window; the **To** and **Subject** fields will be automatically filled out, and the text from the message to which you are replying will remain. Type your reply, and then click the **Send Now** button to send the message immediately. As before, you can spell-check, save, or postpone sending the message.

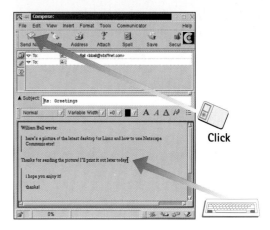

Click

6 Cancel the Reply

To cancel your reply, close the **Compose** window (open the **File** menu, and then choose **Close** to close Messenger or **Exit** to exit Communicator). Before closing, Netscape Messenger will first ask whether you want to save your reply in the **Drafts** mailbox. To discard your reply, click the **No** button.

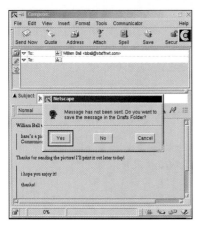

How-To Hints

Save Email or Flush Your Server?

You can configure Netscape to tell your ISP's mail server to hold on to messages after you've retrieved them. To keep your messages on your ISP's computer, open Communicator's **Edit** menu and choose **Preferences**. Click **Mail & Groups** in the **Category** list, and then click the **Mail Server** list item. In the **Mail Server** dialog, toggle the push button for the **Leave Messages on Server After Retrieval** item. Note: As a courtesy, you should periodically flush your mail from your ISP's server (besides, many ISPs impose a limit on the size or number of messages you can store on the remote computer).

End

How to Read Usenet News

Besides browsing the Web and sending and receiving email, Netscape Communicator can also be used to read Usenet news. Usenet news is a worldwide system of computers running software that stores, exchanges, and updates collections of text files, or newsgroups, organized by category and hierarchy. A newsgroup name might look something like **comp.os.linux.x**, which translates to "discussions of using the X Window System for the Linux computer operating system." Usenet news has been around since Prehistoric Times (in Internet years). In 1986, there were about 500 different newsgroups—today there are more than 40,000!

Begin

1 Open Discussions

Select **Message Center** from Netscape's **Communicator** menu. To specify what groups you'd like to join or read, click the **Join Groups** button in the **Netscape Message Center** window's toolbar.

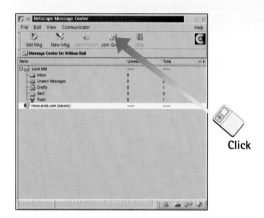

Click

2 Get Discussion Groups

The **Get Discussion Groups** window will appear. Click the **Add Server** button and type the name of your ISP's news server, which is displayed below your mail folders in the previous window. If Netscape Discussions do not start retrieving the list of newsgroups, click the **Get Discussion Groups** button on the right side of the dialog.

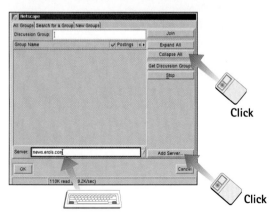

Click

Click

3 Browse Newsgroups

When Netscape finishes retrieving your ISP's list of newsgroups, a list of top-level newsgroup sections will appear. Click the **Discussion Group** field and type **comp.os.linux.a**. Netscape will automatically scroll through the list until it displays the Linux newsgroups, and will then expand the **comp.os.linux** group to show the current groups.

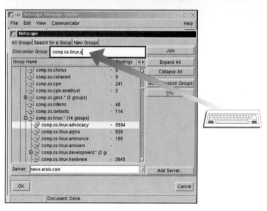

4 Subscribe to Some Newsgroups

Click in the check-mark column on the line of a group's name to subscribe to that newsgroup. A check mark will appear to show that you have joined the discussion group. Continue selecting newsgroups; when finished, click **OK**.

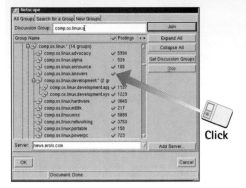

Click

5 Open Discussions Folder

Click the plus sign in front of the news folder name in the Message Center. Your subscribed newsgroups will be listed in the main window. To start reading messages in a newsgroup, double-click the group's listing.

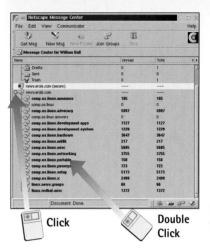

Click

Double Click

6 View Discussion Lists

The lists of messages for the newsgroup will appear in a **Mail & Discussions** window. Click the plus sign to the left of a subject to see the number of messages about a subject. Click **Reply** to reply to the current message. Click **New Msg** to post a new message to the group. When finished, open the **File** menu and then select **Close**.

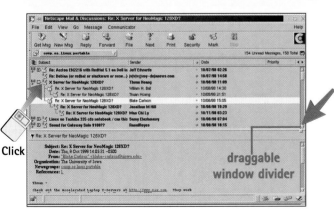

Click

draggable window divider

How-To Hints

Linux Newsgroups?

Here's a short list of Linux newsgroups you should read for more information about using Linux:

comp.os.linux.advocacy

comp.os.linux.announce

comp.os.linux.answers

comp.os.linux.hardware

comp.os.linux.misc

comp.os.linux.portable

comp.os.linux.setup

comp.os.linux.x

End

How to Browse, Download, and Print with Navigator

Netscape Navigator offers one of the most intuitive interfaces for browsing the Web of any Internet software application included with OpenLinux. This friendly program, with its large buttons and multitude of features, is a favorite tool used by millions of people around the world every day. And now you can too! Before you learn how to use some of Navigator's basic features, start KDE, and then start an Internet session with your ISP.

Begin

1 Start Navigator

To start Navigator, click its icon on the taskbar along the bottom of your screen (a lighthouse circled by a ring of fire), or click the **Application Starter** button, choose **Applications**, and then click **Navigator**.

2 Enter an Address

Enter a Web address in the **Location** field of Navigator's main window, such as **http://www.caldera.com/openlinux/index.html**. When the page displays, click a link.

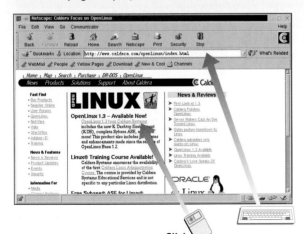

Click

3 Follow a Link

The new page will display. To return to the previous page, click the **Back** button on the Navigator toolbar. Click the **Location** field, erase the current address, and enter a FTP address (such as **ftp://ftp.caldera.com/pub**). Press **Enter**.

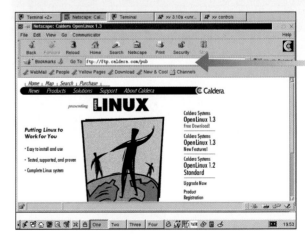

4 Jump to an FTP Site

Navigator will automatically log you in to a remote computer system and display a list of directories you can navigate (such as Web pages) or files you can download. Scroll down through the list until you see a file called **README**. Move your cursor to the file's name, hold down the **Shift** key, and click the file.

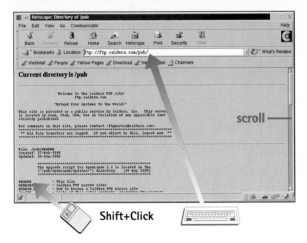

scroll

Shift+Click

5 Download a File

Navigator will display a download dialog and ask you where to save the file. Note the file's name and where it will be saved, and then click the **OK** button. Navigator will download and save the file. Navigator will then display a **Netscape Download** dialog, showing what percent of the file has been downloaded.

6 Print a File

You can use Navigator to print interesting Web pages or to create hard copy of information displayed in Navigator's window. Open the **File** menu, and then click **Print**. Navigator will display a **Print** dialog. Click the **Printer** button in the **Print To** section. If multiple pages will be printed, click the **Last Page First** button in the **Print** section (this will output pages from last to first, so you don't have to reshuffle paper after printing). Select the appropriate orientation, whether you want color, and what paper size to use. When finished, click the **Print** button.

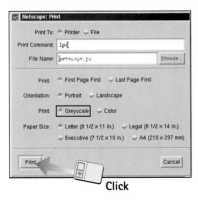

Click

How-To Hints

How to Update Pages

Netscape Communicator saves entire or portions of Web pages in a special cache (pronounced *cash*) memory on your hard drive. If you want to see the very latest version of a Web page, or you want to make sure that what you see is from the Internet and not from cache memory, hold down the **Shift** key and click the **Reload** button in Navigator's toolbar to update the page.

How to Control Storage Space

If your hard drive space is at a premium, you can limit the size of downloaded email and set Communicator to periodically flush old newsgroup messages. Navigate to Communicator's **Preferences** dialog, select the **Advanced** item under the **Category** list, and click **Disk Space**. Set the appropriate settings in the **Disk Space** dialog.

End

Task

9

Sending and Receiving Fax Documents

*M*ost (if not all) modems that work with Linux can send or receive fax documents. This chapter shows you how to configure and use the **efax** family of programs to send and receive faxes. You need to first read Chapter 7, "Connecting to the Internet," to learn how to set up and test your modem.

You don't have to use the X Window System to send, receive, or print faxes, but you do need to use X to view any received pages. Follow the tasks in this chapter and you should be faxing in no time at all!

How to Configure fax

The first step to set up for faxing is to configure the **fax** shell script, found under the **/usr/bin** directory. This command uses several programs included with OpenLinux to prepare documents for faxing. The following tasks show you how to edit and configure this script. You must be the root operator in order to configure **fax**, so log in as root before you begin.

Begin

1 Open the fax Script

Use your favorite text editor, such as pico, to open the fax command (a type of Linux command called a *shell script*). At the command line of your console or an X11 terminal, type **pico -w /usr/bin/fax** and press **Enter**.

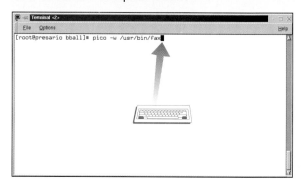

2 Configure Your Modem

Scroll down to the **DEV=** entry and type the device name for your fax modem. For example, if you have your modem on COM2, use **ttyS1**. If you used the **lisa** command to create the **/dev/modem** symbolic link, this entry should be **DEV=modem**.

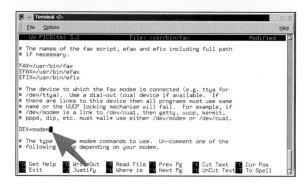

3 Select Modem Class

The **fax** command supports three types of fax protocols: Class 1, Class 2, and Class 2.0. Select the correct class for your modem by removing the pound sign (**#**) in front of the correct class. For example, if your fax modem supports Class 2 protocols, remove the pound sign before the text **CLASS=2**. Check your modem's documentation to see which fax protocol is supported. Make sure that only one protocol is selected and that the other two are preceded with a pound sign.

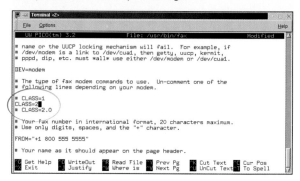

4 Enter Your Fax Number

Scroll down and enter your fax number in the **FROM=** entry. (Substitute your number for the number already present.) For example, if your fax number is 1-703-123-1234, type the entry, without hyphens, in this format: **FROM="1 703 123 1234"**.

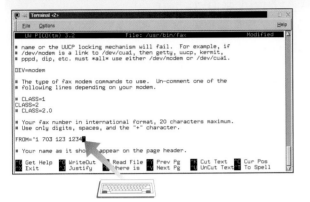

5 Enter Your Name, Save Edits

Scroll down and type your name in the **NAME=** entry. (Substitute your name or your company's name for the existing entry.) For example, if your name is Joseph Piccolo, type the entry so it looks like so: **NAME="Joseph Piccolo"**. When finished, press **Ctrl+X**, and then press **Y** to save the file.

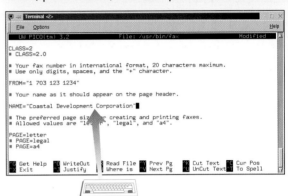

6 View Fax Test

To test your fax setup, save the output of the **fax** command's **test** option. At the command line of a terminal, type **fax test >faxtest**, and then type **less faxtest** to read the test. When finished, press **Q** to quit reading.

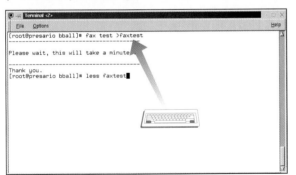

End

How-To Hints

Different Document Sizes

Change the **PAGE=** entry in the fax script to use a different default paper size (such as legal-sized paper) when faxing.

Other Options

You can set other options in the fax script, such as the default command used to print faxes or the default program used to view received faxes. OpenLinux includes all the programs you need if you use the fax script's default settings.

Troubleshooting

Read the **efax** man page for troubleshooting tips when setting up your fax modem (use a command line such as **man efax**). You'll also find a **fax** man page with tips and tricks on using the **fax** shell script.

How to Fax with OpenLinux

This task shows you how to send, receive, view, and print fax documents using the **fax** command. To view a received fax, you must first start an X11 session. In order to print a fax document, your printer must be configured to work with OpenLinux. To set up your printer, see Chapter 16, "Printing Text Files and Graphics," and follow the steps in the "How to Install a Printer" task.

Begin

1 Send a Text File

To send a text fax, use the **fax** command, along with its **send** and **–l** (lowercase *L*) options, followed by a fax number and the name of a text document. For example, to send the file **mydocument.txt** to a fax at 820-7442, type **fax send -l 8207442 mydocument.txt** and press **Enter**. The **–l** is a low resolution setting, which is safer and faster for transmission.

2 Send a PostScript Graphics File

To send a PostScript graphic by fax, use the **fax** command, along with its **send** and **–l** options, followed by a fax number and the name of the PostScript graphic. For example, to send the graphic **tiger.ps** to a fax at 820-7442, type **fax send -l 8207442 tiger.ps** and press **Enter**.

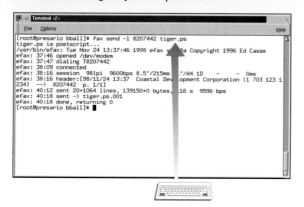

3 Set to Receive a Fax

To wait to receive a fax, use the **fax** command's **wait** option on the command line (type **fax wait** and press **Enter**). The **fax** command waits for any incoming faxes.

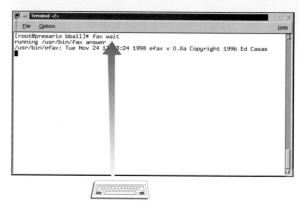

4 Check Fax Status

To check to see whether any faxes have been received, use the **fax** command's **queue** option (type **fax queue** and press **Enter**). The **fax** command lists any files in the **/var/spool/fax** directory. Each page of the received fax document is in a separate file. The first part of the filename (representing the day, month, hour, minute, and second) of each page is the same, but each page has a different extension. For example, the first page of a two-page fax document received November 24 at 1:57 p.m. is named **1124135748.001**, whereas the second page is named **1124135748.002**.

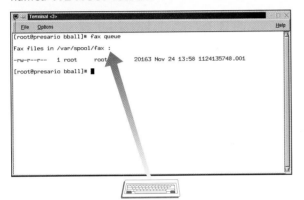

5 View a Fax

To view a fax, you must run the X Window System. Start an X11 terminal program, and use the **fax** command's **view** option, followed by the name of a fax page, to read a received fax. Using the name of one of the files from the previous step, you'd type **fax view 1124135748.001** and press **Enter**. The **fax** command automatically launches the **xv** graphics client to display your fax.

6 Print a Fax Document

To print a fax, use the **fax** command's **print** option, followed by the name of your fax document. Your printer must be configured to work with OpenLinux. Make sure your printer is connected to your computer and turned on, type **fax print 1124135748.001**, and press **Enter**.

How-To Hints

Higher Resolution Faxing

Omit the **fax** command's **-l** option to send faxes at a higher resolution. The low resolution is 98 lines per inch (completely adequate for text documents). The high resolution tries to send your document at nearly 200 lines per inch. Fax resolutions depend on the capabilities of the sending and receiving modems, so check your modem manual for more information.

How Do I Delete Received Faxes?

Use the **fax** command's **rm** option, along with the name of your fax document. Use the asterisk wildcard to delete all the pages of a fax by typing **fax rm 1124135748.*** and pressing **Enter**. Do *not* use the **rm** option without a filename, or you could delete all the files in the current directory!

End

Task

## CHAPTER 10

Word Processing with OpenLinux

Word processing is one of the most important tasks people accomplish with their computers (besides browsing the Web and playing games). You can find a rich assortment of text editors and word processors included on this book's CD-ROM; this chapter introduces you to a few of these programs. You can use these editors to produce simple text files, edit OpenLinux system configuration files, develop computer programs, or produce typeset documents. You also see how to spell check your documents and look up words in your system's dictionary.

It's important to know how to use a text editor with Linux, because you might need, at one time or another, to know how to open an OpenLinux system file and then make and save changes. Some of these editors, such as kedit, require that you use the X Window System, whereas others can be used with or without X. You should also read Chapter 12, "Getting Started with StarWriter," to learn more about word processing with the StarOffice suite of programs.

How to Use the kedit Program

One of the easiest to use editors included with OpenLinux is the kedit text editor included with the K Desktop Environment, or KDE. You need to start an X session, using KDE, in order to run kedit. Start your X session from the command line of a terminal window by typing **kde** and then press **Enter** to begin. Start kedit by clicking the **Application Starter** button, choosing **Applications** and selecting **Editor**.

Begin

1 Enter Some Text

In the **kedit** window, click the blank area and type a short letter.

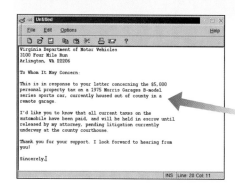

2 Select, Copy, and Paste Text

Click at the beginning of the text and then, holding down your left mouse button, drag to highlight the desired text (to highlight a single word, double-click the word). To copy the text, open the **Edit** menu and click **Copy**. After the selection is copied, click in your document where you'd like paste the text and then paste it using the **Edit** menu.

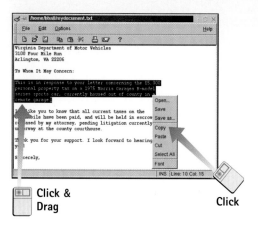

Click & Drag

Click

3 Choose a Font and System

Right-click anywhere in your document and choose **Font** from the pop-up menu. The default font is Courier, but you can use the **Select Font** dialog to change your document's font to a different family, weight, size, or style. Note that you can preview the font in the dialog. When you're satisfied with the font you've selected, click the **OK** button. Your document's text changes to the font you select.

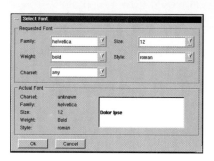

4 Change kedit's Colors

You can change the color of the document's text, as well as the color of kedit's background. Open the **Options** menu, choose **Colors**, and select **Foreground**. The **Select Color** dialog appears. Click a color from the **System Colors** section, or click in the rainbow box to select a color. When finished, do the same for the background color (select **Background** from the **Options | Colors** menu).

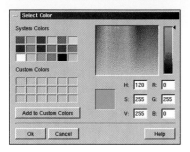

5 Save Your Document

To save your document, click the **Save Document** button on the toolbar or open the **File** menu and choose **Save**. In the **Location** field of the **Save As** dialog, type the name of your document (for example, **newdocument.txt**) and click the **OK** button.

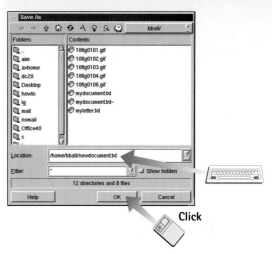

6 Print Your Document

To print your document, open the **File** menu and choose **Print** (alternatively, press **Ctrl+P**). In the **Print** dialog, click **Print directly using lpr** and then click the **Print Document** button. Click **OK**.

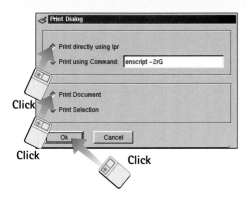

End

How-To Hints

Setting Text Wrap

Although kedit does not have a visible ruler bar with draggable margins, you can set the wrap margin to a certain number of characters per line. Open the **Options** menu and then click **KEdit Options**. In the **kedit** dialog, click **Set Fill-Column at** and type the number of characters you want per line to set the wrap margin. To use word wrap, click the **Word Wrap** button and then click **OK**.

Insert the Date or a File

You can paste text from another file by opening the **Edit** menu and clicking **Insert File**. In the **Open** dialog, double-click the name of another text file; kedit inserts the file at the current cursor location. In addition, you can insert the current date and time by selecting **Insert Date** on the **Edit** menu.

How to Start and Use CRiSPlite

One of the more complex and capable editors available for OpenLinux is the CRiSPlite editor. This program is much more than a simple text editor and offers a wealth of features to computer programmers and other text editor users. In this task, you see how to open a text document, make changes to your text, set print options, and print your document.

Begin

1 Start CRiSPlite

Click the **Application Starter** button, choose **Applications**, and select **CRiSPlite**.

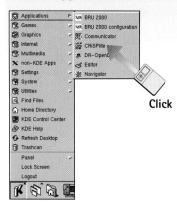

Click

2 Set Line Wrap Mode

The first time you use CRiSP, you see a small window with ordering information. Click the **OK** button to begin. Open the **Options** menu and choose **Setup**. In the **CRiSP Setup Options** dialog, scroll down to the **Language Editing** mode and press **Enter**. The **Setup: Language Specific Editing** dialog appears. To set the right margin, click the **Right Margin** field and type the number of characters you'd like for each line (55, for example). Click the **Autowrap** button to enable word wrapping and click the **Justify** button to enable line justification. Click **OK**.

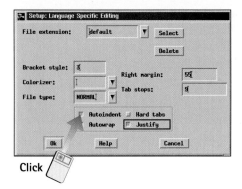

Click

3 Configure for Printing

In the **CRiSP Setup Options** dialog, scroll down to the **Printer** item and press **Enter**. The **CRISP: Printer Setup** dialog appears. Click in the **Print to File** field and type ¦ **1pr** (which is part of an OpenLinux command line used to print text files). Deselect the **Header** and **Line Nos** buttons if you do not want your document printed with line numbers and the date and time at the top of each page. When finished, click **Apply**; in the **Setup Options** dialog, click **Save Setup** to save your changes.

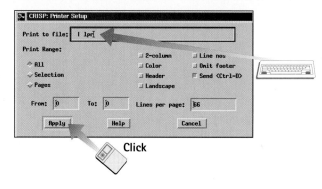

Click

4 Enter Some Text

Type some text—for example, a short letter. To use line numbers in your document, click the **Toggle Line Numbers** button on the toolbar. Line numbers appear to the left of your text. Turn off line numbers by clicking the button again.

Click

5 Save Your File

Open the **File** menu and select **Save File** (alternatively, press **Alt+W**). The **Save File** dialog appears. Type a file name, such as **mydocument.txt**, in the **File** field. Next, click the appropriate file type button—because you're using OpenLinux, click **Text**. CRiSP also creates a backup file with a tilde (~) appended to the end of your file's name. If **Overwrite** is selected in the **File Creation** section, CRiSP overwrites an existing file of the same name.

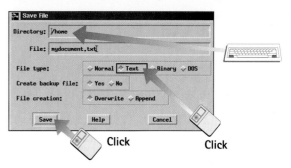

Click   Click

6 Print Your File

To print your file, click the **Print File** button on the toolbar (you can also press the **PrintScr** key on your keyboard). CRiSP sends your document directly to your printer, using the options you selected and prints the short message **File printed to: | lpr** along with the number of pages printed.

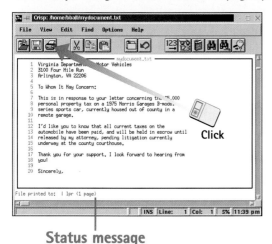

Click

Status message

End

How-To Hints

Word Wrap Won't Work!

Changes to CRiSP's setup usually do not take place automatically. Try pressing **Ctrl+A** followed by **Ctrl+E** to reload your document. If that doesn't work, press the F10 key, type **autowrap**, and click **OK**. CRiSP should print a short message in the lower-left corner of your window, telling you autowrap turned on.

Why Use Line Numbers?

CRiSP is a text editor designed to support computer programmers. Line numbers are important to programmers because programs, such as compilers or interpreters used to create new programs, report errors or problems using line numbers in a program's source code. If you're interested in learning programming, you can find a wealth of software tools on this book's CD-ROM that you can use to write programs—and CRiSP's line-number feature will help you.

How to Start and Use emacs

The emacs editor can be used to edit text, schedule appointments, maintain a diary, browse the Web, read Usenet news, compose and send electronic mail, calculate the phases of the moon, display holidays, write computer programs, play games, and psychoanalyze your moods! You can use emacs with or without the X Window System. To start emacs when using KDE, click the **Application Starter** button in the taskbar, choose **non-KDE Apps**, click **Editors**, and then select **XEmacs**.

Begin

1 Explore the emacs Window

Note that the **emacs** window has a menu bar, along with a toolbar of buttons. The one-line bar at the bottom of the text area is the status bar. As soon as you click the main window, the display clears.

2 Start emacs Tutorial

To start emacs's built-in tutorial, open the **Help** menu, choose **Basics**, and then select **Tutorial**. Note that the **META** key referred to in the tutorial is your keyboard's **Alt** key. To learn more about emacs, follow the tutorial. To stop the tutorial, open the **File** menu and choose **Delete Buffer TUTORIAL**.

3 Configure emacs

To configure emacs for word processing, type the following:

```
(setq default-major-mode 'text-mode)
(setq text-mode-hook 'turn-on-auto-fill)
```

Select **File | Save As**. Erase the **Write File:** prompt and type ~/**.emacs** for the name of your file. Next, select **File | Exit XEmacs**. Finally, start emacs from the command line of terminal window, followed by the name of a new text file, like this: **xemacs mynewdocument.txt &**.

4 Type in Text

When emacs restarts, you see that the status bar contains the name of your document, **mydocument.txt**, along with the words **(Text Fill)**. This means that emacs is now in text mode, with word wrap enabled. To set your right margin, type a word, double-click it, and then press **Esc** and type an **x**. At the command-line prompt below the status bar, type **set-right-margin** and press **Enter**. At the **Set right margin to width** prompt, type a number, such as 55, and press the **Enter** key.

word wrap on

6 Start Spell Check

Click the **Spell** button on emacs's toolbar. The program uses the ispell spelling checker to check your document. A suspect word is highlighted and any suggested replacement word appears above your document. To ignore a suspect word, press the **Spacebar**. To replace the suspect word with a suggested word, type the number or character in parentheses before the suggested word.

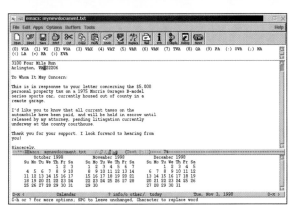

5 Show the Date and Time

If you need to know the date, open the **Apps** menu, choose **Calendar**, and then select **3-Month Calendar**. A three-month calendar appears in a new window below your text, with the current day highlighted. If you would like the time displayed in your document's status bar, press the **Esc** key, type an **x**, and, at the prompt, type **display-time**. Press **Enter**. The time appears in the status bar.

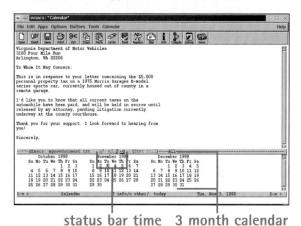

status bar time   3 month calendar

How-To Hints

Oops! I Made a Mistake!

You can undo any mistakes by pressing **Ctrl+X** and then the **U** key. In fact, you can undo various edits repeatedly. If you really screw up a document, press **Esc**, type an **x**, type **revert-buffer** at the command prompt, and press **Enter**. You're then asked whether you want to revert the buffer from the original file on your hard drive. Type **yes** and press the **Enter** key to revert your file.

How Do I Print My Document?

To print your document, open the **File** menu and select **Print Buffer**.

How to Spell Check Documents

This task introduces you to the ispell spelling checker included with your OpenLinux CD-ROM. The program is a flexible, interactive spelling checker with a 30,000 base word dictionary that can also use your system's 45,000-word dictionary. The spelling checker can be used with or without the X Window System and is generally started from the command line, followed by the name of a text document you'd like to spell check, like this: **ispell mynewdocument.txt**.

Begin

1 Start ispell

When ispell starts, the first suspect word is displayed in context. Along the bottom of the screen is a menu of commands. To continue checking, press the **Spacebar**. To replace a suspect word with a suggested one, press the number or character in front of the suggested word.

2 Replace Words

Press the **R** key to replace a word with a correctly spelled word or phrase. At the **Replace with:** prompt, type the correct word. After you press **Enter**, ispell removes the suspect word and replaces it with your entry.

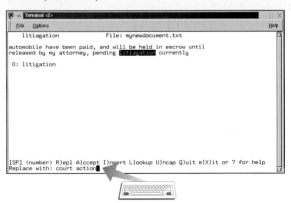

3 Look Up a Word

Press the **L** key to look for words to use as a replacement. At the **Lookup String** prompt, type a portion of a desired word, along with a wildcard (matching) character, and press the **Enter** key. For example, try using **resp*e** to search the dictionary.

4 View Words

After looking for any matches, ispell prints a list of found words. Press the **Spacebar** to continue the spell check.

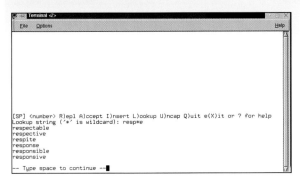

5 Show Help

Press the question mark (**?**) key to get help with ispell. The screen clears and a list of ispell's commands are displayed. Press the **Spacebar** to continue the spell check. When finished, press the **X** key to save your changes or **Q** to quit. When no suspect words are left in your document, ispell quits.

End

How-To Hints

Oops! I Entered a Wrong Word!

Don't worry. When ispell saves your corrected file, it saves a copy of your original document with the same name, but with a **.bak** extension. Your original file remains untouched.

Whoops! I Accepted a Misspelled Word!

When you press the **a** key to accept a word, the word is saved in your personal dictionary, called **.ispell_english** in your home directory. Open this file with your favorite text editor and replace or correct the word. In fact, if you have a list of frequently used words not recognized by ispell, type them in and save the file; ispell uses them the next time you spell check your documents.

The Dictionary Is Too Small

The ispell program comes with six software tools—such as buildhash, munchlist, or findaffix—that you can use to build your own dictionaries. Be warned, however; you have to read the ispell manual pages first, and building the dictionaries can consume more than a little of your computer's resources and time.

Task

11

Getting Started with StarOffice

A number of office-automation productivity suites are available for OpenLinux. An *office suite* is a collection of integrated programs, such as a word processor, spreadsheet, and presentation graphics client. A good office suite's programs use many of the same menu commands (such as for starting a print job), have an integrated "feel," and work well together when sharing data. A great office suite makes your computing experience more efficient and productive.

This chapter introduces you to one of the latest and best office suites for OpenLinux—StarOffice from Star Division GmbH. You can find a copy on the CD-ROM included with this book. You first learn how to install, configure, and use some of StarOffice's basic features, and then move on to more advanced features, such as automatic document creation and using template documents.

In following chapters, you see how to use four out of StarOffice's ten different components, including StarWriter and StarCalc, in more detail using graphic examples. ●

How to Install and Start StarOffice

StarOffice can be installed in a number of ways, but the easiest method is to install from your CD-ROM. Start an X session by typing **kde** on the command line of your console, and press the **Enter** key.

1 Open a Terminal Window

When KDE starts, click the **Application Starter** button, choose **Utilities**, and select **Terminal** to open a terminal window.

Click

2 Start the Installation

Insert your CD-ROM into your computer, and use the **su** command on the command line of the terminal window to mount your CD-ROM like so: **su -c "mount /mnt/cdrom"**. You'll need to enter the root password for your system. Next, use the **cd** command to navigate to the StarOffice setup directory like so: **cd /mnt/cdrom/StarOffice_40/ english/prod_lnx**. Start the installation with StarOffice's **setup** command by typing **./setup** and pressing **Enter**.

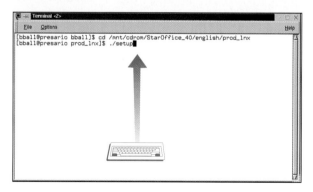

3 Read the License Agreement

Read the StarOffice License Agreement by scrolling through the text, When finished, click the **Accept** button.

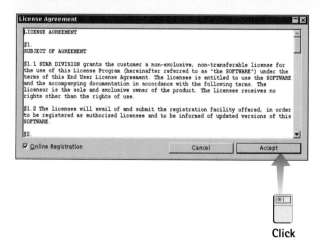

Click

4 Click Continue

A small dialog then appears, saying "Welcome to the installation program." Click the **Continue** button to proceed or the **Cancel** button to cancel the installation.

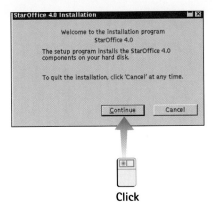

Click

5 Choose an Installation

When the installation type dialog appears, click the box next to the type of StarOffice installation you want. A standard installation is recommended, because this book shows you how to use many features included therein. Note that you'll need at least 171MB of free space on your hard drive for a standard installation.

Click

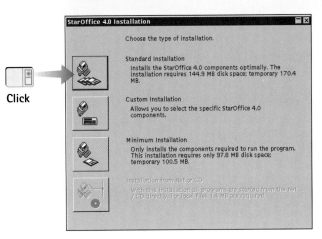

6 Choose a Location

In the next dialog, confirm the directory in which to install StarOffice. This should be your home directory in the form of **/home/youruser-name/Office40**, where **yourusername** is the name you use to log into OpenLinux. Click the **OK** button to continue.

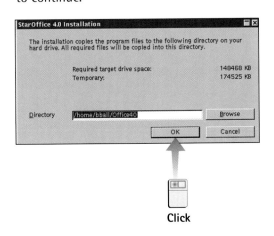

Click

7 Monitor the Install

The StarOffice installation shows a progress bar, along with the estimated time remaining. You have the opportunity to cancel the installation at any time by clicking the dialog's **Cancel** button.

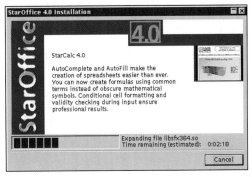

Continues

8 Enter Your Information

StarOffice finishes copying and uncompressing its components into the **Office40** directory in your home directory, and then asks you to fill in your name, address, phone number, and so on. Fill this out as completely and accurately as possible, because much of this information is used in later examples in this book! When finished, click the **OK** button.

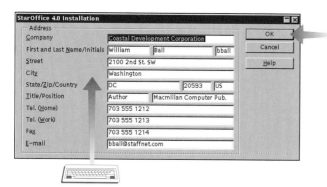

Click

9 Finish the Installation

A StarOffice dialog tells you that the installation is finished. Click the **OK** button to continue.

Click

10 Read the Additional Information!

A dialog appears, containing information about installing, running, and customizing StarOffice. Take the time to read it (if you don't do it now, you can do so later by viewing the **README** file under the **Office40** directory in your home directory). Click the **OK** button, and you're finished!

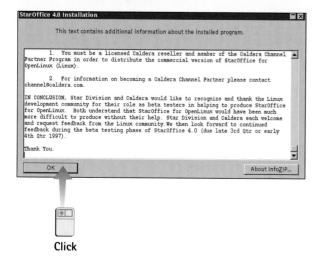

Click

11 Start StarOffice

Start StarOffice with the **soffice** command, found under the **Office40/bin** directory in your home directory. To start StarOffice from your home directory, type the complete path to the **soffice** command (**Office40/bin/soffice &**) and press **Enter**. The StarOffice desktop then appears in your display.

End

How-To Hints

How Much Free Hard Drive Space Do I Have?

To find out how much free space is on your hard drive before installing StarOffice, use the **df** command from the command line of your console or a terminal window. This shows how much free space is on each currently mounted *filesystem* (or hard drive, CD-ROM, and so on). The values are shown in 1024-byte blocks. You can see how large your hard drive is, how many blocks are used, how many are available, what percentage of your hard drive is used, and where the drive is mounted. Note that any mounted CD-ROMs always show **0** for available space (because the CD is read-only).

Okay, I Want to Eject My CD-ROM. How Do I Do This?

In OpenLinux, different *filesystems*, or storage devices such as flash memory cards, CD-ROMs, and different partitions, must first be mounted with the **mount** command at a specific point in your filesystem, or directory structure. The traditional mount point is in a directory under the **/mnt** directory. After mounting a filesystem, unmount the device or partition with the **umount** command, followed by the mount point. So, after mounting your CD-ROM at **/mnt/cdrom**, unmount your CD-ROM by entering `su -c "umount /mnt/cdrom"`. The **su** command is necessary because generally only the root operator, or *superuser*, is allowed to mount and unmount filesystems under OpenLinux (although it doesn't have to be this way—see the **mount** and **fstab** manual pages).

The StarOffice Desktop Is Too Small!

StarOffice is a large complex program with many interface elements in its desktop display. To enlarge the desktop, either click the **Maximize** button in the desktop's title bar or double-click a blank area of the title bar. The desktop enlarges to fit between KDE's taskbar and panel. Need even more room? Configure the panel to Auto Hide by clicking the **Application Starter** button, choosing **Panel**, and then selecting **Configure**. Then click **Hidden** in the **Taskbar** section of the **Panel** tab in the **KPanel Configuration** dialog. Next, click the **Options** tab and select **Auto Hide Panel** and **Auto Hide Taskbar** in the **Others** section. When you maximize the StarOffice desktop, it uses your entire display.

How to Install a Printer for StarOffice

If you intend to use StarOffice to create letters, brochures, spreadsheets, graphics, and so on, and if you have a PostScript printer, one of the first things to do is configure StarOffice for your printer.

Note that if you do not have a PostScript printer, and if you've installed a printer according to Chapter 16, "Printing Text Files and Graphics," the default StarOffice printer configuration should work. However, you should try to print a test page, as described in this task.

Begin

1 Start Printer Setup

Double-click the **Printer-Setup** icon in StarOffice's desktop.

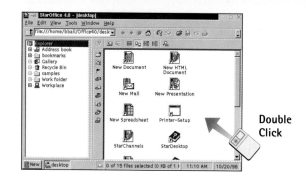

Double Click

2 Add a Printer

A **Printer Installation** dialog appears. Scroll through the list of the existing printer drivers. Add a printer to the list of installed printers by first selecting the printer and then clicking the **Add** button. To remove an installed printer, select it and click the **Remove** button.

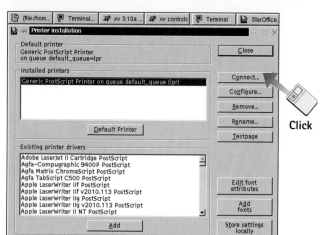

Click

3 Configure Printer Options

To configure an installed printer, select it from the **Installed Printers** list in the **Printer Installation** dialog and click the **Configure** button. The **Configure** dialog enables you to set six different options for your PostScript printer, including paper size and resolution. Margin values are in dots per inch or DPI. When finished, click the **OK** button to apply your changes, or click **Cancel** to reject any changes.

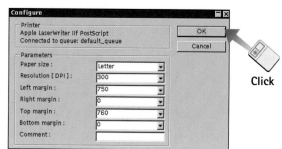

Click

4 Rename Printer

To rename your printer, select it from the **Installed Printers** list in the **Printer Installation** dialog, click the **Rename** button, and enter a new printer name (such as **tree-eater**) in the **Input** dialog. Click the **OK** button to apply your changes.

Click

5 Print a Test Page

Select a printer from the **Installed Printers** list in the **Printer Installation** dialog and click the **Testpage** button. StarOffice sends a test page to your printer after a second or two. A **Testpage** dialog appears, confirming success. See this task's How-To Hints for more information if StarOffice reports an error or if your page does not print.

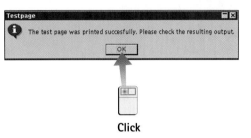

Click

6 Select the Default Printer

After confirming your test page, select the printer you'd like to use with StarOffice from the **Installed Printers** list in the **Printer Installation** dialog and click the **Default Printer** button. Click the **Close** button to exit. Any changes are saved in the file **Xpdefaults** under the **Office40/xp3** directory in your home directory.

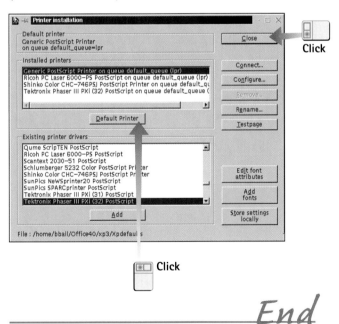

Click

Click

End

How-To Hints

Pursuing Printer Problems

You should have installed a printer during your OpenLinux installation. If you chose not to, see Chapter 16 for details on how to install your printer. If you did install a printer but still have problems, first make sure that your printer is properly connected to your computer and that it is turned on. Make sure that you're not using an Iomega parallel-port Zip drive at the same time. Try to load the parallel-printer kernel module **lp** by using the **su** and **insmod** commands like so: `su -c "/sbin/insmod lp"`. If you hear your printer activate, try printing a test page again. If the **insmod** command reports that a module named **lp** already exists, your kernel supports parallel printing. For detailed troubleshooting tips, read the Printing-HOWTO under the **/usr/doc/HOWTO** directory (type `zless /usr/doc/HOWTO/Printing-HOWTO.gz`).

How to Manage the StarOffice Desktop

The StarOffice *desktop* is the main interface for StarOffice and its component programs. This section introduces you to different desktop elements and shows you how to start a StarOffice project.

Begin

1 Explore the Desktop

The desktop includes a menu bar along with a function bar, which contains a text field showing a path or Web address, followed by various buttons and controls. The left area of the desktop, called the *Explorer*, lists StarOffice's programs and documents. The *work area*, the large area of the StarOffice desktop, contains numerous *links*.

2 Show the Beamer

You can use the *Beamer* to view the contents of directories or graphics files listed in the Explorer window. To open the Beamer, click the **Beamer** icon.

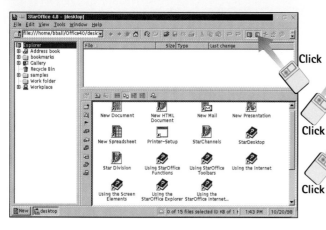

3 View Graphics

Click the plus sign in front of the **Gallery** icon in the Explorer. A list of StarOffice's graphics categories drops down; click a category, such as **Flags & Maps**.

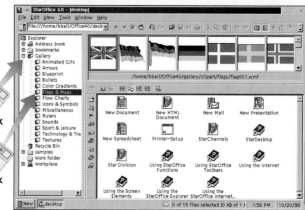

4 Create a Project Folder

To help organize your work, StarOffice supports the grouping of related files into folders, or directories. Create your first project folder by right-clicking a blank area of the work area. A pop-up menu appears; select **New** and click **Folder**. When the folder appears in the work area, give it a name, such as **My Project**. If you make an error typing, right-click the folder and select **Rename** from the pop-up menu

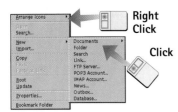

Right Click

Click

5 Put the Folder into the Explorer

The next step is to put the folder into the Explorer. Using the Explorer is a handy way to view and access the contents of your project folders. To put your new folder into the Explorer, select your folder in the work area and, holding down the left mouse button, drag and drop it into a blank area of the Explorer window. Your folder disappears from the work area but is available in the Explorer.

Click & Drag

Release

6 Create a Document

Double-click your project folder in the Explorer, and the work area clears. To create a new document in your project folder, right-click in your project's work area, select **New**, and click **Documents**. A StarWriter text document window appears in the work area; try typing some text in the document.

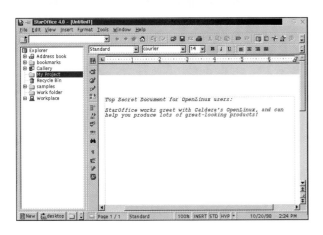

7 Save Your Document

To save your document, press **Ctrl+S**, or open the **File** menu and choose **Save**. A dialog appears, asking you to enter a file name. Enter a file name, such as **mydocument**, and click the **Save** button. To close your new document, open the **File** menu and click **Close**.

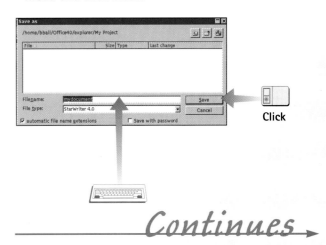

Click

Continues

8 Copy a Document

After you save your document, its icon appears in your folder's work area. To make a copy of your document, right-click its icon, and then select **Copy** from the pop-up menu. Right-click in a blank area and click **Paste** from the pop-up menu. A copy of your document appears in the work area.

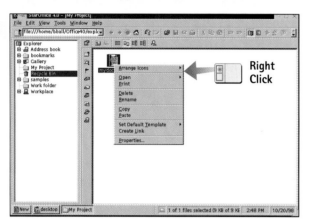

9 Move Documents

To move a file from your work area to a different folder, select the file and then drag and release on a different folder in the Explorer. To copy a file, select it but hold down the **Ctrl** key when you drag and release. You can also copy files from other directories (even filesystems) in your OpenLinux directory by navigating through the Workplace folder in the Explorer. StarOffice asks you to confirm any move and copy operation that could overwrite a file.

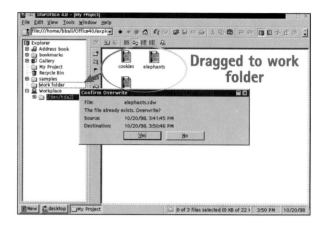

10 Delete One or More Documents

To delete a single document, right-click it and select **Delete** from the pop-up menu. To delete several documents, use multiple selection by holding your left mouse button down in a blank part of the work area and then dragging a rectangle around the documents. Then right-click one of the documents and select **Delete** from the pop-up menu. A **Confirm Delete** dialog appears. Click **All** to delete all documents or **Yes** to delete one document at a time.

11 View the Trash

Deleting StarOffice documents is relatively safe, because you'll get a second chance if you need to retrieve a deleted document (drag it out of the Recycle Bin). To see what files are in the trash, select the **Recycle Bin** in the Explorer, and then click the **Beamer** button on the Function bar.

12 Empty the Trash

After you've worked with StarOffice for some time, you might need to reclaim disk space taken up by documents sitting in the Recycle Bin. To empty the trash, right-click the Recycle Bin and select **Empty Recycle Bin** from the pop-up menu. You'll see a dialog confirming that you want to continue with the deletion. If you want to delete a file from the Recycle Bin without viewing the confirmation dialog, select **Empty Immediately** instead of **Empty Recycle Bin**.

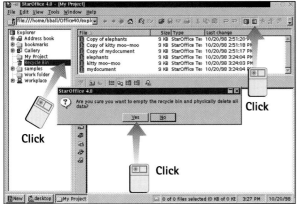

End

How to Use StarOffice Templates

Now that you know how to create, copy, move, and delete documents, you'll learn how to create professional-looking documents with minimum effort. The kind folks at Star Division have gone through a lot of trouble to create 10 template categories with more than 70 handy and ready-to-use template documents. You can even create your own templates from an existing one or from scratch.

1 Access Templates

Navigate to your work area. Right-click a blank area, select **New**, choose **Documents**, and click **From Template** on the menu. When the template dialog appears, scroll through the list of template categories. Each category has a different number and type of assigned templates. Scroll down to the **Miscellaneous** category, select **Newsletter**, and click the **More** button.

Click

2 Preview a Template

The **New** dialog expands to include **Preview** and **Description** sections. Click the **Preview** check box, and after a few seconds, a preview of the Newsletter template appears. To use the Newsletter template, click the **OK** button. The template document appears in a document window in your work area.

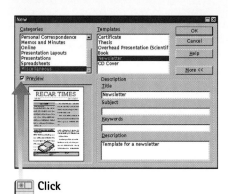

Click

3 Create and Save a Phone Call

You can create your own templates for use with StarOffice documents. Start by creating a new document in your work area. Add a graphic by opening the **Gallery** folder in the Explorer, selecting the **Technology and Transportation** category, and dragging and dropping a telephone onto your document. Then, type the desired text. When finished, select **File | Save as**. In the **Save as** dialog, enter a file name for your new template in the **Filename** field. Click the down arrow at the end of the **File Type** field and select **StarWriter 4.0 Template**. Then click the **Save** button to save your template.

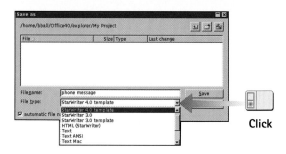

Click

4 Add the Template

From the **File** menu, select **Templates**. The **Document Templates** dialog appears. Select **Standard** from the **Template Categories** list, type the name of your template in the **New Template** field, and click the **OK** button. You now have a new template you can preview and use from the **Document Templates** dialog!

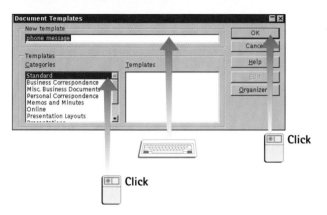

Click

Click

5 Start Template Organizer

If you don't like a template, you can delete (or edit) it. Start by creating a new document or opening an existing document and selecting **Templates** from the **File** menu. In the **Document Templates** dialog, click the **Organizer** button. A dialog of the template categories appears.

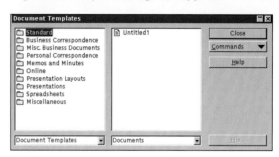

Click

6 Delete or Edit a Template

To delete or edit a template, double-click the template category containing the template. Right-click the desired template, and select **Delete** or **Edit** from the pop-up menu. If you delete the template, you'll be asked to confirm the deletion. If you select **Edit**, the template loads into your work area; edit it as you would a normal document.

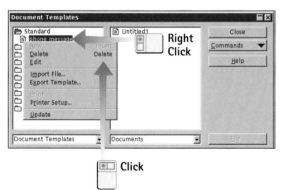

Right Click

Click

How-To Hints

Whoops! I Messed Up StarOffice!

If you accidentally delete an important template, trash StarOffice's clip art, or commit other heinous acts against your installation, don't panic! Open an X11 terminal window and, from the command line, use the **setup** command found under the Office40/bin directory like so: **Office40/bin/setup**. StarOffice asks you to mount your installation CD-ROM and presents you a menu for installation repair—is that cool, or what?

End

How to Use StarOffice's AutoPilot

Using a StarOffice template is only one way to easily create professional documents. Believe it or not, there's an even easier way! With a few clicks of the mouse and a little typing, you can have a great-looking document ready to save, print, or publish. How? Read on, and you'll see how to use the AutoPilot feature from your StarOffice desktop.

Begin

1 Start AutoPilot

Navigate to your project folder by using the Explorer window. Click the **File** menu and choose **AutoPilot**. A submenu of 10 different actions appears; click **Letter** to start.

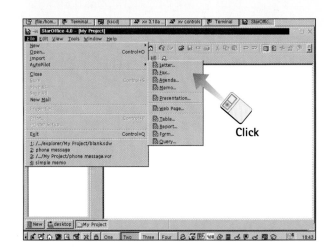

Click

2 Launch a Letter

The **AutoPilot Letter** dialog appears. Select a letter template and style by clicking the appropriate radio buttons. To continue, click the **Next** button.

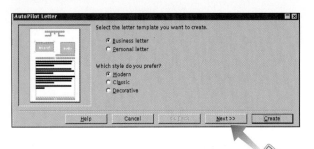

Click

3 Fill In the Details

The **AutoPilot Letter** dialog again appears, but with a preview of your document. To use a logo in your letter, click the **Picture** or **Text** radio buttons. If you choose **Text**, a **Logo Text** field appears, and you can enter text. To get a picture for your letter, click the **Select Picture** button. To continue, click **Next**. (Note that if you change your mind, you can go back by clicking **Back.**)

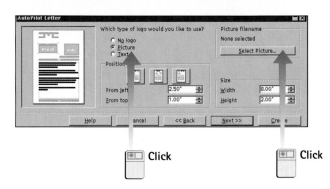

Click   Click

4 Pick a Picture

The **Select Logo** dialog again appears, containing entries for StarOffice's clip-art and sound directories, along with a graphic of a friendly bear. Click the **Preview** button and then select the bear graphic to see what it looks like. Then click the **Open** button. The **AutoPilot Letter** dialog reappears. To continue, click the **Next** button.

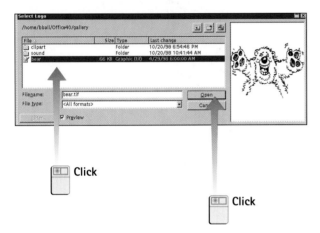

Click

Click

6 Fine Tune Your Letter

The AutoPilot creates and draws your letter in your work area. The picture you chose appears, along with your return address, the day's date, and your salutation. All you have to do is type the addresses and the text of the letter!

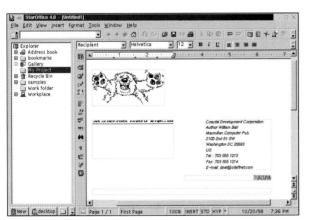

5 Create the Letter

The **AutoPilot Letter** dialog again appears, now asking for the letter's return address. Note that the personal information you entered when you installed StarOffice appears in the **Enter Return Address** field. Although you can continue for several more screens to fill in more details about your letter, you can also click the **Create** button now to create your letter.

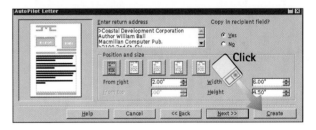

Click

How-To Hints

Help Is Only a Click Away

If you're using an non-commercially licensed version of StarOffice, you'll have to rely on built-in help—or you can read its user guide. This guide, called **user_guide.pdf**, is in Adobe Acrobat Portable Document Format, and can be found under the **StarOffice_40/english/documentaton** directory on your CD-ROM. You can read this guide directly from a mounted CD-ROM by using the xpdf X11 client. First, mount the CD-ROM. Then, from the command line of an X11 terminal window, type **xpdf /mnt/cdrom/StarOffice_40/english/documentation/user_guide.pdf**.

AutoPilot Can't Always Fly Solo

StarOffice's AutoPilot can quickly create a number of professional documents with minimal help. However, some types of AutoPilot documents, such as reports, require an existing database or table of data in order to work. See StarOffice's Advanced Tips, available through the desktop's **Help** menu item.

End

Task

## CHAPTER 12

Getting Started with StarWriter

StarWriter is the word processor portion of the StarOffice office-automation productivity suite for OpenLinux. This program is integrated into the StarOffice desktop, and shares information with other parts of StarOffice, such as StarCalc or StarOffice Presentations. In order to use StarWriter, you need to install StarOffice and run the X Window System. Before you begin this chapter, take a moment to read Chapter 11, "Getting Started with StarOffice"; this will help familiarize you with some of the elements and features of the StarOffice desktop.

This chapter introduces you to StarWriter. You start by using StarWriter's basic features but then move on to more advanced tools, such as using spell check or the thesaurus. Finally, you see how to create professional-looking documents easily through the use of templates and AutoPilot.

Begin by starting StarOffice from the command line of a terminal window. Type **Office40/bin/soffice &**, press the **Enter** key, and begin! ●

How to Create, Format, and Save a StarWriter Document

This task leads you through the basic steps of creating, formatting, and saving your first StarWriter document.

Begin

1 Create a Document

Double-click the **New Document** icon in the StarOffice desktop.

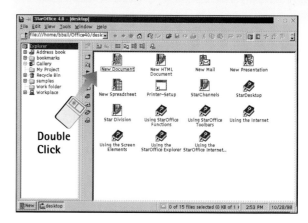

Double Click

2 Enter Text

Click in the blank page and start typing. Note that the ruler above the work area is used to set margins and tab stops, and the formatting toolbar is used to set the font, font size, attributes (such as bold, italic, or underline), and justification (such as left, centered, right, or filled). The vertical toolbar to the left of the work area can be used to insert tables, fields, graphics, or drawn objects; start spell checking; do search and replace; show hidden characters; and perform other actions.

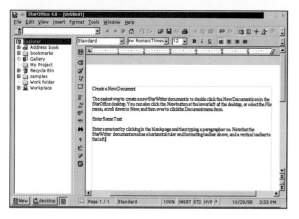

3 Highlight Some Text

One way to format your text is to highlight it and click the appropriate toolbar icon. Another way is to right-click the text and select the attributes from a pop-up menu. Double-click to select a word; triple-click to select a line. To select to the end of a line, press **Shift+End**. To select multiple lines, click an insertion point and, holding down your left mouse button, drag up or down to highlight the desired text.

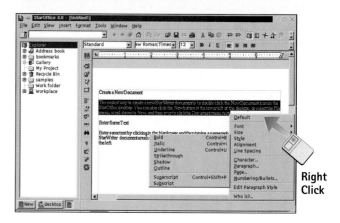

Right Click

4 Use Character Formatting

Select the desired text. Next, open the desktop's **Format** menu and choose **Character**. When the **Character** dialog appears, scroll and click the desired font under the **Font** section. Select the desired style, size, or effect, and then choose one of more than 90 colors. The effect of your choices is displayed in the **Preview** area. To choose more effects, such as spacing, caps, position, or more sophisticated controls, such as kerning, click the **Font Effects** tab. To choose a colored background, click the **Background** tab. When finished, click **OK**.

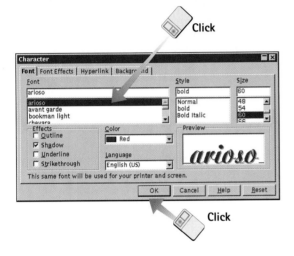

Click

Click

6 Save Your Document

To save your document, open the **File** menu and choose **Save**. The first time you save a new document, you see the **Save as** dialog. Note where the document will be saved by checking the path listed at the top of the dialog. By default, new documents are saved in the desktop's **Work** Folder. Type a filename, such as **mydocument**, and click the **Save** button. To close your document, open the **File** menu and choose **Close**.

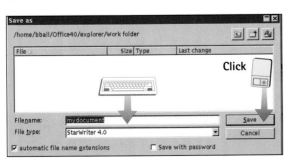

Click

5 Copy and Paste Text

To copy a section of text, highlight it, and then open the **Edit** menu and choose **Copy**. To paste the copied text, click an insertion point where you'd like the copied text to appear, and open the **Edit** menu and choose **Paste**. You can also paste copied objects from other StarOffice documents, such as graphics or spreadsheet charts.

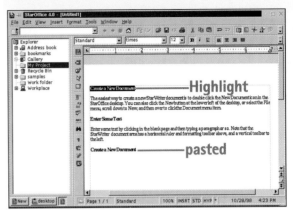

Highlight

pasted

End

How-To Hints

Why Won't My Backspace Key Work?

Many programs—or *clients*—for the X Window System automatically recognize and use the backspace key. But if you find that your backspace key does not work in the way you expect, first make sure that you have not disabled the **XKEYBOARD** extension in your **XF86Config** file (found under the **/etc** directory). If the **XkbDisable** item in the **Keyboard** section of this file is not preceded with a pound sign (**#**), log in as the root operator, open **XF86Config**, and put one in! You'll need to restart X11 to use any changes. If **XF86Config** is okay, try using the **xmodmap** command from the command line of terminal window like so: **xmodmap -e "keycode 22 = BackSpace"**.

How to Open, Spell-Check, and Print Your Document

Before you begin this task, make sure that you've installed a printer for StarOffice, or that you've verified that your printer works by printing a test page, as shown in Chapter 11. This task shows you how to open a document, check its spelling, and then print.

1 Open a Document

There are several ways to open a document. The first is to click the document's folder in the Explorer, and then double-click its icon in the work area. Alternatively, you can press **Ctrl+O** or select **Open** from the **File** menu, select your document from the **Open** dialog, and click the **Open** button.

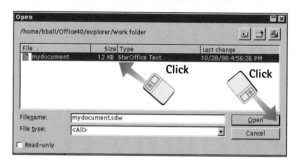

2 Enable Auto Spellcheck

After your document opens, tell StarWriter to automatically underline any misspelled or suspect words by enabling Auto Spellcheck. Open the **Tools** menu, select **Spelling**, and then click **Auto Spellcheck**.

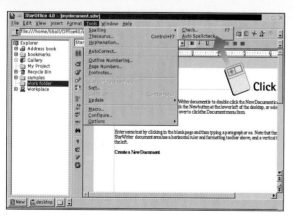

3 Check Spelling

To spell-check your document, open the **Tools** menu, select **Spelling**, and then click **Check**. The **Spelling** dialog opens, displaying the first suspect word. Note that the word also is highlighted in your document. Click the appropriate button to ignore, replace, globally ignore, or globally replace the word in your document. If you are certain that the word is spelled correctly, click the **Add** button to add the word to StarWriter's dictionary.

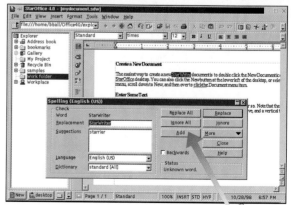

4 Correct Spelling

To correct a misspelled word or phrase, select a suggested word and then click the **Replace** button. If no suggestion appears in the **Spelling** dialog's **Suggestions** list, either click **Ignore**, or click in the **Replacement** field, correct the spelling, and click the **Replace** button. Continue through the document (or, if you started at the end of the document, click the **Backwards** check box to spell-check back through to the beginning of the document.

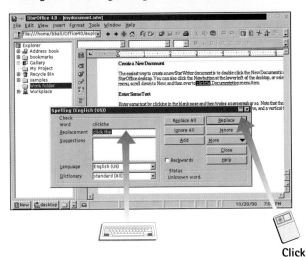

Click

5 Preview Printing

When you finish the spell check, save the document by choosing **Save** from the **File** menu or by pressing **Ctrl+S**. To preview your document, open the **File** menu and choose **Page View**. Click the **Close** button above the work area to return to normal view.

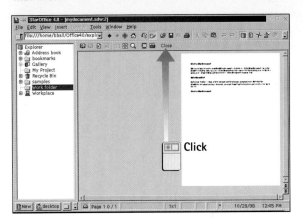

Click

6 Print the Document

To print your document, select **Print** from the **File** menu, or press **Ctrl+P**. The **Print** dialog lists the current printer (which should be **Generic PostScript Printer**). If you want more than one copy of your document, change the number in the **Copies** section of the dialog by clicking the up or down arrow button. To print a portion of your document, enter a range of pages in the **Print Range** field. To start printing, click the **OK** button.

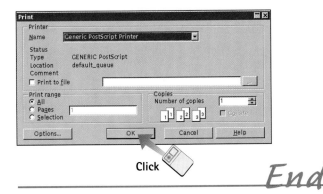

Click

How-To Hints

Spell Check Tips

Make sure to read the **Advanced Tips** section of StarOffice's help documentation to get the most out of spell check. Open the **Help** menu, and then click **Contents**. In the Explorer index in the left side of the work area, click **Advanced Tips**, then **Advanced Tips for Text Documents**, and finally, **Spellcheck, Thesaurus**, and **Hyphenation**.

I Added a Misspelled Word During Spell Check!

To remove a word from the dictionary, open the **Tools** menu, click **General**, and then click the **Linguistic** tab. Next, click the middle button (called **Edit**) on the right side of the dialog. The **Edit Custom Dictionary** dialog appears. Scroll through the list of words until you find the misspelled word, select the word, and then click the **Remove** button.

End

How to Create a Business Letter

This task lead you through the process of entering an address into your StarOffice Address book and creating a professional business letter using a StarOffice template. After going through this task, you'll be able to easily create other documents you can use for your personal or professional business.

Begin

1 Add to Your Address Book

Before you create a business letter, enter your addressee into your StarOffice address book. Open the **Edit** menu and click **Address Book**. In the **Address Book** dialog, click the **New** button, and enter as much information as possible about your addressee. Click the **Close** button.

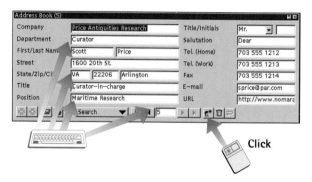

Click

2 Select a Business Letter Template

Open the **File** menu, select **New**, and choose **From Template**. When the New dialog appears, click the **Business Correspondence** entry in the **Categories** list and click the **Professional Letter** entry in the **Templates** list. To see more information about the template, click the **More** button. Check the **Preview** check box to see a preview. Click **OK** to continue.

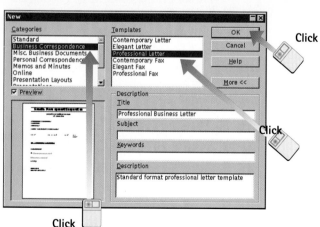

Click

3 Select the Addressee

StarOffice automatically creates a professional letter in the work area. In the **Address Book** table above the work area, click in the far left column of buttons to select your new addressee (scroll as needed). A black triangle, pointing to the right, appears.

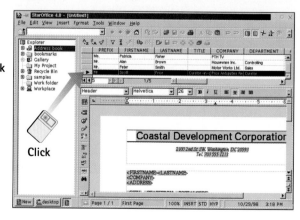

Click

4 Edit Your Letter

Replace <Please enter the subject here> with the subject of your letter, and replace <Please enter your text here> with your letter's body text. Note that StarOffice has used your personal information to create the letterhead and closing. When you finish entering your body text, spell-check and save your letter.

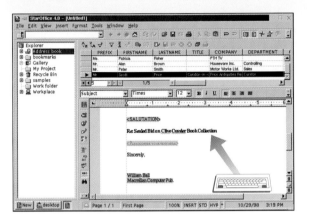

5 Save, Merge, and Print

Before you can print your letter, you must merge your addressee with the letter. Click the **Mail Merge** button, located above the **Address Book** table and to the left of the printer button. In the **Mail Merge** dialog, specify the records you want to merge and the output of the operation, and then click **OK**. The **Print** dialog appears; click **OK** to print.

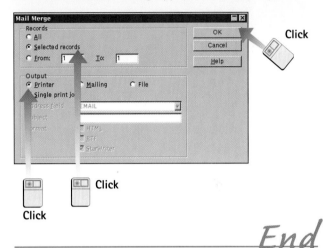

Click

Click

Click

End

How-To Hints

Got the Urge to Merge?

Your address book is a handy tool for saving addresses for later use. By holding down the **Shift** key while you select different addressees in your book, you can then merge and print customized letters from a single form letter. If you want to select someone at the beginning of your address book and someone from the middle or end of your address book, hold down the **Ctrl** key when you click each addressee's entry.

Time Stamping Made Easy

You can quickly and easily insert the current date and time—as well as other bits of information—into your document. Open the **Insert** menu, choose **Field**, and click **Other**; you'll find more than 30 different statistics and bits of information you can paste into your document.

Feel the Need for Change?

Don't like the personal information StarOffice uses when it creates your customized letters? You can change your information by opening the **Tools** menu, choosing **Options**, and clicking **General**. Click the **User Data** tab in the **General Options** dialog ; you can then edit your personal information.

How to Customize a Personal Letter

Now that you know how to create a letter from a template, you'll now see how to customize a personal letter with a graphic or other information.

Begin

1 Select a Template

Open the **File** menu, select **New**, and choose **From Template**. When the **New** dialog appears, select the **Personal Correspondence** entry in the **Categories** list and choose **Personal Letter** in the **Templates** list. Click **OK**.

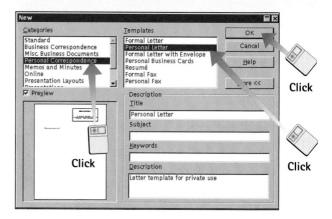

Click

Click

Click

2 Insert a Frame

A blank personal letter, with your return address, fills the work area. To make room for a graphic in the upper left corner of your letter, you must insert a frame. Open the **Insert** menu and click **Frame**.

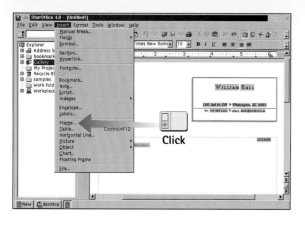

Click

3 Configure the Frame

In the **Frame** dialog, set the width and height of the graphic in the **Size** section and select the appropriate position for your frame. The preview shows where the frame will appear in the document window in your work area. You can set various options by clicking the appropriate tabs at the top of the **Frame** dialog. When finished, click **OK**.

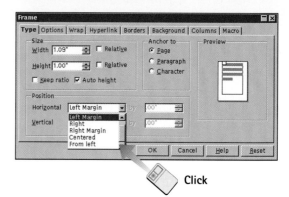

Click

4 Open the Clip Art Gallery

The frame appears in your document. Click a blank area of the document to deselect the form and click inside the frame to activate an insertion point (blinking vertical cursor). Next, click the plus sign to the left of the **Gallery** folder in the Explorer and double-click the **Icons & Symbols** folder. The Beamer opens to display the various pieces of clip art in the folder. To use a piece of clip art, scroll through the Beamer, click a desired picture, drag the picture onto the new frame, and release it.

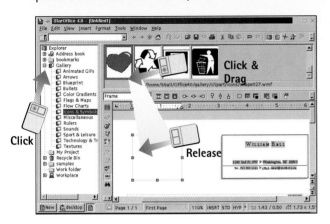

5 Resize and Move a Picture Frame

The picture appears inside your frame. Click and drag one of the eight anchor points to make your picture larger or smaller. When finished, click in a corner of your frame and drag the frame around your document. Note that the picture and any text typed into the frame go along for the ride! Set the frame where you want it and finish typing your letter; then spell-check, save, and print.

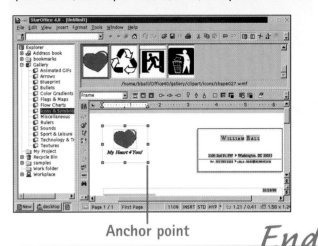

Anchor point

End

How-To Hints

My Pasted Graphic Looks Funny

The best way to resize a graphic is to use proportional resizing. Hold down the **Shift** key when you click and drag a resize anchor point in a graphic's frame. Proportionally sized graphics look more natural when printed; of course, you can always distort the image for a special effect!

You'll Flip Over Graphics

If your graphic is facing toward the left, and you'd like it facing right, flip it! Double-click the graphic in your document and, in the **Pictures** dialog, click the **Graphics** tab. Select either **Vertical** or **Horizontal** to flip the artwork. Of course, this won't work for text (unless you like reading backwards or upside down).

Create Your Own Graphics

StarOffice has numerous graphics capabilities. You can select one of thirteen different drawing tools from the **Draw** pop-up menu on the vertical toolbar to the left of the work area. You can import graphics files from your OpenLinux directories and copy and paste graphics from other StarOffice documents. See Chapter 14, "Getting Started with StarOffice Presentations," for more information.

How to Import and Export a Document

Besides quickly creating complex documents, StarWriter can also read, or import, documents from different types of word processors. You can also use StarWriter to export, or save, your document in different formats. This task shows you how to import and export documents in several different formats.

Begin

1 Import a Foreign Document File

Start StarOffice and click the **Work** folder in the Explorer. StarOffice documents are represented by a document icon with a vertical blue stripe. Other word-processing document icons can be recognized and shown. To open a foreign document, double-click its icon.

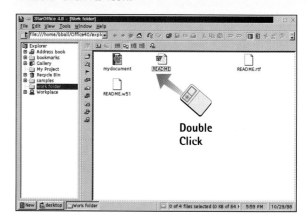

2 Select a Document Filter

If StarWriter is not sure about the file's type, it shows the **Select Filter** dialog, listing different types of documents. Scroll through the list to select the correct type, and then click **OK**.

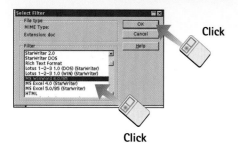

3 Edit a Foreign Document

After the document opens, edit the text as needed. You can use any StarOffice tools with the new document, such as formatting, styles, or drawing.

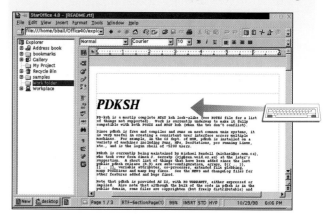

4 Export a Document

To export a StarWriter document to another file type, open the document, and then open the **File** menu and choose **Save as**. The **Save as** dialog appears. To export your document, open the **File Type** drop-down menu (click the small black arrow at the end of the **File Type** field), and scroll through it until you find the file type you want to use to save the document. Note that if the **Automatic File Name Extensions** check box is enabled, a period and a three-letter extension are appended to the document's name. Rename the document if you'd like, and then click the **Save** button to export it.

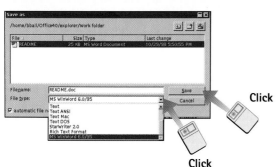

Click

Click

5 Export an HTML Document

StarWriter can import Hypertext Markup Language, or HTML documents. However, your choices are somewhat limited when exporting HTML. Open an HTML document, such as the Linux Commercial-HOWTO, and select **Save as**. Click the **File Type** drop-down menu. Note that you can export HTML documents to a more limited number of formats.

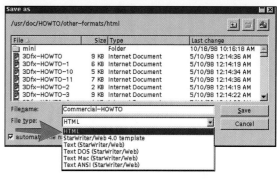

End

How-To Hints

How Do I Get Files into the Work Folder?

In order to open files directly from the **Work** folder, you must first navigate to the folder and then copy files into it. If you use KDE, drag files from the desktop or other folders into the **Office40/explorer/Work** folder. To do this from the command line, use the **cd** (change directory) command like so, where *myusername* is the name of your home directory: **cd /home/*myusername*/Office40/explorer/Work***.

Then, use the **cp** command to copy files into the **Work** folder like so: **cp /*wherethefileis*/*filename* ..** (*wherethefileis* and *filename* are the directory path and filename of the document). The period (**.**) means to copy the file here, or the current directory.

How Many Types of Documents Can I Read?

StarOffice can read at least 68 different types of documents. (Undoubtedly, by the time you read this, many more document types will have been added.) Do you need to use all these types of documents? Most people won't. If you plan to trade documents with other people, stick to a document format most word processors (even on other computer operating systems) can read: Rich Text Format, or RTF. You'll still be able to use many formatting features, and there's a much smaller chance of losing formatting than with other document types.

Task

13

Getting Started with StarCalc

*S*tarCalc is the spreadsheet component of the StarOffice office-automation productivity suite for OpenLinux. This program is integrated into the StarOffice desktop and can share information with other parts of StarOffice, such as StarWriter or StarOffice Presentations. StarOffice must be installed, and you must be running the X Window System in order to use StarCalc. Definitely read Chapter 11, "Getting Started with StarOffice," before starting tasks in this chapter; doing so makes your StarOffice desktop sessions a lot more fun!

This chapter introduces you to StarCalc. You start by using some basic StarCalc features; you then move on to creating more complex sheets and graphing your spreadsheet data. Next, you see how to quickly create custom documents using templates. Finally, you see how to share your spreadsheet data to create professional-looking documents.

Start StarOffice from the command line of a terminal window. Type **Office40/bin/soffice &**, press the **Enter** key, and get started! ●

How to Create, Format, and Save a StarCalc Spreadsheet

Spreadsheets are handy tools for storing and tracking information, quickly visualizing many numbers, and forecasting, or providing "what if" calculations.

Begin

1 Create a Spreadsheet

The easiest way to create a new StarCalc spreadsheet is to double-click the **New Spreadsheet** icon in the StarOffice desktop. Alternatively, you can click the **New** button in the lower-left portion of the desktop, or open the **File** menu, choose **New**, and then click **Spreadsheet**.

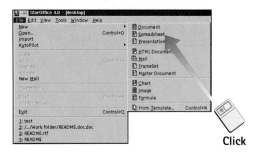

Click

2 Enter Some Data

Enter some data—text or numbers—by clicking in a blank spreadsheet cell. The data in the current cell appears in the data entry field above the work area. Press **Enter** to move to the cell below the current cell; press **Tab** to move to the cell to the right of the current cell. In addition, you can use the cursor keys to move to different cells in your sheet.

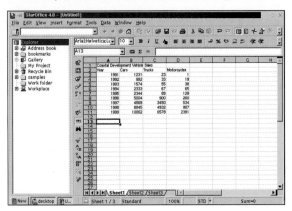

3 Format Your Data

To format a single cell, click it and choose formatting options from the formatting toolbar above the work area. To select multiple cells, select a cell and then drag. To format two or more areas of your spreadsheet at the same time, click the first cell and drag to select the first area. Then, holding down the **Ctrl** key, click and drag to select another area, and then format the cells as needed.

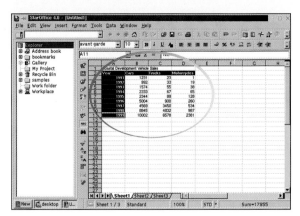

4 Total a Column of Numbers

StarCalc performs quick totals of your data. Click in the bottom cell of a column of numbers and click the **Sum** button (the button marked with a Σ next to the equal sign in the data-entry field above your work area). Two new buttons, one with an X and another with a check mark, appear next to the data entry field, which has the SUM formula inserted. Click the check mark button to accept the entry, or click the X button to cancel.

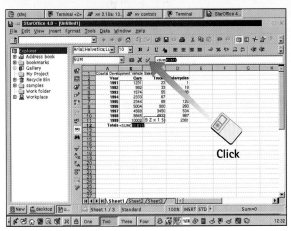

Click

5 Total Columns of Numbers

StarCalc can also quickly total two or more columns of data. Click in the cell at the bottom of one column of numbers, drag to select an adjacent cell and click the **Sum** button. The sums of both columns appear, and each cell contains the SUM formula.

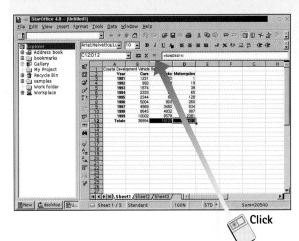

Click

6 Save Your Spreadsheet

Open the **File** menu and choose **Save**. The first time you save a new spreadsheet, the **Save as** dialog appears. By default, StarOffice spreadsheets are saved in StarCalc format, but by using the drop-down menu in the **File Type** field, you can export, or save, your sheet in a format used by other spreadsheet programs.

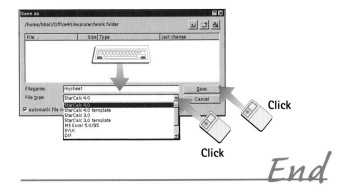

Click

Click

End

How-To Hints

Quick Totals Works Horizontally, Too

You can also use the **Sum** button to total a row of numbers. Click and drag to the left or right across a row of numbers to an empty cell, and then click the **Sum** button. The sum appears in the empty cell. This is a handy feature to build simple spreadsheets quickly.

Quick Copies of Data

Don't want to use the keyboard or menu commands to copy sections of your spreadsheet? Click and drag to select the desired cells, then hold your left mouse button down, press the **Ctrl** key, and drag the cells to a new area. When you release your mouse button, voilà! The original cells are copied and placed in the new area.

How to Graph Your Spreadsheet Data

Use StarCalc to create complex graphs of your spreadsheet's data. This task shows you how to build a chart quickly and easily, using the previous data as an example. Start StarCalc and open your spreadsheet to begin.

Begin

1 Highlight Text and Numbers

Select the spreadsheet data you'd like to graph. Include any columns or rows you'd like to use as labels for your numbers. Then, click the **Insert Object** button on the vertical toolbar. The cursor turns into a plus sign with a tiny chart icon. Click and drag on a blank area of your spreadsheet to set the initial size of your graph. When you release your left mouse button, the **AutoFormat Chart** dialog appears.

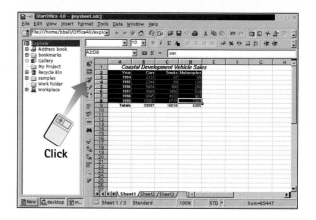

Click

2 Set Autoformat Options

The **AutoFormat Chart** dialog leads you through the steps to create your chart. If your data has row and column labels, make sure to click the **First Row as Label** and **First Column as Label** check boxes. Click the **Next** button to continue.

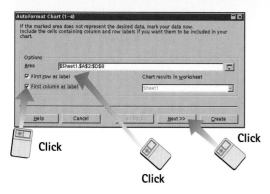

Click

Click

Click

3 Choose a Chart

Scroll through the chart types and select a chart. Note that that the **Preview** area of dialog shows how your data will look. When finished, click the **Next** button to continue.

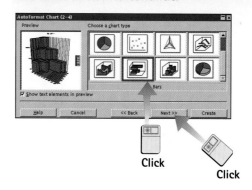

Click

Click

4 Set Grid Lines or a Variation

Click the **X Axis**, **Y Axis**, or **Z Axis** check boxes to add lines to your chart. If you want, click a chart variation, and then click the **Next** button to continue. Note that you can also return to previous dialogs if you change your mind about the chart; simply click the **Back** button.

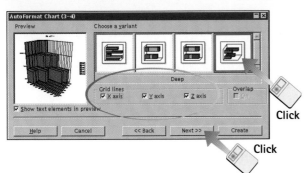

Click
Click

5 Set Chart Title

Enter a name for your chart in the **Chart Title** field. You can also add titles to the X, Y, or Z axes. To add a legend, click the **Yes** radio button, and then click the **Create** button to have StarCalc draw your chart.

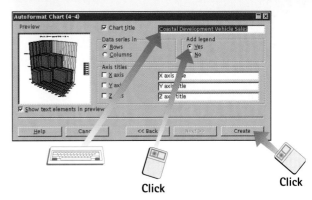

Click
Click

6 Preview, Move, or Resize Your

The chart appears in your spreadsheet. Click in a blank area of the spreadsheet, and then click the spreadsheet again to enable the chart's eight resize anchor points. To resize your chart, click and drag an anchor point while holding down your left mouse button. To delete your chart, press the **Backspace** key or **Delete** button when the anchor points are displayed. When finished, save your spreadsheet by selecting **Save** from the **File** menu.

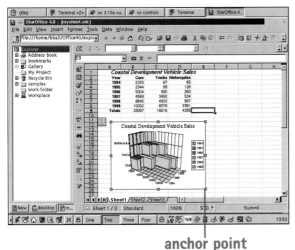

anchor point

End

How-To Hints

Changing Chart Fonts

You can change the font used in your chart by right-clicking the chart element whose font you want to change. For example, if you want to change the font of the chart's title, click the title to select it, right-click it, and choose **Object Properties** from the pop-up menu. A **Title** dialog appears. Click the **Character** tab and set the font, style, size, effect, and color of the font. This also works for the legend. To change the axis fonts, open the **Format** menu, choose **Axis**, and then click the axis for which you want to change the font.

Using Different Chart Views

Three-dimensional charts are attractive, but they sometimes need to be rotated or stretched to better display data. To change the view of your chart, open the **Format** menu and choose **3-D View**. A **3-D View** dialog appears. Change the X-, Y-, or Z-axis orientation by increasing or decreasing the degree of the angle.

How to Create a Personalized Calendar

This task shows you how StarCalc can help you quickly create a custom calendar for any month or year. You can use StarOffice's template feature to create these calendars, which can then be edited, saved, or printed.

Begin

1 Choose a Calendar Template

Start by opening the **File** menu, choosing **New**, and then clicking **From Template**. In the **New** template dialog, click the **Spreadsheets** category and the **Yearly/Monthly Calendar** template. Click the **Preview** check box, and then the **More** button to see a preview and short description. Click **OK**.

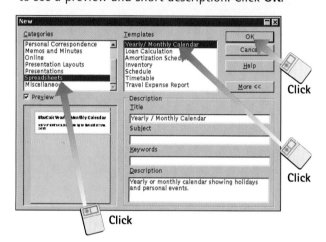

Click

Click

Click

2 Select a Calendar Type

In the **Calendar Template** dialog, click **Year Overview** or **Month** in the **Calendar** section. You also need to enter a year—or the desired month and year—in the **Time Frame** section. Next, click the **Personal Data** button.

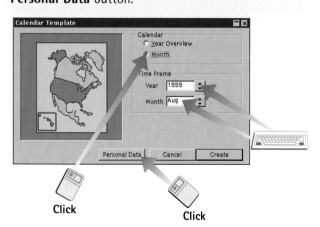

Click

Click

3 Enter Personal Data

Click in the **Event** field and type the name of an event. Then type the day and month of the event in the appropriate fields. If this is a one-time event, click the **One-Time** check box, which enables you to enter a year. Click the **Insert** button to submit the event and to enter another one. To delete an event, click it in the list, and then click **Delete**. When finished, click **Create**.

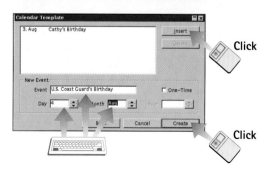

Click

Click

4 Select Graphics for Your Calendar

StarCalc then creates your calendar. To add a graphic, click the plus sign to the left of the **Gallery** entry in the Explorer and double-click **Miscellaneous**. The Beamer opens and displays rows of graphics.

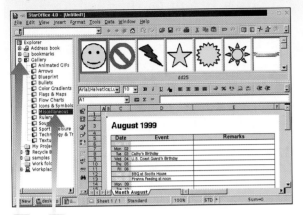

Click **Double Click**

5 Insert a Graphic in Your Calendar

Click a graphic you like. Then, holding down your left mouse button, drag the graphic from the Beamer to your spreadsheet and release. Resize the graphic by holding down the **Shift** key and clicking and dragging. Move the graphic by dragging it around the sheet. Save or print your calendar by selecting the appropriate command from the **File** menu.

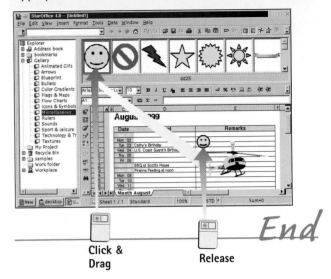

Click & Drag **Release**

End

How-To Hints

Graphics on My Display Lose Color!

Don't worry if graphics lose color on your display. When you print StarOffice graphics to your color printer, they look okay. A lack of color probably means that you're using only 256 colors, or an 8-bit pixel depth during your X session. If your computer's graphics card supports more than 256 colors, and the XFree86 XF86_SVGA server supports your graphics card, use a greater color depth for your X session. For example, to use X and the K Desktop Environment, use **kde** and the **–bpp** option followed by a color depth like 16 by typing **kde – -bpp 16**.

What's the Day?

OpenLinux comes with many other tools you can use to create weekly, monthly, or annual calendars. From the command line of your console or an X terminal window, use the **cal** command, which prints the current month's calendar. If you use **gcal**, the current month is printed, but the current day is highlighted. If you use **tcal**, tomorrow's day is highlighted. To set appointments for a weekly, monthly, or annual calendar, try the **ical** X11 client. If you like to use a day planner, try the **plan** X11 client.

How to Share Spreadsheet Graphs

You can share your spreadsheet graphs with other StarOffice documents. In this task, you see how to copy and paste spreadsheet graphs into a StarWriter document. Start by opening a StarCalc spreadsheet graph.

Begin

1 Copy a Graph to the Clipboard

Create and click on a new graph (or click on an existing graph), and then open the **Edit** menu and choose **Copy**. (Note that you can also select the graph and then press **Ctrl+C**.) The graph is now in the StarOffice clipboard.

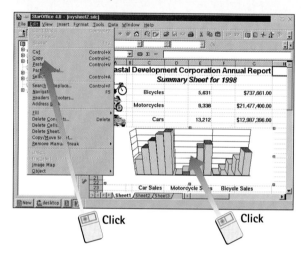

Click   Click

2 Open the Frame Dialog

Open an existing StarWriter document or create a new one. Then open the **Insert** menu and choose **Frame**. The **Frame** dialog opens. By default, your frame has a thin, black border. Click the **Borders** tab and then click the far left box in the **Presets** section to specify that no border be used. When finished, click the **OK** button.

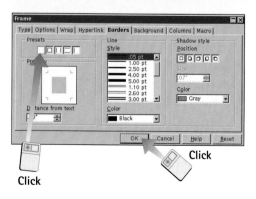

Click

Click

3 Select Paste

The new frame appears in your document. Resize the frame by clicking and dragging one of its eight anchor points. When finished, click a blank area of your document and then click inside the frame—you see a blinking insertion cursor. Open the **Edit** menu and choose **Paste**.

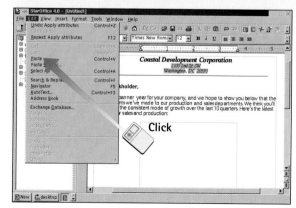

Click

4 Edit the Frame

Your graph appears in the frame. To resize the graph in the frame, click and drag one of the graph's eight anchor points. You can move the graph within the confines of the frame; you can also add text to the frame by clicking in a blank frame area. Move the graph to make room for any regular document text.

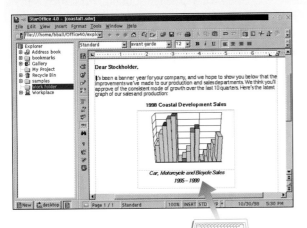

5 Add Background

To add a color background to your frame, right-click inside the frame and choose **Paragraph** from the pop-up menu. Click the **Background** tab on the **Paragraph** dialog, and click a background color, such as **Gray 10%**. Click **OK**. When finished, save or print your document by choosing the appropriate command from the **File** menu.

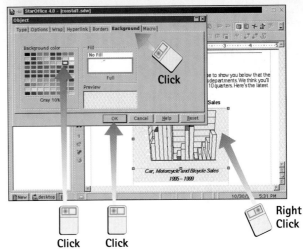

End

How-To Hints

Working Around Frames

With your frame selected, choose **Frame** from the **Format** menu to determine how the frame interacts with text. When the **Frame** dialog appears, click the **Wrap** tab, and then select the type of text wrapping you desire. By choosing different values in the **Spacing** section, you can change how much space is between your text and each side of the frame.

Working Around Pictures

If you insert a graphic into your StarOffice document, choose **Picture** from the **Format** menu to determine how text interacts with your picture. When the **Pictures** dialog appears, click the **Wrap** tab and choose the type of text wrapping. An exciting feature under the **Options** section is the **Contour** check box. If you click **Contour**, text flows around the outside edges of your picture and not just around its box!

How to Share Spreadsheet Data

You can share spreadsheet data between StarCalc and StarWriter. This task shows you how to insert spreadsheet data into your word-processing documents.

Begin

1 Copy a Spreadsheet

Open a spreadsheet document. Click and drag to select the desired data and select **Copy** from the **Edit** menu.

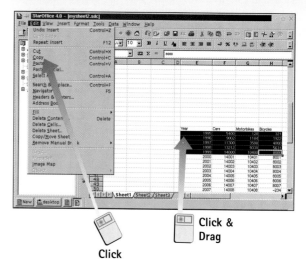

Click

Click & Drag

2 Select Paste Special

Open your StarWriter document, and then select **Paste Special** from the **Edit** menu.

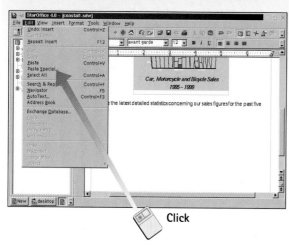

Click

3 Select Data Type

In the **Paste Contents** dialog, click the **StarCalc Spreadsheet** item as the clipboard contents type. Then click the **OK** button.

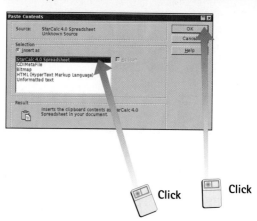

Click   Click

4 Review Data

The pasted spreadsheet data appears in a box with eight anchor points. You can resize the pasted data like a graphic by clicking and dragging the different points. Move the pasted data by pressing the left mouse button and dragging the box around the page.

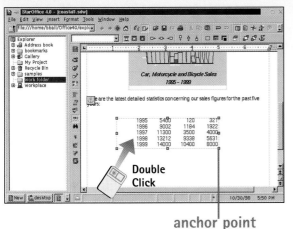

Double Click

anchor point

5 Edit Data

You can even edit the data! Double-click your left mouse button on the pasted data; a StarCalc window appears on your document's page. You can make changes to the data by clicking on different cells and typing new information. When finished, click outside the data area. Then resume editing and save or print your document.

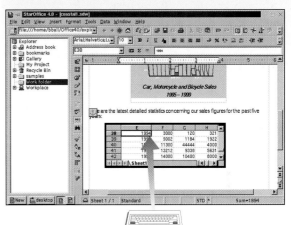

End

How-To Hints

How Do I Put Other Pictures into My Document?

To put a graphic (other than one from StarOffice's **Gallery** folder in the Explorer) into your document, open the **Insert** menu, choose **Picture**, and then click **From File**. In the **Insert Picture** dialog, navigate through your folders to select a picture and click the **Open** button.

How Many Types of Graphics Can I Use?

You can insert one of at least fifteen types of graphics into your StarOffice documents, including scanned images, Macintosh graphics, and Windows bitmaps. Click the drop-down menu in the **File type** area of the **Insert Picture** dialog to see the different types of graphics you can insert.

Changing Chart Data on the Fly

If a pasted chart's data is incorrect, you don't have to reopen its spreadsheet and go through the whole process of re-creating the chart! Select the chart's graphic, and then select **Edit | Object | Edit**. A thick, black bar appears around the chart. Select **Chart Data** from the **View** menu; a dialog with the chart's spreadsheet data appears. Change the desired values, and then click the **Transfer data** button (to the right of the input field). You see your chart's graphic updated on your document's page!

Task

14

Getting Started with StarOffice Presentations

*S*tarImpress is the presentation application included with the StarOffice suite of programs. Use this program, along with StarOffice's gallery of art, to quickly create presentation slides or graphics. Using StarImpress and the StarOffice AutoPilot feature, you can also create complex documents with minimal effort.

This chapter shows you how to create a formal presentation, a certificate, and a business report. Because StarOffice requires the X Window System, you need to start an X session. Start StarOffice from the command line of a terminal window by typing **Office40/bin/soffice &**. ●

How to Use the Presentation AutoPilot

This task leads you through the essential steps of creating an AutoPilot presentation with StarImpress. When you've finished creating the document, you can save your work or print the final product.

Begin

1 Start a Presentation AutoPilot

Open the StarOffice window's **File** menu and choose **AutoPilot | Presentation**. The AutoPilot's **Welcome** dialog appears; click **Next** to continue.

Click

2 Enter Information

In the **Basic Ideas** dialog, click each field and enter the appropriate information. Click **Next** to continue.

Click

3 Select the Type of Presentation

Click the radio button next to the type of presentation you'd like to create. As you click each type, a new description of the presentation appears in the **Description** field. Pick one best suited for your purpose, and then click **Next**.

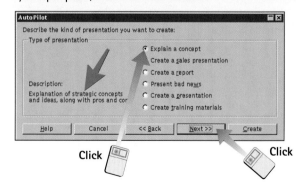

Click   Click

4 Select the Design and Duration

Choose a design for your presentation under the **Presentation Design** section, and then choose a duration. Click **Next** to continue.

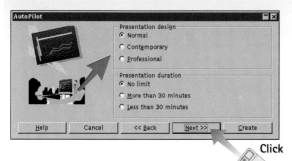

Click

5 Select Presentation Medium

Click the type of medium for your presentation—whether it's paper, overhead, or slide—and then click **Next**.

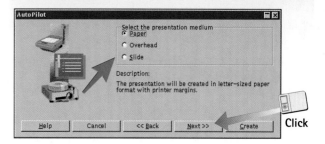

Click

6 Create the Presentation

The next dialog tells you that you're finished. Click **Create**. StarOffice then creates your StarImpress document, using the parameters you specified in the AutoPilot.

End

How-To Hints

Flying on AutoPilot

StarOffice comes with a number of different AutoPilot documents. To see how to create a personal calendar, see Chapter 13, "Getting Started with StarCalc." To see how to create a business letter, see Chapter 12, "Getting Started with StarWriter."

Using the Desktop

To learn more about using the StarOffice desktop, see Chapter 11, "Getting Started with StarOffice." You can also get a bit more information from the StarOffice **Help** menu.

PowerPoint 97 Users

To open a PowerPoint 97 document, open the **File** menu and click **Open**. Click the **File Type** drop-down menu and select MS PowerPoint 97, and then click your PowerPoint document and click the **Open** button.

Using Slides

To learn more about creating your presentation as a slide show, read the StarOffice user guide's chapter on working with presentations and graphics. You can find the StarOffice user guide on your OpenLinux CD-ROM under the **Star Office** directory. You need the Acrobat or xpdf X11 client to open and read the guide, because the document is in Adobe Acrobat format.

How to Create a Certificate

You can use StarOffice templates to create other types of StarImpress documents. This task shows you how to create a simple certificate using one of StarOffice's miscellaneous templates.

Begin

1 Select Template Menu Item

Open the **File** menu, choose **New**, and select **From Template**.

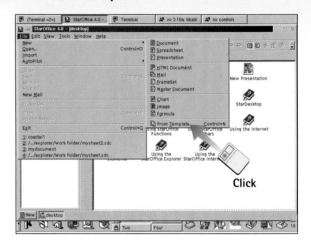

Click

2 Select Certificate Template

In the **New** dialog, click the **Miscellaneous** entry in the **Categories** list, and then click the **Certificate** entry in the **Templates** list. Check **Preview** to see a picture of a sample document. When finished, click **OK**.

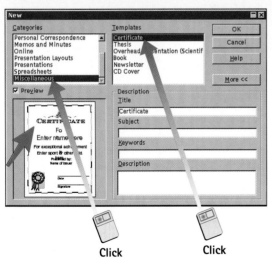

Click   Click

3 Enter a Title, Select a Layout

Click the **Name** field and type a title for your certificate. You can select a different type of layout, but for the purposes of this exercise, use the default type selected by StarOffice. Click **OK**.

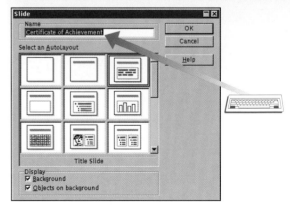

4 Enter the Recipient's Name

Click the **Enter Name Here** item on the certificate page and type the recipient's name.

5 Type the Endeavor

Click the **Enter Sport or Other Field Here** item on the certificate and type an endeavor.

6 Enter Issuer

Click the **Name of Issuer** item and enter a name. When finished, click a blank area to the side of the certificate to view your work.

End

How-To Hints

Other Fun Templates

Look for other templates, such as the greeting card template, that you can use to create fun documents.

Sharing Documents

You can share your StarImpress documents with other applications. See "How to Export Your Impress Document," later in this chapter, to learn how to create and save documents for other programs, such as the GNU Image Manipulation Program (GIMP). To learn more about using graphics clients with X11, see Chapter 15, "Capturing and Creating Graphics."

Printing in Color

Of course, you want to print your certificate in color if you have a color printer. Make sure you've used the **lisa** command to configure OpenLinux for color printing. See Chapter 16, "Printing Text Files and Graphics," for more information.

How to Create a Business Project

Use StarOffice's templates to create more complex documents, such as a business project presentation. This task shows you how to quickly create a presentation, including charted data, without using StarCalc.

Begin

1 Select Business Project Template

Open StarOffice's **File** menu, choose **New**, and then select **From Template**. In the **New** dialog, click the **Presentations** entry under the **Categories** list and choose the **Business Project** item under the **Templates** list. Click **OK**.

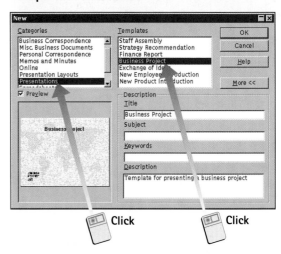

Click   Click

2 Enter a Name, Select a Layout

Click the **Name** field, and type a name for the report. Scroll through the layout field and click a layout that has a chart object. Note that when you move your mouse over a layout, a small window appears with information about the layout. When finished, click **OK**.

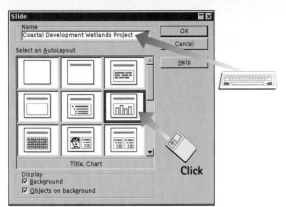

Click

3 Select Presentation View

StarOffice creates a StarImpress presentation. Note that if you choose **Master View** from the **View** menu, you can look at the presentation in different ways. Click **Outline**.

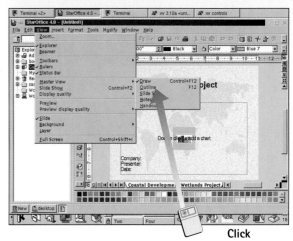

Click

4 Edit Presentation Text

Your presentation's outline, in text form, appears. StarImpress automatically generates the outline according to the type of presentation you specified in steps 1 through 3. Edit the text under each slide's headline (denoted by a small rectangle) and type your presentation's outline. When finished, open the **View** menu, choose **Master View**, and select **Draw**.

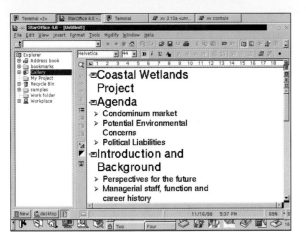

5 Add a Chart

Double-click the chart box on the slide; a dummy chart appears. Open the **View** menu and select **Chart Data**.

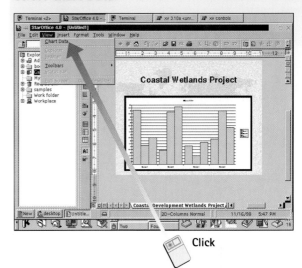

Click

6 Edit and Update Chart

Click each item in the **Chart Data** dialog, and edit the data to fit your projects. Use the different buttons to change your data or the number of rows and columns. When finished, click the **Transfer Data** button to update your chart. When finished, click the × button in the upper-right corner of the **Chart Data** window.

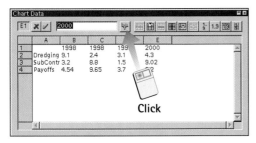

Click

End

How-To Hints

Using Data Charts

This task shows how to create a chart by changing the dummy chart's data. To see how to create your own charts, see Chapter 13. You learn how to create your own spreadsheets, and have StarCalc graph your data.

Spell Check Too!

Because StarImpress is part of the StarOffice suite of programs, you can use spell check to make sure there are no misspelled words! Choose **Spellcheck** from the **Tools** menu to check your documents when editing your presentation in outline mode.

How to Export Your Impress Document

This task shows you how to export your StarImpress documents for use by other programs, such as graphics editors.

1 Select Template

Click **File**, then **New**, and then **From Template**. Click the **Miscellaneous** entry in the **Categories** list, and choose the **CD Cover** item in the **Templates** list. Click **OK**.

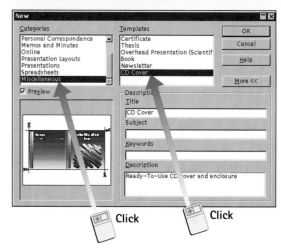

Click   Click

2 Enter Name

Enter a name for your main graphic page, and then click **OK**.

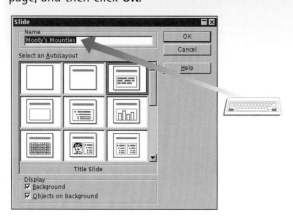

3 Edit Document

Type relevant information, such as a title, a name, or songs. Then choose **Export** from the **File** menu.

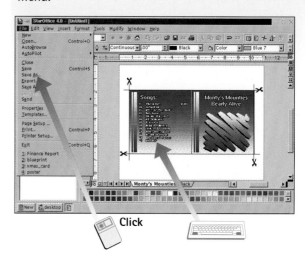

Click

4 Export Document

In the **Export** dialog, type a file name, such as **monty**, for your document. Then choose a file type (such as JPEG) from the **File Type** menu. Click **Save** (the file be named **monty.jpg**).

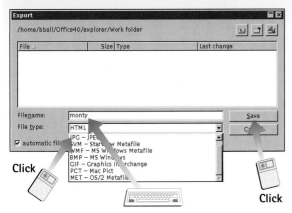

Click

Click

5 Select Graphic Options

In the **JPEG Options** dialog, type a quality percentage, click **Grayscale** or **True Colors**, and then click **OK**. When finished, quit StarOffice by choosing **Exit** from the **File** menu (save the document first if you want to export it again).

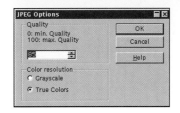

6 Load the Graphic with GIMP

You can then load the graphic using GIMP. From the command line of an X11 terminal window, type `gimp Office40/explorer/Wor*/monty.jpg`. GIMP loads your graphic for editing.

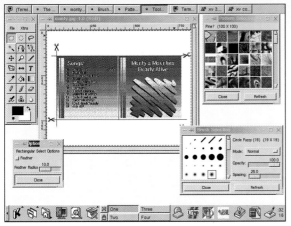

End

How-To Hints

Converting Graphics

If you'd like your StarImpress document in a graphics format other than those supported by the Export function, see Chapter 15. You learn how to use other programs for OpenLinux that convert your graphic into one of more than seventy graphics formats.

Graphics Formats

StarImpress can export each slide's page as an HTML, JPEG, WMF, BMP, GIF, PICT, or MET graphic. The most popular formats are JPEG and GIF, although other formats, such as BMP and PICT, are used by Windows and Macintosh users.

Creating Graphics

Exporting your presentation or StarImpress document is only one way to create graphics. All StarOffice documents have drawing tools available from the vertical toolbar on the left side of the work area that you can use to draw simple graphics. When working with StarImpress, use the **Draw** view to gain access to these tools.

Task

15

Capturing and Creating Graphics

Graphics are an important part of using Linux. Graphics are used in icons, in programs' toolbars, in the desktop, and in documents. Using graphics can make using Linux more fun and interesting.

This chapter shows you how to capture, create, and convert graphics files. You'll see that OpenLinux comes with a wealth of graphics editors and conversion utilities, some of which—such as GIMP—rival commercial software applications.

You need to run the X Window System to use many (but not all) of these programs. Read on and see how you can get started with your own graphics! ●

How to Capture a Window or Desktop

Several programs installed with OpenLinux can be used to capture and save graphic files off your display. This task starts with one of the simplest capture programs and then shows you how to use **xv**, a more flexible utility.

Begin

1 Start xwd

The **xwd** (X Window dump) command is started from the command line of an X terminal window. Type the command and, using output redirection with the shell's > operator, redirect **xwd**'s output to the name of a graphic file, like this: **xwd > capture.xwd**. When you press the **Enter** key, your cursor turns into a cross-hair.

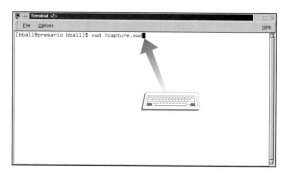

2 Capture a Window

To capture a window, move the cross-hair cursor to a window and click with your left mouse button. To capture the entire desktop, use **xwd** with the **-root** option. You can also use the **-out** option, followed by a filename for the captured graphic. From the command line of a terminal window, type **xwd -root -out desktop.xwd**. When you press the **Enter** key, a picture of the entire desktop is saved in file **desktop.xwd**. The file is saved in the X Window dump format.

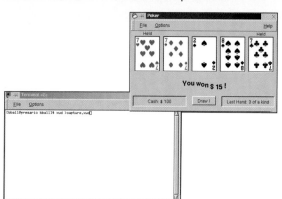

3 Start xv

The **xv** client is a capable graphics utility included with OpenLinux. Start **xv** from the command line of an X11 terminal window like by typing **xv &**. A splash screen appears; right-click the display to open the **xv Controls** dialog. Click the **Grab** button to begin.

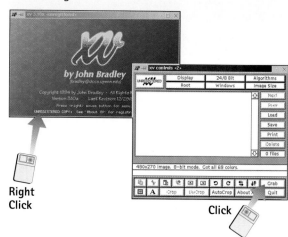

Right Click

Click

4 Grab a Window or Desktop

To grab a window or the entire desktop, click the **Grab** button in the **xv Grab** dialog and click a window or a blank area in your desktop to capture a graphic of the window or the desktop, respectively. Click the **Hide XV Windows** check box before you click the **Grab** button. This hides **xv**.

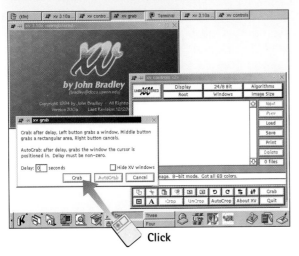

Click

6 Specify Graphics Type

When the **xv Save** dialog appears, click the **Save File** field and type a name, such as **mygraphic**. To save the graphic in one of fourteen different formats, click the **Format** button, and then select a graphic type from the drop-down list. Don't forget to use an appropriate extension for the filename. For example, when saving a Graphics Interchange Format, or GIF, graphic, type **.gif** at the end of your file's name. When finished, click the **OK** button.

5 Save a Grabbed Graphic

A captured window appears in a new **xv** window. To save the graphic, click the **Save** button on the **xv Controls** window.

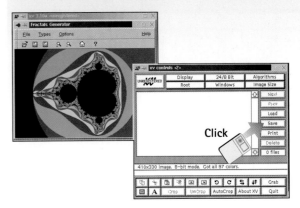

Click

How-To Hints

Is There a KDE Capture Program?

Yes! Browse to **http://www.kde.org/applications.html** and download ksnapshot. This handy tool captures an image of a window or the desktop and can save the capture in five different graphics formats.

Is xv Free?

No! Unlike the majority of software included with OpenLinux, **xv** is shareware. For personal use, **xv** is free, but if you use it for work, you must pay a $25 registration fee. For more information, click the **About XV** button in the **xv Controls** dialog, or read the **xv** documentation under the **/usr/doc** directory.

End

How to View Graphic Images

There are many different ways to view graphics with Linux. This task shows you how to view the screenshots captured in the previous task and shows what you can do with them.

Begin

1 Undump a Window Dump

When you capture and save a graphic using the **xwd** command, use the **xwud** (X Window undump) command to display the graphic. On the command line of a terminal window, use the **xwud** command and its **–in** command line option, followed by the name of your **xwd** graphic, like so: **xwud -in capture.xwd**. After you press the **Enter** key, the graphic is displayed in a window on your desktop.

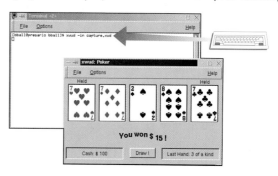

2 Display a Graphic

The **xloadimage** command included with OpenLinux can display nearly 20 different graphics file formats. From the command line of a terminal window, type **xloadimage mygraphic.gif** (where **mygraphic.gif** is the name of your graphic). After you press the **Enter** key, the graphic is displayed in a window on your desktop.

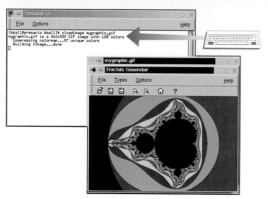

3 Load an Image into the Desktop

One of the fun things you can do is load an image into the desktop, or root window. Use the **xloadimage** command, along with its **–onroot** and **–fullscreen** options, followed by the name of the graphic, like this: **xloadimage -fullscreen -onroot mygraphic.gif**. The image enlarges to fill the background, or root display, of your desktop.

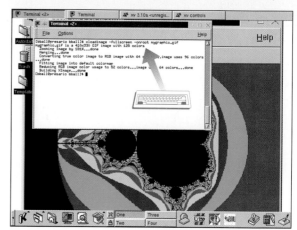

4 Change a Capture

OpenLinux comes with a number of programs you can use to change the appearance of your graphic. For example, to rotate an image 45°, use the **display** command along with its **–rotate** command-line option like this: `display -rotate -45 mygraphic.gif`. The **display** command has many other options for changing graphics! See the **display** man page to learn how to create other effects with your graphics.

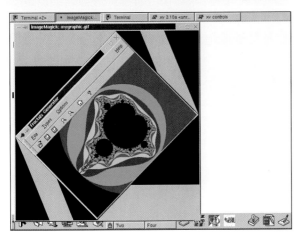

5 Magnify an Icon

Another nifty utility to display and capture a portion of a window or your desktop is the **xmag** client. From the command line of a terminal window, type **xmag** and press the **Enter** key. Your cursor changes to a backward 7. Click a part of your display, and **xmag** captures and magnifies the area you clicked.

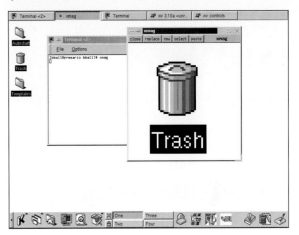

6 View a Graphic with kview

KDE fans will definitely want to use the **kview** utility to view graphics. This program supports drag and drop to display graphics. Click the **Application Starter** button on your desktop's panel, choose **Graphics**, and then click **Image Viewer**. The **kview** window appears. If you have your home folder open in your desktop, select a graphics file, and drag it into **kview**'s main window. Double-click the graphic's name in **kview**'s window; **kview** displays it in a separate window. Use **kview**'s toolbar buttons to shrink, enlarge, or resize the graphic.

Double Click

End

How-To Hints

I Don't Use KDE, but I Want a Root Image!

If you don't use KDE, but you'd like to use a graphic as the background, you'll have to put the **xloadimage** command line into your **.xinitrc** file in your home directory. For more details about using **.xinitrc**, see Chapter 2, "Getting Started with the X Window System."

My Graphic Looks Awful!

Although the problem could be that the graphic is low resolution, or an enlargement of a small picture, it might be that your color depth isn't high enough. Use as many colors as possible for your X sessions. Use the **startx** or **kde** commands to start your X session. Type **kde — -bpp 16** to enable your X session to support thousands of colors or **kde — -bpp 24** for millions of colors.

How to Open a Graphic with GIMP

The *GNU Image Manipulation Program*, or *GIMP*, is one of the latest and best graphics tools for Linux, with features that rival commercial graphics applications. GIMP has many different menus, tools, and filters, but, in this task, you learn how easy it is to use. Start GIMP from the command line of a terminal window by typing **gimp &**. A dialog appears, telling you that GIMP will install a configuration directory in your home directory. Click the **Install** button to continue. A second dialog shows what has been installed. Click the **Continue** button to start editing.

Begin

1 Read the Tip of the Day

After GIMP installs its directory and displays a few splash screens, you see the GIMP tip of the day. Click the **Close** button.

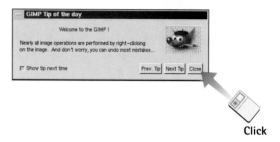

Click

2 Show Tool Dialogs

If you plan to spend some time editing, open the **File** menu, choose **Dialogs**, and click **Brushes**. Repeat this step until each item listed in the **Dialogs** submenu is displayed.

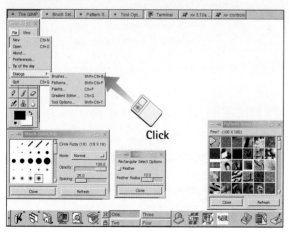

Click

3 Open a Graphics File

Display a graphics file by clicking the **File** menu and choosing **Open**. Scroll through your directories, click a graphics file's name, and click the **OK** button.

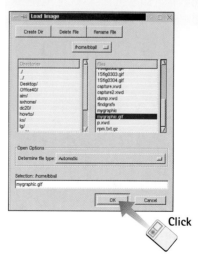

Click

4 Select a GIMP Menu

The image is displayed in a GIMP window. Use GIMP's floating toolbar to select different tools, such as the pen, pencil, airbrush, fill bucket, or eraser. To access the full set of GIMP menus, right-click your mouse and hold the button over the image. A series of pop-up menus appears.

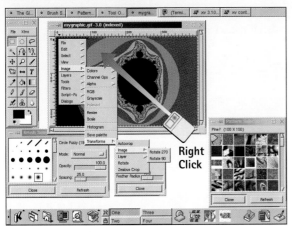

5 Save a GIMP Graphic

To save your graphic, right-click it and choose **File** | **Save as** from the pop-up menu. In the **Save Image** dialog, click the **Selection** field and type a filename. To select a different graphics format in which to save your graphic, open the drop-down list in the **Save Options** section of the dialog, and click a graphics format. When finished, click **OK**.

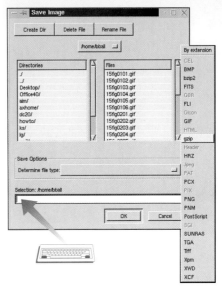

End

How-To Hints

How Do I Learn More About GIMP?

GIMP is a complex graphics application, but if you take the time to read about its features, you'll be on your way to creating great graphics in no time at all. However, in order to learn more (besides the information in its short man page), you must go to **http://www.gimp.org** for the details. You'll find a GIMP FAQ, numerous tutorials, and a wealth of information about the various GIMP tools.

How Do I Configure GIMP?

Start GIMP, open the **File** menu, and choose **Preferences**. You'll find many different settings you can change, such as the default image size and type, how many levels of undo are supported (five is the default), or what directories to use.

My System Slows Down When I Open a Graphics File!

You should be warned that opening large graphics with GIMP can eat up a lot of your system's memory. When this happens, Linux uses the swap file you created, and if memory gets "tight," you have a lot of disk swapping. Let's put it this way: The more memory, or RAM, you have, the better off you'll be if you need to edit large graphics files.

How to Edit Graphics with the kpaint Client

This section introduces you to the **kpaint** program, which comes with the K Desktop Environment (KDE) and reads five different graphics formats. You can use this program to create your own graphics or to edit graphics files to use with KDE.

Begin

1 Start kpaint

Click the **Application Starter** button, select **Graphics**, and choose **Paint**.

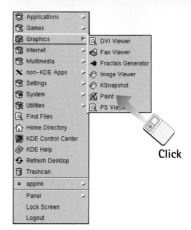

Click

2 Open a File

Note that **kpaint**, like other KDE applications, has a menu bar and a toolbar. The program has an additional toolbar, containing basic drawing tools. Open the **File** menu and choose **Open Image**; an **Open** dialog appears. Navigate through your folders and scroll through your graphics files. Click a filename and then click the **OK** button to open the file.

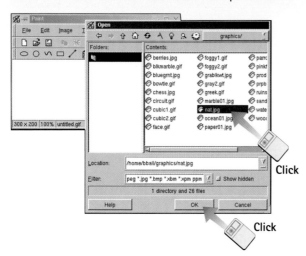

Click

Click

3 View a Graphic

Your graphic file appears in **kpaint**'s main window. To enlarge your graphic to work on it more easily, click the **Zoom In** button on **kpaint**'s toolbar.

Click

4 Edit the Graphic

The graphic enlarges. Click one of the color selector buttons on the right side of the display to set an outline or fill color. Then choose a drawing tool, such as the spray can. When you're finished "spraying" your image, click the **Zoom Out** button to view your work.

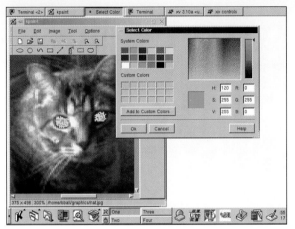

5 Save the Graphic

To overwrite the original file, choose **Save Image** from the **File** menu. To save the file with a different name, choose **File | Save Image as**; **kpaint**'s **Save** dialog appears. Type a filename in the **Location** field. Note that although **kpaint** can read five different formats, you must save the file in JPEG (Joint Picture Experts Group) format. Graphic files of this type usually have a name ending in **.jpg**. When finished, click the **OK** button.

End

How-To Hints

Freedom of Choice

You'll find many other graphics tools included on your OpenLinux CD-ROM. For technical drawing, try the **xfig** or **tgif** clients. Another paint program to try is **xpaint**. You can also use the **display** command as a graphic's file editor.

How Many Graphics Formats Exist?

This is a good question. The answer is that you probably don't have to worry about using different graphics when using Linux. Why? Because your OpenLinux CD-ROM comes with programs that can read, convert, or write nearly 100 different graphics formats. Some programs, such as **xv** and the ImageMagick suite of commands discussed in the next task can convert nearly 70 different formats.

Kpaint Can Save Only JPEG Graphics?

At the time of this writing, **kpaint** was still in beta release (although quite useable). This means that by the time you read this, **kpaint** might have additional features and tools and better documentation. Check **http://www.kde.org** for details about the latest versions of any KDE application. Besides, you can always convert a **kpaint** graphic to another format by using another graphics utility!

How to Convert Graphics

This task shows you how to convert different graphics formats. By using a couple of different graphics programs, you should be able to read, process, and convert 70 different graphics formats. You'll see how to use the **xv** and ImageMagick clients to convert files.

Begin

1 Start xv

Start **xv** and open a graphics file, such as a KDE wallpaper JPG file. From the command line of a terminal window, type **xv /opt/kde/share/wallpapers/ruins.jpg &**. The graphic appears in a window. Right-click the window to display the **xv Controls** dialog.

2 Convert and Save the Graphic

Click **xv**'s **Save** button, and the **xv Save** dialog appears. To convert the graphic to a different format, such as TIFF (Tagged Image File Format), click the **Format** button and choose **TIFF** from the drop-down list that opens. Note that the file's name in the **Save File** field now has an extension of **.tif**. When finished, click the **OK** button. Then, **xv** asks whether you would like to save the file in one of three different TIFF formats. Click one, and then click the **OK** button.

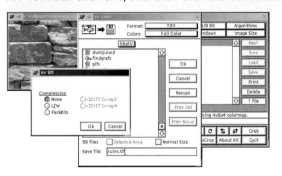

3 Start ImageMagick

ImageMagick is a collection of graphics software tools you can use to edit or convert graphics. Start ImageMagick by using running its **display** command from the command line. Type **display &**; ImageMagick's splash screen appears, along with its **Open File** dialog.

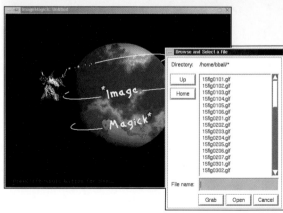

4 Open a Graphics File

Navigate through your directories by clicking the **Up** or **Home** button. The **Home** button takes you to your home directory. If you click the **Grab** button, ImageMagick performs a screen capture. Select a graphics filename, and then click the **Open** button.

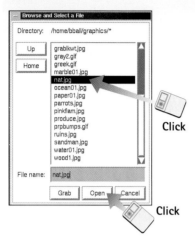

Click

Click

5 Save the Graphic

The graphic appears in a window. Right-click the window to open ImageMagick's menu. To convert your graphic, choose **Save** from the **File** menu.

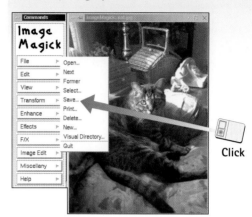

Click

6 Select the Graphic Format

Click the **Format** button in the **Browse and Select a File** dialog. Another dialog appears with a list of graphics formats. Scroll through the list, select a format such as **ZSoft PC Paintbrush** or **pcx**, and then click the **Select** button. The format dialog disappears. Next, click the **Save** button in the **Browse and Select a File** dialog to convert and save your graphic.

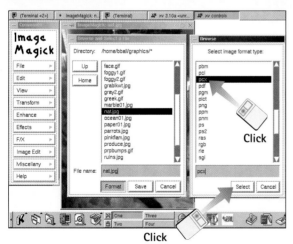

Click

How-To Hints

Use a Visual Directory

To see a window containing miniature images of all the graphics files in a directory, use ImageMagick's visual directory feature. Navigate to the graphics directory, and then start ImageMagick. Choose **Visual Directory** from the **File** menu. When the directory dialog appears, click the **Directory** button. In a few moments (maybe more, depending on the number and size of your graphics), a window appears with your images. To open a file, right-click its image.

Is There a Faster Way to Convert Graphics?

You betcha! Use ImageMagick's **convert** command. By specifying a file's extension, the **convert** command translates and saves a new graphic. For example, to convert the file **mygraphic.gif** to the PCX format, use a command line like **convert mygraphic.gif mygraphic.pcx**.

End

Task

## CHAPTER 16

Printing Text Files and Graphics

One of the most important tasks you perform when using OpenLinux is installing and configuring printing support. If you have a parallel-port printer that works with other operating systems and isn't a "WinPrinter," chances are very good that you can print text and graphics using OpenLinux.

Your time and effort in configuring printing support is quite rewarding, because you end up with a printing system that supports PostScript document preparation, including color PostScript graphics! Combine this capability with the low cost of today's color inkjet printers, and you can see why many people think OpenLinux is a bargain.

Log in as the root operator, because you need permission to configure your OpenLinux system. Some of programs discussed here also require the X Window System, so it's best to start an X session before you begin. ●

How to Install a Printer

Boot OpenLinux and log in as the root operator. Although you don't have to, you can start X. This task shows you how to configure OpenLinux to support your printer. The magic of printing with Linux happens in the background. When you print, your document is converted to the PostScript printing language, saved in your system's printer spool directory, **/var/spool/lpd**, and then fed to your printer through your computer's parallel port.

Begin

1 Plug in the Printer

Make sure your printer is plugged into your computer's parallel port and turned on.

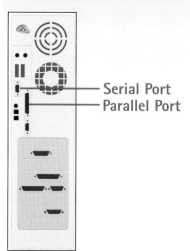

— Serial Port
— Parallel Port

2 Detect the Printer Device

On the command line of an X11 terminal window, type **dmesg ¦ less**. Scroll through the information until you find a line that looks something like **lp1 at 0x0378, (polling)**, which indicates that OpenLinux detected your printer as device **/dev/lp1** (which is one of three devices, such as **lp0** or **lp2**, under the **/dev** directory).

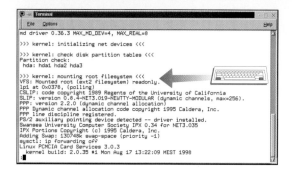

3 Check for Printer Device Support

You can check whether you have printer device support (**lp**) by listing devices in the **/proc** directory. Use the **cat** command to list the current devices and pipe the output through the **fgrep** command to print any matches (look for **lp**). Type

```
cat /proc/devices ¦ fgrep lp
  6 lp
```

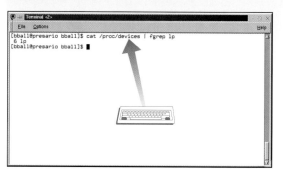

4 Check for Printer Support Module

Finally, you can check to see whether the printer support module, **lp.o**, is loaded into the kernel by typing the following:

```
lsmod ¦ fgrep lp
lp                    2           0
```

Look for a line containing **lp** after you pipe the output of the **lsmod** command (which lists currently loaded software modules).

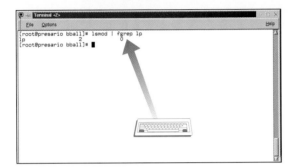

5 Start System Configuration

To begin installing your printer, start the Linux Installation and System Administration (**lisa**) tool from the command line of your terminal window by typing **lisa**. Use your keyboard's **down-arrow** key to cursor down, select **System Configuration**, and press **Enter**.

6 Select Hardware Configuration

In **lisa**'s **System Configuration** dialog, select **Hardware Configuration** and press **Enter**.

7 Select Configure Printer

In the Hardware Configuration dialog, cursor down using your **down-arrow** key and highlight item 6, **Configure Printer**. Press **Enter**.

Continues

8 Select a Printer Driver

In the **Select Printer Driver** dialog, use your cursor keys to scroll through the list of nearly 40 printer types to specify which printer driver you need to use. If you don't see your printer type listed, select a printer that most closely resembles yours (for example, if you have an HP400 deskjet, select HP deskjet). When finished, press **Enter**.

9 Select a Printer Port

In the **Configure Printer Connection** dialog, scroll through the list of printer ports and select the port—parallel or serial—to which you've connected your printer. Press **Enter**.

10 Set the Default Printer Resolution

Some printers offer different resolutions or dots per inch. Select the default resolution for your printer (check your printer's manual) in the **Default Printer Resolution** dialog and press **Enter**.

11 Select the Default Paper Size

In the **Default Paper Size** dialog, select the paper size usually used for your printer, and press **Enter**. Your printer is now configured and installed.

12 Test Your Printer

To test your new printer, try sending a directory listing to the printer using the **ls** command. Use the pipe (|) shell operator and the line-printer command, **lpr**, to send the listing to your printer; type **ls -l | lpr**. Your printer activates and a long-format listing of your directory is printed.

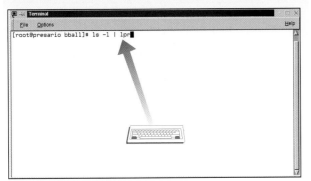

End

How-To Hints

My Printer's Not Printing!

Before you do anything else, make sure your printer is turned on. If **lpr** reports an error, the problem could be that the printer spooling system, **lprNG**, is not set up correctly, or that the printer daemon, **lpd**, is not running. For more information, see the **lpr** man page, and read the documentation under the **/usr/doc/LPRng** directory.

What About Epson Printers?

Certain models of Epson printers, such as the Stylus Color printers, require special setup procedures in order to work with OpenLinux. To find directions on setting up your Epson printer, mount your OpenLinux CD-ROM, and then use Netscape Navigator to read Caldera's Technical Support pointers:

```
mount /mnt/cdrom
netscape
/mnt/cdrom/OpenLinux/doc/col13/ind
ex.html
```

Where Else Can I Get Help on Printing?

For more information on printing, navigate to the **/usr/doc/HOWTO** directory, and read the Printing-HOWTO and the Printing-Usage-HOWTO. An easy way to peruse this information is to start Netscape Navigator, click the **Home Page** button, and browse through the HOWTO document links. Don't forget to check Caldera's Web site (**http://www.calderasystems.com**) for the latest errata or fixes. Finally, if you get stuck, join the Caldera users mailing list and ask for help (see Appendix C, "Internet Resources for Linux and OpenLinux," for details).

How to Print Text Files

There are several ways to print text files using OpenLinux. This section shows you how to print text documents using the command line, as well as using different programs included with OpenLinux.

Begin

1 Print from the Command Line

The best way to print a document from the command line is to send the file through the line-printer spooler, **lpr**, by typing `cat file.txt | lpr`.

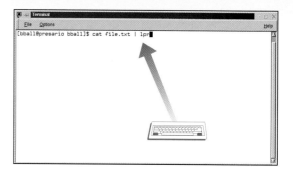

2 Print a Text File with Emacs

To print a document that has been created with or imported to the emacs text editor, open the document and select **Print Buffer** from the **File** menu. To use emacs' commands to print a document, press **Esc** and then press **X**. At the prompt, type **lpr-buffer** and press **Enter**. To print only highlighted text, press **Esc** and then **X**, and type **print-region**. To send a PostScript version of your document directly to the printer, press **Esc** and then **X**, and type **ps-print-buffer** at the prompt.

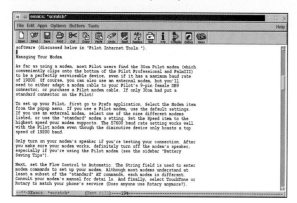

3 Import a Text File with LyX

To use the LyX editor to print text files, you must first import the file you want to print to LyX. To start LyX, type **lyx** on the command line and press **Enter**. To import a file you must create a new file and "pour" the contents of the file you are importing into it. Select **New** from the **File** menu. In the **Filename** field of the **new document** dialog, give the new file a name and click **OK**. Select **Import ASCII File** from LyX's **Insert** menu and click **As Lines**.

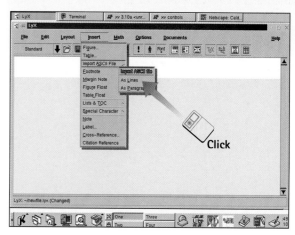

4 Select the File You Want to Print

In the **File to Insert** dialog, type the name of file whose contents you want to print and click **OK** (alternatively, you can simply double-click the file's name).

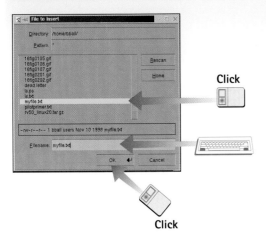

Click

Click

Click

6 Preview a PostScript Text File

You can use the **mpage** command to create PostScript documents with multiple pages on a single printed page. Printing multiple pages of text on a single page not only conserves trees, but also saves you time. To generate a PostScript file that prints two pages side-by-side in landscape format (with no border), type **mpage -2 -o myfile.txt >myfile.ps**. Although you can print directly from the command line, consider using the **gv** PostScript previewer to preview your document. Simply type **gv myfile.ps**. To send the file to your printer, choose **Print Document** from gv's **File** menu and click **Print**.

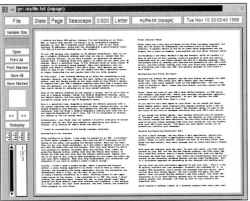

5 Print the File

Use LyX to format your document with different fonts and styles. When finished, choose **Print** from the **File** menu. In the **Print** dialog, click **Printer**, type **ps** in the **Printer** field, and click **OK** to start printing.

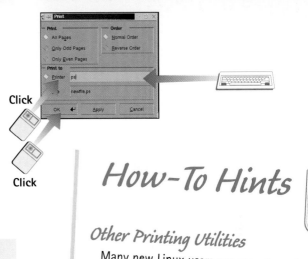

Click

Click

How-To Hints

Other Printing Utilities

Many new Linux users are accustomed to formatting text documents with a word processor. You'll be pleased to know that you can use many different typesetting software packages with OpenLinux to produce attractive documents. For starters, see the **groff** or **tex** man pages.

What About Commercial Word Processors?

For more information on creating and printing professional documents using commercial software, see Chapters 11–14, which cover the StarOffice suite of programs. In addition, Corel (**http://www.corel.com**) offers the WordPerfect word-processing system for Linux free for personal use, and a company called Applix (**http://www.applix.com**) markets an office suite called Applixware.

Print Management

Use the **lpq** command to see how many print jobs are waiting to be printed, the **lprm** command to kill any waiting print jobs, and the **lpc** command to control your printers. Make sure to read the man pages for these commands!

End

How to Print Graphic Images

Many different programs included with OpenLinux print graphics. This section shows you how to print graphic files using three different applications. You see how to preview PostScript graphics and prepare other files for printing.

Begin

1 Select Print Mode with xv

Start **xv** and load a graphic file. The graphic's image appears onscreen. Right-click the image to see the **xv controls** dialog and click the **Print** button. In the **xv prompt** dialog, click a print mode, such as grayscale.

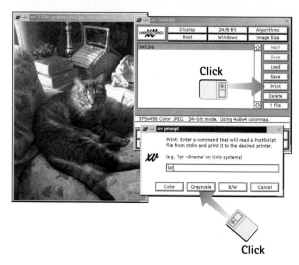

Click

Click

2 Select Print Options

In the **xv postscript** dialog, click the desired orientation and paper size. Click the **Center**, **Origin**, or **Max** button to adjust the image's size on the printed page and click **OK** to print your document.

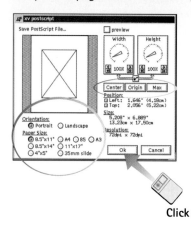

Click

3 Load a Graphic with tgv

To start **gv** from the command line and load a sample image (in this example, **tiger.ps**), type **gv /usr/share/ghostscript/4.03/examples/ tiger.ps**.

4 Print a PostScript Graphic

Choose **Print Document** from **gv's File** menu and click **Print** in the dialog that opens.

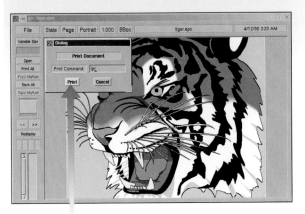

 Click

5 Load a Graphic

Start the **display** command, specifying the name of a graphic image like so: **display /usr/ share/ghostscript/4.03/examples/tiger.ps**. Press **Enter**. When the graphic appears, click the image to display ImageMagick's menu and choose **Print** from the **File** menu.

 Click

6 Select Geometry and Print

Click the page size used by your printer and then click the **Select** button. A small print dialog appears. Click **Print** to print your graphic.

Click

End

How-To Hints

Other Graphics Programs

See Chapter 15, "Capturing and Creating Graphics," for information about GIMP. This professional graphics tool can also be used to send images to your printer. To create and print technical drawings and other images, try the **xfig** or **tgif** clients. To print other graphic images, such as bitmap files, try the **xpaint** program. All these software packages are included with OpenLinux.

Converting Graphics

You can find more than 175 different graphics-conversion programs on your OpenLinux CD-ROM. These programs, part of the portable bitmap, pixmap, graymap, and anymap software packages, are used from the command line of your console or X11 terminal window. For details, see the **pbm**, **ppm**, **pnm**, and **pgm** man pages.

Task

17

Setting Schedules and Using Productivity Programs

*T*his chapter shows you how configure and use various productivity programs with OpenLinux, X11, and the K Desktop Environment. You'll see how to start and configure calculators, set appointments, maintain an address book, use sticky notes on the desktop, track your time, and use different calendars.

You use the K Desktop Environment for this chapter's tasks, so first start an X11 session using KDE. On the command line of your console, type **kde** and press **Enter**. ●

How to Start and Configure Calculators

This task shows you how to start and configure the xcalc and kcalc calculators included with OpenLinux.

Begin

1 Select Calculator

Click the **Utilities** button on your desktop's panel, and then click **Calculator** to start the kcalc client.

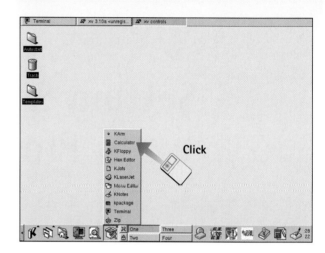

2 Select a Base

Click **Dec** to perform calculations in decimal, or base 10, mode. kcalc can also use hexadecimal (base 16), octal (base 8), and binary (base 2).

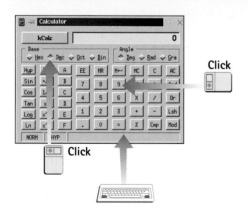

3 Enter and Translate a Number

By clicking kcalc's number pad, enter the number **32767**. The preferred method is to use the keypad of your keyboard. If you have a laptop or a keyboard without a keypad, turn on **Num Lock** and use the keypad numbers printed on your keyboard. As a last resort, you can use the numbers and characters %, *, -, +, /, and = on your keyboard (**Backspace** or **Del** clears all results). Click **Hex** to translate **32767** into hexadecimal.

4 Configure kcalc

Click **kCalc** (the button above the **Base** buttons) to view the **KCalc Configuration** dialog. Click **Statistical Mode** to change kcalc's buttons to perform statistical calculations (the default is trigonometry mode).

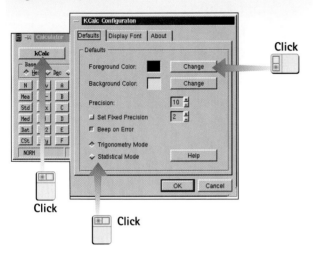

Click

Click

Click

5 Select a Color

Click the **Change** button next to Foreground Color to change the color of kcalc's LEDs. Then, click the **Change** button next to Background Color to change the background color. When finished, click **OK**.

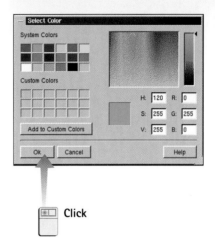

Click

Click

6 View Results

kcalc then implements your changes. Click **OK** to exit KCalc Configuration, and then click the close button (×) in the upper-right corner of kcalc's window to quit. Your changes remain in effect the next time you use kcalc.

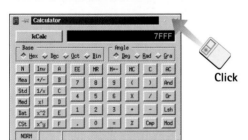

Click

End

How-To Hints

Limits

Number translation to binary is limited to 32,767 decimal. If you try to convert a number larger than this, you get an error.

Other Calculators

The XFree86 distribution of X11 also includes another graphic calculator called **xcalc**. Type **xcalc** at the command line of a terminal and press **Enter** to start this calculator. If you don't use X, try the interactive **dc** calculator. To program with a calculator-like language, try the **bc** calculator, which reads calculating operations from a file.

How to Use KJots

This task shows you how to quickly take notes with the KJots program. Use this program to jot down information and save indexed notes in different "books" on your hard drive. You should know that although you can save a lot of information using KJots, it's not a word processor[md]but you save notepaper!

Begin

1 Start KJots

Click the **Utilities** button on your desktop's panel and click **KJots**.

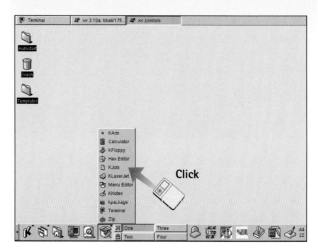

Click

2 Create a New Book

The **KJots** window appears. Open the **File** menu and click **New Book**.

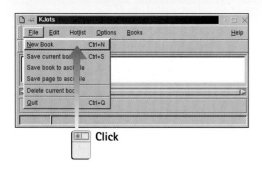

Click

3 Name the Book

Click the **Book Name** field and type a subject, date, or other mnemonic (such as **Pets**) for your new KJots book and click **OK**.

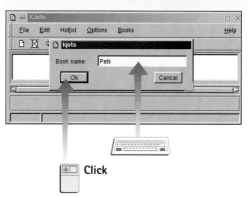

Click

4 Enter a Subject

Click the blank field next to the book's name and enter a short, more specific subject, such as **Feeding Schedule**. Next, click the blank field and type your note.

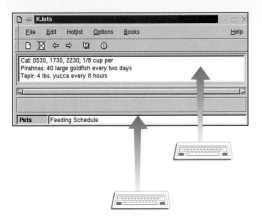

5 Add a Page

Open the **Edit** menu and click **New Page** to add a page to the current book. Repeat the previous step with a different subject and text.

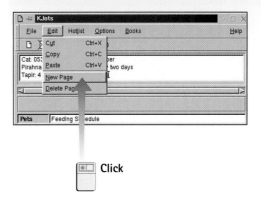

Click

6 Save Book and View Subjects

When you've finished taking notes, press **Ctrl+S**, or open the **File** menu and click **Save Current Book**. To view the list of subjects for the current book, click the **Subject List** button. A **kjots** dialog appears with a list of subjects. Double-click a subject to add more text, or click **Close**.

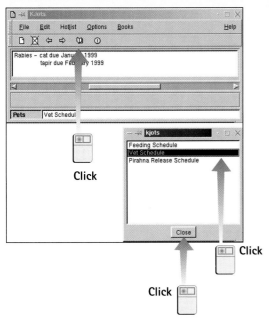

Click

Click

Click

Click

How-To Hints

KJots Keyboard Quickies

Press **Ctrl+A** to add a new subject, or page, to the current book. To switch to different subjects, click the **Next** or **Previous** buttons in KJots's toolbar. To show the list of subjects in the current book, press **Ctrl+L**.

Improvements

Periodically check **http://www.kde.org** to see whether a new version of KJots has been released.

Other Features

KJots also has a HotList feature that you can use to switch to different books. Open the **Help** menu and click **Contents** to read about how to use this and other features.

End

How to Take Notes with KNotes

This task shows you how to use KNotes, which is used for quick note-taking. It also has some unique features you can use to save or share information.

Begin

1 Start KNotes

Click the **Utilities** button on your desktop's panel then click **KNotes**.

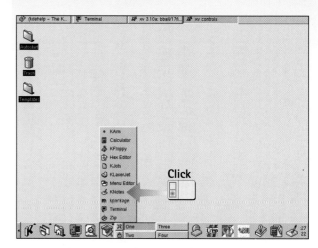

2 Insert the Date

Right-click the **knote** window, click **Insert Date**, and enter text.

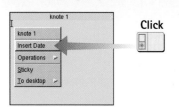

3 Open Menu to Rename

Right-click the **knote** window, and then click **Operations | Rename Note**.

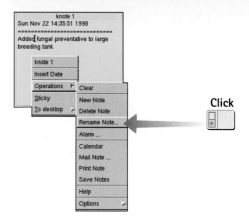

4 Rename Note

Click and type a name in the blank field, and then click **Rename**.

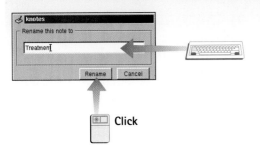

Click

5 Set Alarm

Right-click the **knote** window, and then click **Operations | Alarm**. To set an alarm, click the appropriate buttons or up and down triangles for the day, month, year, and time, and then click **Set**. When the alarm triggers, your computer beeps three times and a small dialog with a notification appears. KNotes also starts and shows your note.

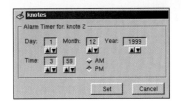

6 Mail Note

Right-click the **knote** window and click **Operations | Mail Note**. A small dialog appears. Type an email address and click **Mail**.

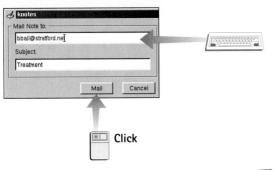

Click

End

How-To Hints

Sticky Notes

Right-click your note and click **Sticky** to make your note appear in each KDE desktop. Click **To Desktop**, and then click **One, Two, Three,** or **Four** to send KNotes to a particular desktop. To unstick the KNote from your desktops, right-click the **knote** window and click **UnSticky**.

Options

Click **Options** under KNotes's **Operations** menu to set different options such as the font, background color, foreground color, or commands used to mail and print notes.

Resize knote

Move your mouse to a corner of a **knote** window, press **Alt** and your right mouse button, and drag to resize the **knote** window. This lets you create or read larger notes.

How to Track Time with KArm

This task shows you how to keep track of time for selected tasks with KArm. This program is handy for measuring the progress of different tasks or for accounting billable hours for different projects.

Begin

1 Start a New KArm Task

Click the **Utilities** button on your desktop's panel, and then click **KArm**. A blank window appears, containing a menu bar and a toolbar. The toolbar boasts **Start Clock**, **Stop Clock**, **New Task**, **Delete Task**, and **Edit Task** buttons. Open the **Task** menu and click **New**.

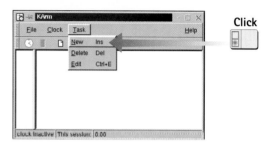

Click

2 Add New Task(s)

Click the **Task Name** field, type the name of a new task, and click **OK**. Repeat this step to add a list of tasks (such as for a project). If time has been spent on a task before you add it, enter the time (in minutes) in the **Accumulated Time** field.

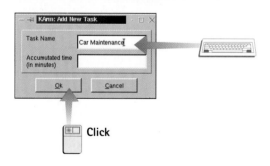

Click

3 Delete a Task

Click a task name in the list of tasks, open the **Task** menu, and click **Delete**.

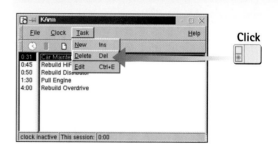

Click

4 Confirm the Deletion

Click **Yes** to delete the task.

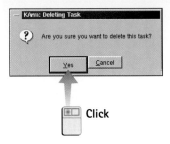

Click

5 Track a Task

To track a task, click the task name in the list, and then click the **Start Clock** button (alternatively, open the **Clock** menu and click **Start**). To track a different task, click the **Stop Clock** button and highlight another task, or click another task while the clock is running.

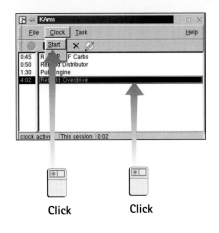

Click   **Click**

End

How-To Hints

How to Schedule Tasks

See the next task, "How to Use the **plan** Client," to find out how to create schedules for your projects or appointments.

Scheduling at Reminders with OpenLinux

Use the **at** command to send yourself reminders. For example, to remind yourself about a dental appointment at 1 p.m., type **at 12:45** and press **Enter**. Then type **xmessage -display :0.0 "Time for the dentist!"**, press **Enter**, and press **Ctrl+D** to save the reminder. You can also use the at command to run other programs at a scheduled time, such as tape backups at the end of the day. Use the **atq** command to see your scheduled jobs, and use **atrm** to remove jobs. Read the **at** man page for details.

Setting Routine Schedules

Use the **crontab** command to schedule repetitive tasks. As the root operator, you can set these schedules in your OpenLinux system's **crontab** file, found under the **/etc** directory. Individual users can set programs to run at regular times by using the **crontab** command with its **-e** option. Make sure to read the **crontab** man page.

How to Use the plan Client

OpenLinux comes with several calendar programs you can use to see the current date, set a schedule, or plan appointments. This task shows you how to start and use the plan client for X11.

Begin

1 Start the plan Daemon and plan

Start a terminal program. At the command line, type **pland** and press **Enter** to start the plan daemon (used to track appointments). Next, type **plan** and press **Enter**.

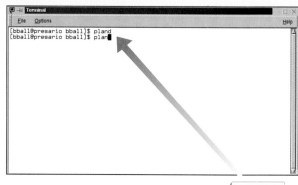

2 View Current Month

The **plan** window appears. By default, **plan** shows the current month. To view past or future months or years, click the left or right arrow, respectively. The current day is highlighted. Open the **Config** menu, and then click **Adjust Time**.

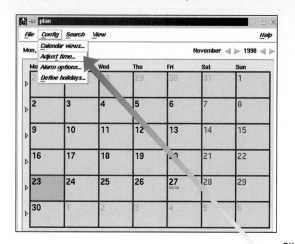

Click

3 Set the Time

Click the **Timezone Is GMT** field and enter the number of hours that your time zone is offset from Greenwich Mean Time (GMT). For example, if you use EST, or Eastern Standard Time, enter **5**. (PST, or Pacific Standard Time would use **8**.). Next, click your Daylight Saving preference. Click **Automatic** to have **plan** automatically guess what days to turn Daylight Savings Time on and off. When finished, click **Done**.

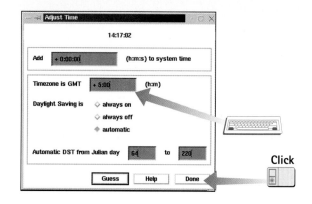

Click

4 Set Appointment

Click a future day in the monthly calendar to set an appointment. The **Schedule** dialog appears. To set a one-time appointment, click a box under the Time column and enter a time in the form **hh:mm(a,p)**. For example, to enter an alarm for 10:07 in the evening, type **10:07p**. Next, click the **Note** field and enter a short description (the text appears when plan notifies you of the appointment). When finished, click **Done**. Repeat this step to enter any other appointments.

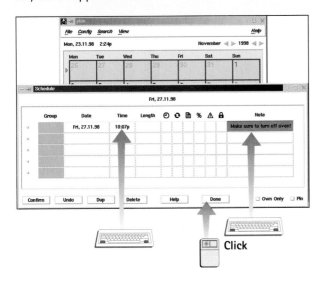

Click

5 Select Print

Your **plan** calendar lists each appointment and time on the selected day. To start to print a calendar, open **File** and click **Print**.

Click

6 Print the Month's Calendar

Click **Month**. Next, click the **Spooler String** field and erase any existing entry. Type **lpr**, and then click **Print** to send the calendar to your printer.

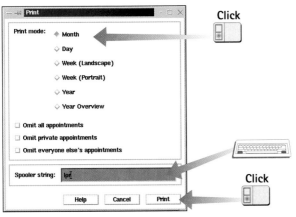

Click

Click

How-To Hints

I Can't Set an Appointment Time!

If **plan** does not accept **hh:mm(a,p)** appointment times, you must configure it to use 12-hour time instead of the default 24-hour time. Open the **Config** menu, and then click **Calendar Views**. Under **Global Options**, click **12-hour am/pm**.

I Missed an Appointment!

The pland daemon must be running in order for plan to notify you with alarms. Create a text file call **.xsession**, and then type **pland** and save the file. The next time you use X, the pland daemon launches.

End

Task

18

Playing Music and Watching TV

*M*any people enjoy listening to the radio or watching TV, and OpenLinux users are no exception! This chapter shows you how to pop a music CD into your computer and listen to your favorite tunes. If you like listening to the radio or watching TV, you also see how to install and use RealPlayer software for Linux.

You must configure Linux to work with your computer's sound card in order to use the programs discussed in this chapter. See Appendix B, "Adding Miscellaneous Hardware," for more information about configuring Linux for sound.

Some programs discussed here also require the X Window System and an active Internet connection, so it's best to start an X session and log in to your ISP before you begin.

How to Play a Music CD

Playing music CDs with Linux is not only easy, but also convenient and fun! This task shows you how to use the kscd player. It's best to have an active Internet connection when you use kscd (although you don't have to). Why? Because if you do, when you insert a music CD and start kscd, the player goes out to the Internet, queries a remote computer, and retrieves the name of your music CD, the artist's name, the number of tracks, and the name of each track. You can then save this information on your hard drive.

Begin

1 Detect the CD-ROM Device

Make sure that OpenLinux found your CD-ROM drive when you started Linux. On the command line of an X11 terminal window, type **dmesg ¦ less**. Scroll through the information until you find a section that looks like the section circled below.

The **hdc: TOSHIBA CD-ROM XM-1802B, ATAPI CDROM drive** line means that device **/dev/hdc** represents your CD-ROM drive. If you have a SCSI CD-ROM, the device listed is different.

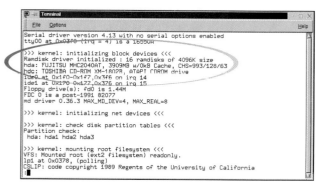

2 Look for cdrom in the /dev

Check to make sure a device named **cdrom** exists in the **/dev** directory by typing **ls -l /dev/cdrom**. The **/dev/cdrom -> /dev/hdc** portion of your output indicates that the default CD-ROM device correctly points to your CD-ROM drive.

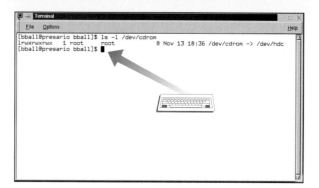

3 Check the Settings

Just to make sure that everything is set correctly, use the **chmod** command to change the permissions of your CD-ROM so that anyone can read your CD. Typing **su -c "chmod 664 /dev/cdrom** runs the **chmod** command as root and sets your CD-ROM device to the correct permissions (otherwise, you get an error message from the CD player software).

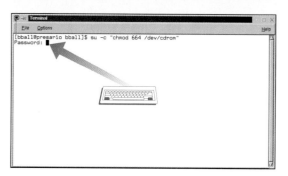

4 Start the kscd Player

Before you begin, connect to your ISP, and start X. Open your computer's CD-ROM bay and insert a music CD. Next, click the **Application Starter** button on your desktop's panel, choose **Multimedia**, and select **CD Player**.

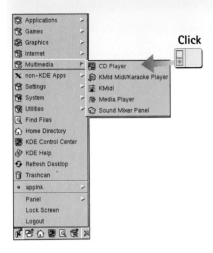

Click

5 Select the Artist and Title

The kscd player automatically goes out to the Internet and tries to locate your CD's artist and title. You don't have to do anything! In the **Kscd** dialog, click the CD from the list and then click the **OK** button.

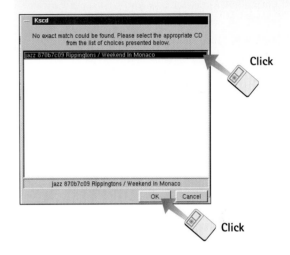

Click

Click

6 View kscd's Controls

The **kscd** main window appears. Note that the artist and title of your CD appears in the window; note also that kscd has many of the familiar controls of a hardware audio CD player, including the **Play**, **Stop**, **Previous Track**, **Next Track**, and **Eject** buttons, and a sliding volume control. Click the **Play** button to start playing your CD and click the **Configure** button to set various options.

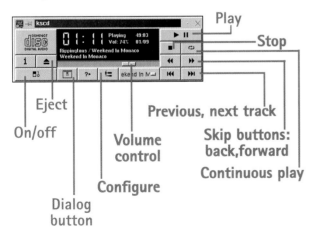

Play

Stop

Eject

On/off

Volume control

Configure

Dialog button

Previous, next track

Skip buttons: back,forward

Continuous play

7 Configure kscd Remote Search

When the **kscd Configuration** dialog appears, note that the **Enable Remote CDDB** button is selected. If kscd has trouble connecting to a particular remote Internet database, click a different server in the **CDDB Server** list. If you don't want kscd to check for database entries, deselect the **Enable Remote CDDB** button.

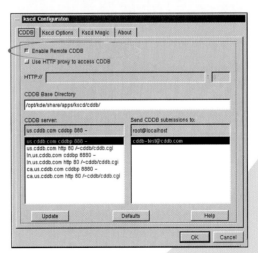

Continues

8 Configure kscd Display

Click the **Kscd Options** tab. To change kscd's LED color, click the **Change** button to the right of the **LED Color** dialog item. In the **Select Color** dialog, click a color box under **System Colors** and click **OK**. To save your change, click **OK** in the **kscd Configuration** dialog.

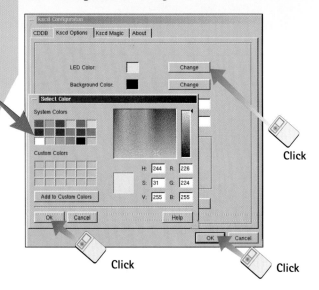

Click

Click

Click

9 View Your Tracks

Click the **CDDB Dialog** button to view your CD's tracks. The **CD Database Editor** dialog appears; kscd fills out most of the information about your CD, such as the disc artist and title.

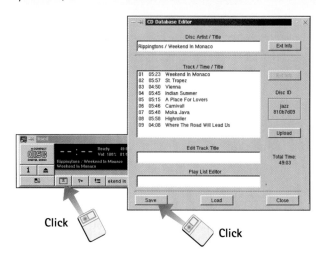

Click

Click

10 Save Your Tracks

Click the **Save** button on the **CD Database Editor** dialog. In the **Kscd** dialog, click the music category, and then click the **OK** button to save your tracks. Then, kscd saves your CD's information in a file under the path you select.

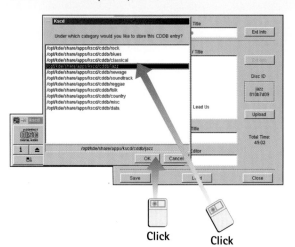

Click

Click

11 Toggle Display

Click the **Compact Disc** button to toggle how **kscd** displays information. The amount of elapsed play time for the current track is shown by default; you can toggle this to the amount of time remaining for the current track, the current total elapsed time, or the time remaining for the CD.

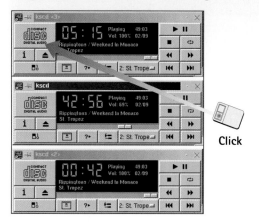

Click

12 Select a Track by Name

To select a track by name, click the track name menu and choose the desired track.

End

How-To Hints

OpenLinux Won't Recognize My CD-ROM!

Take a look at the CDROM-HOWTO under the **/usr/doc/HOWTO** directory. You will find lots of tips and pointers on troubleshooting problems with CD-ROM drives.

Are There Other Music CD Players for OpenLinux?

Oh yes. Try cdplay, xplaycd, or WorkMan. You're sure to find at least one you like. There are also many other audio CD players for Linux. Browse to **ftp://sunsite.unc.edu/pub/Linux/apps/sound/cdrom** for pointers to dozens of players.

Why Only 11 Categories for Music?

This is a decision by CDDB, Inc. For more information about the CDDB Internet database (which contains entries for 263,000 music CDs at the time of this writing), browse to **http://www.cddb.com**. You can also use this site to search for long-lost CDs, to see lists of the most popular music artists, or to download other CDDB-aware CD players.

How to Play MIDI Karaoke Music

Your OpenLinux system comes with several musical instrument digital interface (MIDI) players. MIDI files, usually distinguished by the file extension **.mid**, contain information needed by your computer's sound card to play different musical instruments. This section introduces you to the kmid player, which not only plays MIDI files, but also shows lyrics so you can sing along!

Begin

1 Start the kmid Player

Click the **Application Starter** button on your desktop's panel, choose **Multimedia**, and then click **KMid Midi/Karaoke Player**.

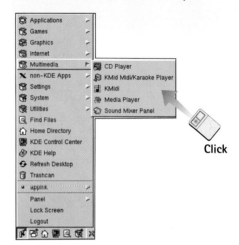

Click

2 Open kmid's Organizer

The kmid player has a menu bar, a toolbar of player controls, and a sliding control for MIDI songs. To create a collection of songs to play, open the **Collections** menu and choose **Organize**.

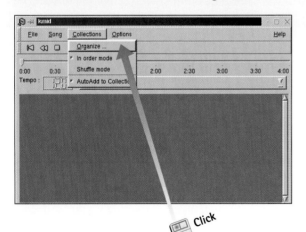

Click

3 Create a Collection

When kmid's **Collections Manager** dialog appears, click the **New** button. In the **New Collection** dialog, enter a name for your collection, such as **mysongs**, and click the **OK** button.

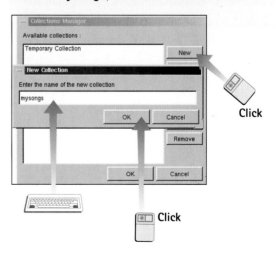

Click

Click

4 Add Songs

Click the **Add** button in the **Collections Manager** dialog, and kmid's **Open** dialog appears. Click the **Location** field, press the backspace key, type **/opt/kde/share/apps/kmid/**, and press **Enter**. A list of sample **kmid** files appears. Click a filename, such as **AlwaysLookOnTheBrightSideOfLife.kar**, and then click the **OK** button. Repeat until you've added all the songs you want. When finished, click the **OK** button in the **Collections Manager** dialog.

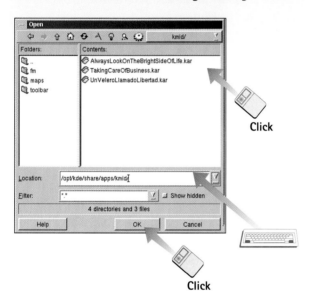

Click

Click

5 Play a Song

Click the **Play** button to start playing the first song in your collection. As kmid plays the song, each word in the song's lyrics is highlighted.

Click

End

How-To Hints

What About Other MIDI Players?

Several MIDI players are included with OpenLinux. Try playmidi or timidity (highly recommended) to play MIDI files without using X Window. KDE users also should try the KMidi player, which has an interface similar to kscd. Try the xplaymidi client for X, or use timidity with its **-ik** command-line option to play MIDI files using a Tcl/Tk graphical interface.

Where Can I Get More kmid Files?

One place to try is the home page of kmid player's author at **http://www.arrakis.es/~rlarrosa/midifiles.html**. To look for regular MIDI files, use your favorite Web search engine.

How to Play Animations or Movies

OpenLinux comes with several programs you can use to watch animations or movies. This section introduces you to some of the animation players included on this book's CD-ROM. You see how to run several demonstration programs.

Begin

1 Start a gnuplot Animation

The gnuplot mathematical modeling and plotting program can be used for simple animations. To see a demonstration, run the following commands and press **Enter**:

```
cd /usr/X11R6/lib/gnuplot/demo
gnuplot animate.dem
```

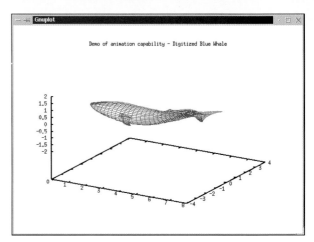

2 Play an Illustrated Audio File

You can play synchronized computer slide shows and audio tracks in Illustrated Audio format by using the iaplay client included with OpenLinux. To play a demonstration clip, **cd /usr/share/data/illustrated-audio iaplay**

After you press **Enter**, an eight-second demo is played.

3 Play an MPEG Video

Use the mpeg_play client to play Moving Picture Expert Group (MPEG1) video animations on your desktop. To play a demo video clip, use the **mpeg_play** command followed by the name of the demo video clip. For example, type **mpeg_play /usr/share/data/mpeg/RedsNightmare.mpg**, and press **Enter**.

4 Play an MPEG Video in Grayscale

You can also use the xmpeg client to play MPEG1 video animations. This program has a single control window but can be used to play video in a variety of display modes, such as grayscale. To play a demo video clip, use the **xmpeg** command followed by the name of the demo video clip. For example, type **xmpeg /usr/share/data/mpeg/RedsNightmare.mpg** and press **Enter**. Click xmpeg's main window to open xmpeg's color control dialog. Select a video display mode by clicking on its name, and then click the **OK** button.

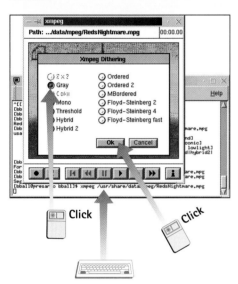

Click

Click

5 Play a QuickTime or Active Movie

Use the xanim client to play files in one of fifteen different formats, including QuickTime MOV files or Active Movie AVI files. On the command line of an X11 terminal, use xanim followed by the name of a video file. For example, type **xanim upandaway.avi &**. The xanim client has several controls, including **Pause**, **Frame-by-Frame**, and **Play** buttons.

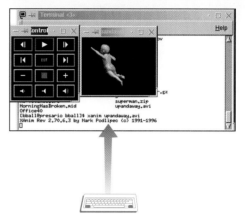

End

How-To Hints

Where to Learn About Making Movies

To learn more about how to make MPEG movies, browse to the U.S. Army's High Performance Computing Research Center's Graphics and Visualization Laboratory at **http://www.arc.umn.edu/GVL/Software/mpeg.html**. This site has numerous links to movie-making software and offers tutorials on using different graphics software to make movies.

Movies Look Awful on My Display!

Start your X session at a higher color depth than the default 256 colors to see better renditions of all graphics. Use the **startx** or **kde** command from the command line of your console. For example, type **kde − -bpp 16** to start X using thousands of colors. If your computer and the XFree86 software support greater depths, you can try **-bpp 24** or even **-bpp 32**.

How to Install, Configure, and Use RealPlayer

You can use the RealPlayer client from Real, Inc. to listen to live radio or watch live TV from stations all over the world. You need to run the X Window System and install Netscape Communicator from this book's CD-ROM before you can use RealPlayer. You also need to open an Internet connection and browse to **http://www.real.com** to download RealPlayer for Linux. Follow the prompts at Real Inc.'s site, and then download RealPlayer (about 1.6MB) to your hard drive.

Begin

1 Install RealPlayer

On the command line of a terminal window, type **tar xzf rv50_linux20.tar.gz** and press **Enter**. Next, run Netscape from the command line to read RealPlayer's installation notes by typing **netscape rvplayer5.0/ index.htm &** and pressing **Enter**.

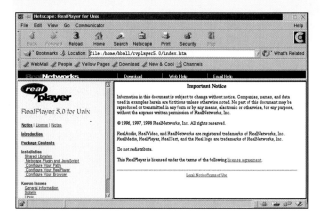

2 Configure Your Environment

Open the file **.profile** in your home directory. For example, if you're using **pico**, type **pico -w .profile**. Scroll to file end and type:

```
LD_LIBRARY_PATH=$HOME/rvplayer5.0
export LD_LIBRARY_PATH
PATH=$PATH":$HOME/rvplayer5.0:"
```

From the command line of your terminal, read in RealPlayer's environment variables by typing **source .profile**.

3 Configure Netscape Navigator

Choose **Preferences** from Netscape's **Edit** menu. Click the **Navigator** item in the **Category** list, and then choose **Applications**. In the **Applications** dialog, click the **New** button.

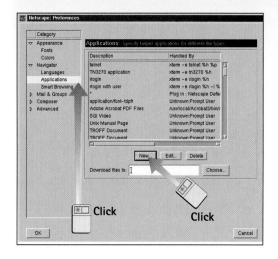

4 Add RealPlayer

In the **Description** field, type **RealPlayer 5.0**; in the **MIMEType** field, type **audio/x-pn-realaudio**. In the **Suffixes** field, type **.rm,.ra,.ram**. Click the **Application** button in the **Handled By** section, and type **rvplayer %s** in the **Application** field. Click **OK** once in the **Netscape: Application** dialog and again in the **Netscape: Preferences** dialog.

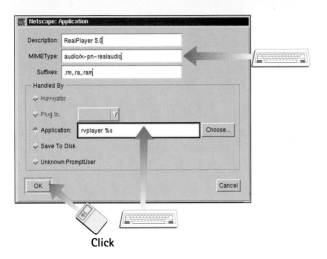

Click

5 Configure RealPlayer

Start RealPlayer from the command line of your terminal by typing **rvplayer &**. Choose **Preferences** from RealPlayer's **Edit** menu. When the **Preferences** dialog appears, click the **Connection** tab. In the **Bandwidth** box, click the type of Internet connection you use (for example, **56K Modem**) and click **OK**. Finally, click the **Exit** menu item of RealPlayer's menu to exit.

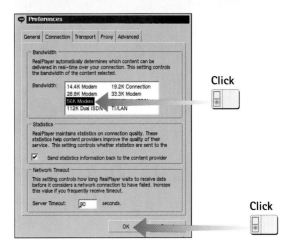

Click

Click

6 Watch TV!

Log in to your ISP, start Netscape from the command line of your terminal window, and navigate to a Web site (such as **http://www.foxnews.com**) that provides RealPlayer video. When you click a video icon, Netscape launches RealPlayer so you can watch TV.

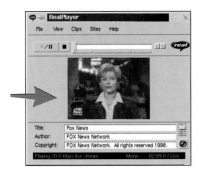

End

How-To Hints

Netscape Says It Can't Find rvplayer!

If Netscape says it can't find **rvplayer**, the best approach after editing your **.profile** file is to log out of Linux and then to log back in. Use the **env** command from the command line of your console to see whether the path to the **rvplayer** command is listed and active. Make sure that you follow the directions included with RealPlayer for installation, and that you configured Netscape's application preferences correctly. You can also try typing **rvplayer rvplayer5.0/welcome.rm &** from the command line to see whether RealPlayer is working correctly on your system.

Task

Playing Games

It's time to take a break and relax! This chapter shows you how to play a small sampling of the nearly 100 games included with OpenLinux. The chapter starts with a selection included with the K Desktop Environment (KDE), and then introduces you to some traditional board games. Next you'll see how to start and run the LinCity city and country simulator. At the end of this chapter, you'll learn about some popular action games for Linux.

These games require the X Window System, so you need to start an X session. You should also configure OpenLinux to work with your computer's sound card to fully enjoy the raucous sounds included with some of these games. If you haven't configured X for your computer's graphics card, see the last section of Appendix A, "Installing Caldera OpenLinux," to learn how. To configure OpenLinux to work with your computer's sound card, read Appendix B, "Adding Miscellaneous Hardware."

Now get ready to have some fun!

How to Start and Play KDE Games

This task introduces you to several games included with KDE. You need to start an X session using KDE. If you logged into OpenLinux at the command line of a console, type **kde** and press **Enter**.

1 Start the kasteroids Games

Click the **Application Starter** button on your desktop's panel. Click **Games**, and then click **Asteroids**.

Click

2 Play kasteroids

The **Asteroids** window appears. Open the **File** menu and click **New Game**. Press **Enter** to play. The four controls are as follows: Press the **Spacebar** to fire; cursor up to thrust; cursor left to rotate counterclockwise; and cursor right to rotate clockwise. You have four lives. Shooting a large asteroid breaks it into pieces (which you also have to shoot). The number of asteroids and their speed increase with each level.

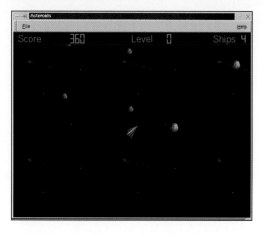

3 Play SameGame

Click the **Application Starter** button on your desktop's panel. Click **Games**, and then click **SameGame**. The object of this addictive game is to remove all the balls from the screen. Move your cursor over a set of at least two same-colored balls, and they rotate. Click to remove the set of rotating balls. If you click a set of balls at the bottom, the ball on top falls down, creating new sets (or unlike sets) of balls. Continue until all balls are gone.

Click

4 Play Mahjongg

Click the **Application Starter** button on your desktop's panel. Click **Games**, and then click **Mahjongg**. The object of this game is to click a tile, and then click a matching tile to remove the two tiles. Try to remove as many tiles as you can. Only rarely are you able to remove all the tiles—but it is possible!

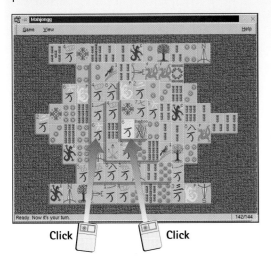

Click   Click

5 Play Reversi

Click the **Application Starter** button on your desktop's panel. Click **Games**, and then click **Reversi**. The object of this game is to capture and reverse the opponent's colored buttons. Your color is blue by default. Click a blank square on the other side (diagonally, horizontally, or vertically) of a red button to flip the color of any red button between the blank square and your blue button. Here's a hint: Try to capture at least three corners of the grid to win.

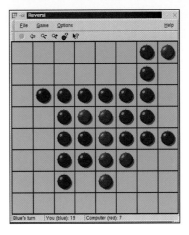

6 Play Patience

Click the **Application Starter** button on your desktop's panel. Click **Games**, and then click **Patience**. This offers not one, but *nine* solitaire card games. The default game is the familiar Klondike solitaire. To play a different type of solitaire, open the **Game** menu, select **Choose New Game**, and then click one of the nine different card games.

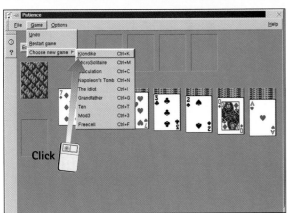

Click

End

How-To Hints

What Other Games Come with KDE?

You'll also find several other games included in the KDE distribution. These include the games Abalone, Minesweeper, Poker, Shisen-Sho (similar to Mahjongg), Snake Race (which requires a display larger than 800×600), and a version of the popular falling blocks game, Tetris.

Getting Help Playing Games

Each KDE game has a menu bar with a **Help** menu at the far right of the bar. Open the **Help** menu, and then click **Contents** to read about the game.

How to Start and Play Board Games

This task introduces you to several board games included with OpenLinux. These games range from more traditional board games, such as chess and backgammon, to more complex games, such as frisk.

1 Start an xboard Chess Game

Start an X11 terminal. At the command line, use the **xboard –size** option, followed by a size such as **small**. Type **xboard -size small &**, and press **Enter**. This starts the xboard chess game. To play, click and hold a white chess piece and drag and release the piece on a legal square of the chess board (you must make legal moves). If you have an active Internet connection, you can play chess games with remote computers and players in real time (live) or by electronic mail.

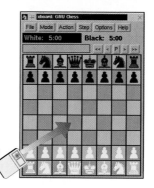

Click & Drag

2 Play XGammon

Type **xgammon &** at the command line of a terminal and press **Enter** to start the XGammon backgammon game. XGammon starts, like backgammon, with the roll of the dice to determine who goes first. If XGammon goes first, it moves its pieces and waits for you to click the blank dice to determine your roll.

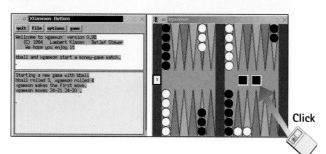

Click

3 Start xpat2 Solitaire

Type **xpat2 &** at the command line of a terminal and press **Enter** to start the **xpat2** solitaire card game. This X11 client features 15 different built-in card games. Click **Rules**, and then drag down and click a solitaire game to start. Click a card, and **xpat2** moves it.

Click

4 Start the xsok Board Game

Type **xsok &** at the command line of a terminal and press **Enter** to start the simple-but-infuriating game of Sokoban for X11. The object of this game (which is more like a puzzle) is to push square blocks with your cursor keys or mouse to a scoring area. But you have to figure out how to get around other blocks first! This game includes multiple levels with different mazes, springing blocks, one-way corridors, and other traps.

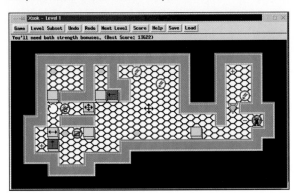

5 Start frisk

The frisk board game (a game of world domination) requires two programs to run: the **friskserver** and the **xfrisk** client. Type **friskserver &** at the command line of a terminal and press **Enter** to start the server. To open the game, type **xfrisk localhost &** and press **Enter**. When **xfrisk** starts, click **Add Player** in the **Player Registration** dialog. The **Add Player** dialog appears. Click the **Name** field, type your name, and click **OK**. Repeat these steps at least once to add another player, because **frisk** requires at least two players. To start a game, click **Start Game** in the **Player Registration** dialog.

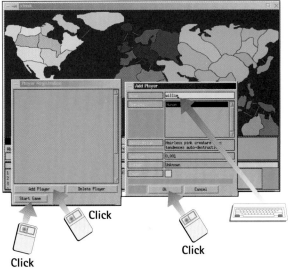

Click

Click

Click

Click

End

How-To Hints

xboard Uses a Black and White Board

KDE or other X11 programs might be using nearly all the available colors for your display. Start your X11 session with more colors than the default 256 colors by using the **-bpp** option. For example, typing **kde — -bpp 16** starts KDE with thousands of colors.

How Do I Play xfrisk?

You can play xfrisk, a complex multiplayer game, either at your computer or over a network. Click **Help** in the main **xfrisk** window, or read the xfrisk man page included with the game.

How to Start and Play LinCity

This task shows you how to play the wonderful LinCity simulation game. This game, similar to commercial simulation games, provides hours of fun as you control and build your own city or country. You can play this game with or without the X Window System by using the xlincity client or LinCity program. The X11 version of this game is used in this task.

1 Start xlincity

At the command line of an X11 terminal, type **xlincity &** and press **Enter**. The first time you run LinCity, it asks whether it can create a directory called **.Lin-city** in your home directory. Press **Y**.

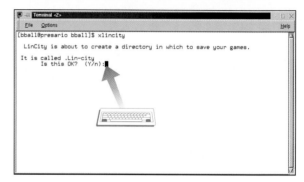

2 Load a Scene

The LinCity splash screen appears. Press any key to continue. In the main LinCity window are three buttons you can use to start a simulation: **Load a Built In or Saved Scene**, **Start—with Random Village**, and **Start—with Bare Board**. When you save your simulation, start a game by loading a saved scene. To play a random game, click the random village button. To build your own city to start a game, click the bare board button. For now, click the built in or saved scene button.

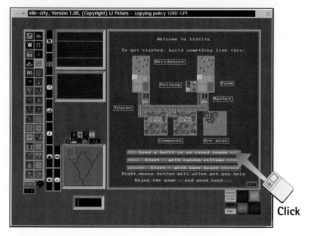

Click

3 Load Good Times

The window clears, and you'll have a choice between starting a built-in Good Times or Bad Times game. Click **Good Times**.

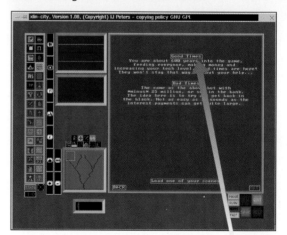

 Click

4 Watch and Play!

You're presented with an active, healthy community. The report at the bottom of the screen shows that there's plenty of food and very low unemployment. The main controls for the game are in the lower-right corner of the window. You can click **FAST** to speed up the simulation rate, **SAVE** to save the game, or **HELP** to read about using LinCity (click the close button—the × in the upper-right corner of the window—to quit the game). Click **HELP** to see the help screen.

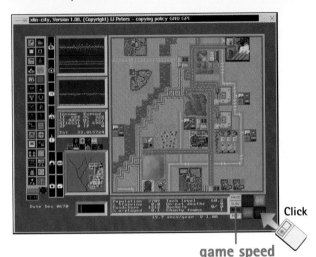

Click

game speed

5 Select Help

LinCity offers help with the keyboard, the buttons (which are along the left side of the window and are used to create or demolish structures, roads, farms, housing, airports, seaports, and so on), and the opening screen (shown in step 2). Click the **Click Here to See Button Index Page** button.

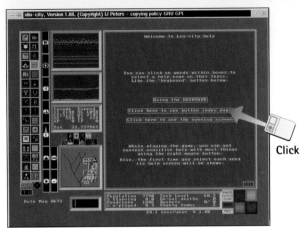

Click

6 Read Help

The first of three pages of indexed help on LinCity's buttons appears. To get a full description of a button, such as the **Farm** button, click it in the list. To quit help, click **OUT**.

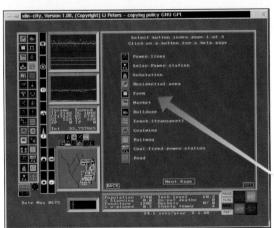

Click

How-To Hints

The Colors Go Berserk on My Display!

Again, this is a problem when running some X11 clients on a 256-color display. Try to start your X11 session with more colors by using the **–bpp** option. For help on configuring X11 to support more than 256 colors, also read the **XF86Config** man page.

How to Find Out More About LinCity

Read the **lincity** man page. You'll find a pointer about how to join the LinCity electronic mailing list. You'll also find a short FAQ under the **/usr/doc/lincity** directory.

End

How to Start and Play Action Games

This task shows you how to start and play several action games with OpenLinux and X11. You'll find a number of fast-action arcade games on this book's CD-ROM.

1 Start the XGalaga Game

Type **xgal &** at the command line of a terminal and press **Enter**. The game's splash screen appears. Press any key to start. The object is to shoot the ships streaming down your screen. Use your mouse to move left or right. Click your mouse to shoot.

2 Start the Koules Game

Type **xkoules &** at the command line of a terminal and press **Enter**. Press any key and the main Koules screen appears. Press **Enter** to start a game. The object is to bat the tiny balls into the sides of the game window until none are left. But be careful you don't touch the sides of the window!

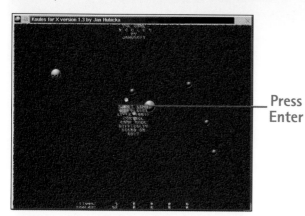

Press Enter

3 Start the XBoing Game

This game requires an X11 display of at least 1024×768, but repays the cost of a new graphics card and monitor for OpenLinux with hours of fun. Type **xboing -speed 1 -sound &** and press **Enter** to start this awesome breakout game at a slow speed and with sound turned on.

4 Start the X Scavenger Game

This game is similar to an old game from the early days of personal computers. Type **scavenger &** and press **Enter** to start this game from the command line of a terminal. The object is to run around the screen picking, digging, and climbing. The game controls are on your keyboard's numeric keypad. Press the spacebar to see the main menu, **F8** to see different levels, **F4** to start a game, and **Alt+X** to quit.

6 Play XPacman

To play a complex version of an old favorite game, type **xpacman &** at the command line of a terminal and press **Enter**. The object, of course, is to eat as many dots as possible before your character gets caught by roving ghosts. Directions for playing are in the game window's title bar.

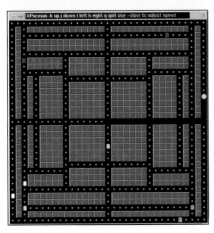

5 Play 3D Blockout with xbl

Type **xbl &** at the command line of a terminal and press **Enter** to start the XBlockOut game. This is a three-dimensional game of dropping blocks. The object is to build and complete flat levels (similar to falling-block games).

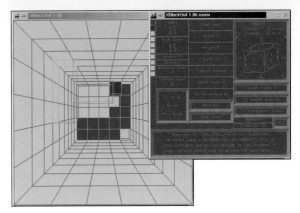

How-To Hints

About Other Games

Another excellent game included with OpenLinux is abuse. Type **abuse &** at the command line of a terminal and press **Enter** to play this fascinating arcade game. The screen is small, but the action is fast and the sounds are loud. Don't like loud games or don't care for blasting aliens? Try the **oneko** X11 client. Your cursor turns into a mouse, and a small cat chases it around the screen. Use **oneko**'s **-dog** option to turn your cursor into a bone.

What About Doom or Quake?

If you're a veteran PC game player, you'll also find versions of Doom and Quake for Linux. Browse to **http://www.idsoftware.com** to download a copy for OpenLinux.

End

Task

20

Starting and Running DOS Programs with DR-OpenDOS

O penLinux comes with Caldera's DR-OpenDOS, a disk-operating system (DOS) that runs under the **dosemu** emulator program. You can run DOS from the console or in a window during your X sessions. DR-OpenDOS can run older or legacy DOS programs, perform network connections, and even build a bootable DOS system disk for your PC.

This chapter shows you how to configure **dosemu** so you or other users can start DR-OpenDOS. You'll also see how to read the DR-OpenDOS manual and get help with DOS commands. Using **dosemu** during an X session is a convenient way to run two operating systems at the same time. To do this, first start X from the command line of your console.

Configure dosemu and DR-OpenDOS

This task gets you started with configuring **dosemu**. OpenLinux uses the **rpm** command to install and set up **dosemu** on your computer's hard drive. Although the files are correctly copied from your CD-ROM, you still need to edit a system file in order to use **dosemu** and DR-OpenDOS. The default configuration is very restrictive; aside from the root operator, no one can use a floppy drive or create and delete files on the DOS drive.

Begin

1 Start a DR-OpenDOS Session

Click the **Application Starter** button on your desktop's panel, choose **Applications**, and click **DR-OpenDos**.

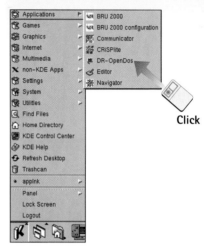

Click

2 Read Error Message

The **xmessage** command reports an error and tells you to contact the system administrator. Who's that person? Why you, of course! Click the **okay** button.

Click

3 Open the User Configuration File

At the command line of a terminal window, log in as the root operator and open **dosemu**'s configuration file with the **pico** text editor (type **su -c "pico -w /etc/dosemu.users"**). Press **Enter** to edit the file.

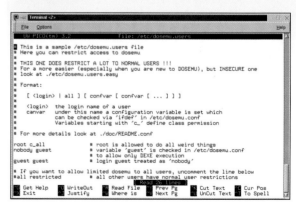

4 Add a User

Scroll down to the **guest** entry and add your username (in this example, I've typed **bball**). Press the spacebar. To give yourself access to your computer's floppy drive, type **c_normal**. To give yourself full access to all of **dosemu**'s features, type **c_all**. When finished, press **Ctrl+X** to save the file.

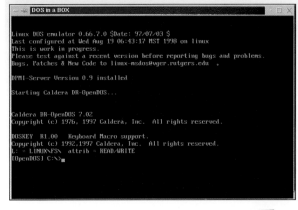

5 Start a DR-OpenDOS Session

Repeat step 1. This time, an X window appears with the name **DOS in a BOX**. You're now running DR-OpenDOS!

End

How-To Hints

Change Your Computer

The default configuration used by **dosemu** and DR-OpenDOS gives you an 80386-type computer with 1MB of system memory, 650KB available for DOS programs, and a 7.7MB hard drive. You can change these settings to add memory or use an 80486 Central Processing Unit (CPU) by editing, as the root operator, the file **dosemu.conf** under the **/etc** directory. You can also build a new hard drive (the hard drive is actually a 7.7MB file called **hdimage.od** under the **/var/lib/dosemu** directory) if you need more storage for DOS programs.

How Do I Quit a DOS Session?

The C: drive used by **dosemu** and DR-OpenDOS contains two directories called **EMUBIN** and **OPENDOS**. Use the **EXITEMU.COM** command under the **EMUBIN** directory to quit your DOS session.

How Do I Find Out More About dosemu?

Read the file **README.txt** under the **/usr/lib/dosemu/doc** directory for details about how to use **dosemu**, configure custom settings, and create larger hard drives using the **setup-hdimage** command.

How Do I Access My Floppy or Linux Directories?

A single-floppy computer has drive A: assigned to the first floppy. Drive B: presents the second floppy on a two-floppy system. Drive L: is defined as your Linux directory. Type **L:** and press **Enter**. You'll then be at your root, or **/** directory. Use the **cd** command to navigate to your home directory like so: **cd home\yourusername**.

How to Use DR-OpenDOS Help

Help is only a few keystrokes away when you use DR-OpenDOS. This task shows you how to read about OpenDOS using the **DOSBook.EXE** command. Start a DOS session using DR-OpenDOS.

Begin

1 Start Help

At the **C:** prompt, type **help** and press **Enter**. The **help** command is a DOS batch file called **HELP.BAT** under the **C:\OPENDOS** directory, and runs the **DOSBook.EXE** command. You'll see **DOSBook**'s main table of contents. Note that **DOSBook** has three menus and four buttons. Click the **CONTENTS** entry in your DOS window (or press your down-arrow key until the word is highlighted), and press **Enter**.

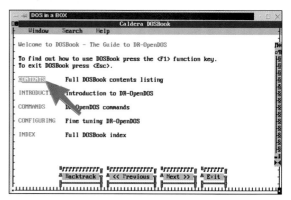

2 Navigate the Table of Contents

A table of contents appears. Use your cursor keys to scroll through the list. Scroll down to the Commands section of Chapter 4, and then click the word **Commands**.

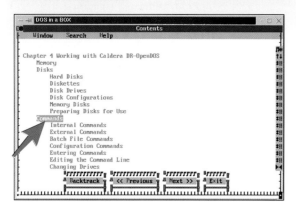

3 Read About Commands

Text about using commands appears. To search for information about a certain command, open the **Search** menu and choose **Search Index**.

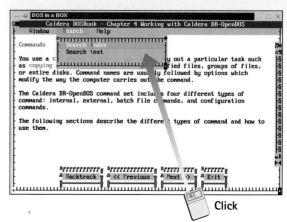

Click

4 Run the Search Index

Click at the blinking cursor and enter a search term, such as **format**. Then click **Search**.

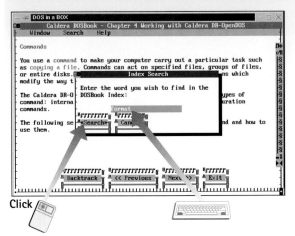

Click

5 Click the Command Word

The **FORMAT Command** index item is highlighted. Click the item to display its help page.

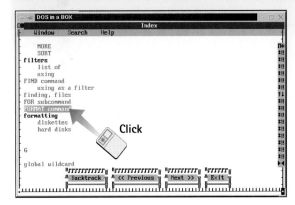

Click

6 Read Help

The help page for the **FORMAT** command appears. Click **Exit** to quit Help.

End

How-To Hints

How Do I Use My Serial Port or Printer?

As root operator, open the file **dosemu.conf** under the **/etc** directory using your favorite text editor. You'll find separate sections, each relating to keyboard, serial port, networking, video, memory, hard disk, printer, and floppy access. Although the configuration file is full of helpful comments, make sure to read the **/usr/lib/dosemu/doc/README.txt** file for specific details.

Do I Have to Use DR-OpenDOS?

No! OpenLinux also comes with FreeDOS, a free version of DOS similar to DR-OpenDOS. You'll find a preconfigured small hard drive image in the file **hdimage.test** under the **/usr/lib/dosemu/etc** directory. To use FreeDOS instead of DR-OpenDOS, change the line in **/etc/dosemu.conf** that says **disk { partition "/var/lib/dosemu/hdimage.od" }** to **disk { partition "/usr/lib/dosemu/etc/ hdimage.test" }**.

Installing Caldera OpenLinux

*L*inux is the kernel of an operating system released to the world in 1991 by Linus Torvalds while he was working as a graduate student at the University of Helsinki, Finland. Remember: Linux is the kernel—the thousands of programs and support software packages that come with the Linux kernel make up what is called a *Linux distribution*. Caldera's OpenLinux is Caldera System's distribution of Linux. There are other Linux distributions from a variety of companies, organizations, and even individuals.

You can find Caldera's OpenLinux on this book's CD-ROM. This appendix shows you one way of installing OpenLinux on your computer. However, you should keep in mind that there are a number of ways to install and run Linux on a PC. You can find all the documentation and technical details about installing Linux on this book's CD-ROM.

If you want to read more about OpenLinux before starting your installation, browse to **http://www.calderasystems.com** and follow the various links to OpenLinux. To read the OpenLinux Getting Started Guide, browse to **http://www.calderasystems.com/doc/index.html** and click the **Getting Started Guide** link. You can read the guide in German, English, Spanish, French, and Italian. Read Chapter 2 of the guide for specific information about installing OpenLinux. ●

Will Linux Run on My Computer?

*I*f you can run DOS or Win9*x* on your computer, you can install and run Linux. There are versions of Linux for other computers, such as those from Sun Microsystems, or computers using other Central Processing Units (CPUs) such as the Alpha chip. To read more about other distributions of Linux for other computers besides those based on the x86 architecture, browse to **http://sunsite.unc.edu/LDP**.

The general requirements for installing OpenLinux are

- ✓ 386 or better equivalent CPU
- ✓ 16MB of random access memory (RAM)—although Linux works with 8MB
- ✓ 1.44MB 3.5-inch floppy drive
- ✓ CD-ROM drive
- ✓ Minimum of 60MB hard drive space. Up to 1GB might be required for a complete installation of the contents of this book's CD-ROM

How Do I Install OpenLinux?

There are several ways to install OpenLinux. This section gives you an overview of various methods you can use. It does not cover installing Linux using a network or a Parallel Line Internet Protocol (PLIP) interface (for details about these methods, see Caldera System's Web site).

The Easy Way: Using the OpenLinux CD-ROM

The easiest way to install Caldera OpenLinux is to insert the OpenLinux CD-ROM in your computer, reboot, and follow the prompts. Booting from a CD-ROM drive might require you to reset your computer's BIOS to change the order of boot disk recognition (usually done by pressing a particular function key after starting your computer—see your computer's manual for details).

The Harder Way: Using a Boot Floppy

You can create a boot floppy disk, insert your OpenLinux CD-ROM, and boot from your floppy to start an installation. You need to use the **RAWRITE3.COM** program under DOS to create the floppy if you cannot boot the OpenLinux CD-ROM. First, note the drive letter (such as **D** or **E**) for your CD-ROM. To create a boot floppy, do the following:

1. Insert the OpenLinux CD-ROM, and then reboot to DOS. At the DOS command line, type each of the following lines and press Enter:

   ```
   D:
   CD \COL\LAUNCH\FLOPPY
   RAWRITE3
   ```

2. After the RAWRITE3 programs starts, it asks you to enter the source filename. Type **INSTALL.144** and press **Enter**.

3. RAWRITE3 then asks you to enter the destination drive (A or B); type the drive letter of your floppy, such as **A**, and press **Enter**.

4. RAWRITE3 then asks you to install the target disk in the disk drive. Insert a blank disk into your drive and press **Enter**.

5. RAWRITE3 copies the file INSTALL.144 onto your floppy.

6. When finished, either remove the disk or reboot to start the installation.

To start the installation, insert your OpenLinux CD-ROM in your computer, insert your boot floppy into its drive, and reboot.

Other Ways

You can also install Linux on an existing DOS partition. This is a safe way to install Linux. For details about this type of installation, see the file **README** under in the OpenLinux CD-ROM's **col/launch/dos** directory.

Alternatively, you can buy Linux preinstalled on a brand new laptop or computer. This can be costly, but if you want a computer completely configured out of the box, this is the way to go. Browse to **http://sunsite.unc.edu/LDP/HOWTO/ VAR-HOWTO.html**.

Get by with a Little Help from Your Friends

If all this seems way too daunting, ask a friend with Linux experience to come over and install Linux for you! This is a great way to share information, and having someone on hand to help can make the installation process easier.

Alternatively, go to a Linux User Group (LUG) InstallFest! Check your local computer club to find out whether a LUG meets near you. LUGs regularly hold installation meetings, and you'll have Linux installed and configured in no time at all! Browse to **http://www.linux.org/users/index.html** to find a LUG near you. And if there isn't one, start a LUG yourself!

Tip If you have a PCMCIA CD-ROM drive or need other specialized support, repeat teh preceding steps with a separate floppy, but use MODULES.144 instead of INSTALL.144. This creates a second disk with software you need to help OpenLinux recognize your external CD-ROM during the first installation steps.

How Do I Start Linux?

There are different of ways to start Linux:

- ✓ LILO   The Linux loader (LILO) is a small program used to jumpstart Linux. It can be installed in the Master Boot Record of a DOS partition, or in the root partition of a Linux partition on your hard drive.

- ✓ LOADLIN.EXE   You can use the LOADLIN program from DOS to boot Linux. This means that you do not have to install LILO if you use this program and you can also install Linux on a DOS partition. Booting from DOS can enable you to make certain that "Plug-and-Pray" hardware works correctly.

- ✓ Boot disk   You can easily create a boot disk to start Linux. You have an option during installation to save LILO on disk.

- ✓ Floppy   Don't want to install Linux? Browse to **http://sunsite.unc.edu/LDP** and search for Linux distributions that fit on a floppy. You can boot to Linux with a single floppy (but you won't get the X Window System).

- ✓ System Commander   This is a commercial program you can use to boot multiple operating systems from a single computer. Browse to **http://www.systemcommander.com** for details.

- ✓ BootMagic   Included with PowerQuest Corp's PartitionMagic, BootMagic can be used to boot multiple operating systems from a single computer. Browse to **http://www.powerquest.com** for details.

Installing Linux

This appendix describes installing and using the Linux loader, or LILO, to boot Linux. This section does not cover booting Linux over a network.

A Preflight Checklist

Here's a list of things you should know before installing OpenLinux. Unfortunately, many manufacturers don't document the technical characteristics of their computers, so you might have to dig through your computer manual, call the manufacturer, or browse to the manufacturer's Web site for this data. You won't need all this information to install Linux, but you might need some of it later in order to configure any PC cards, set up sound, and so on.

- ✓ Type of CPU (386, and so on).
- ✓ Amount of system RAM (in megabytes).
- ✓ Size of hard drive (in megabytes).
- ✓ Size of hard drive for Linux swap (twice the size of system memory, or your computer's RAM).
- ✓ Size of hard drive for Linux (in megabytes).

- ✓ Type of hard drive controller (IDE/SCSI, and so on).
- ✓ Type of CD-ROM controller (ATAPI, and so on).
- ✓ Number of serial ports (note: there was no USB support in Linux at the time of this writing).
- ✓ Type of keyboard (PS/2 most likely).
- ✓ Number of keys (101, 102, 104, and so on).
- ✓ Type of mouse (PS/2, serial, and so on).
- ✓ Infrared port. (COM1–COM4, shared, and so on. Note: Linux currently fully supports networking and printing via infrared; serial communication is anticipated in the near future.)
- ✓ Serial port assignment (COM1–COM4).
- ✓ Type of Modem. (Fax, voice, and so on. Note: Winmodems do *not* work with Linux. These pieces of junk should be immediately discarded or donated to users of "another operating system." If you have one, get rid of it. If you have a Winmodem built in to your computer, you're out of luck (an unfortunate and nasty trend in the laptop industry of late). Get a real modem (one that works with any operating system).
- ✓ Parallel port assignment (0x378, IRQ 5, and so on).
- ✓ Type of printer (PostScript, HPCL, and so on).
- ✓ PC cards used (modem, flash memory, and so on).
- ✓ Type of PCMCIA controller (TI, and so on).
- ✓ Type of sound card (SoundBlaster, ESS, and so on).
- ✓ I/O address of sound card (0x220, and so on).
- ✓ DMA values (0, 1, and so on).
- ✓ Sound card IRQ (5, 7, and so on).
- ✓ Miscellaneous addresses (such as for MPU, and so on).
- ✓ Type of graphics card (chipset used, such as TGUI9680, and so on).
- ✓ Amount of video memory (1MB, 2MB, 4MB, and so on).
- ✓ Color depth capability (256, 16-bit, 24-bit, and so on).
- ✓ Monitor Horizontal Refresh (31.5–60, and so on).
- ✓ Monitor Vertical Refresh (70–100, and so on).
- ✓ Monitor Maximum Resolution (800×600, 1280×1024, and so on).

Other Considerations

Linux is a complex and capable operating system, but don't raise your hopes too high, and don't expect everything to work correctly at the get-go. Although new Linux users can easily install and adapt to Linux, you might experience an occasional problem. The basic hurdles to a successful Linux installation are

- ✓ Partitioning the hard drive   This is one of the reasons many people think Linux is hard to install. Not many people accustomed to the other operating system have had to partition a hard drive to install a different operating system. Many experienced Linux users don't partition the hard drive at all, and merely install Linux as the sole operating system. Installing Linux is a breeze if you don't have to deal with partitioning.

✓ Configuring X11   The X Window System is the default graphical interface for Linux—but it is *not* Linux. X11 runs on many different types of computers. Luckily, Linux users benefit from the efforts of the XFree86 Project, and the XFree86 distribution of X11 is much better than many commercial offerings. You have a much better chance of configuring X11 to work with your graphics hardware if you have a graphics card that's been around in the market for at least two years. Having the latest and greatest graphics card lessens your chances of being able to use X— although you can still use Linux.

✓ Configuring sound   After Linux is installed and your X11 display is working, configuring Linux to work with your computer's sound card could be the next task. Caldera OpenLinux comes with loadable code modules you can use to get sound working, or you can recompile the Linux kernel to work with your sound card. You can also browse to **http://www. 4front-tech.com** and download an evaluation copy of the OSS drivers. This inexpensive set of sound drivers works with hundreds of different sound systems, and using OSS can be the easiest way to configure sound.

✓ Getting connected   Connecting to the Internet through your ISP using Linux is an important step. Make sure you have a real modem. If you want to avoid trouble, get an external modem for your computer that doesn't depend on software drivers to function. To make the job of connecting to the Internet easier, use the Red Hat **netcfg** tool or the **kppp** client to set up your account. Make sure to read the PPP-HOWTO and ISP-Hookup-HOWTO if you have trouble.

Starting the Installation

Before you begin, make sure you've backed up any important data. Or if you plan to only use Linux, don't worry! You can wipe out any existing partitions and reformat your hard drive during installation. Set your computer to boot from CD-ROM. Do the following:

1. Insert the OpenLinux CD-ROM in your computer and reboot.

2. When your computer restarts, you see Caldera's splash screen and a prompt like this

        boot:

    Press the **Enter** key to begin.

3. OpenLinux starts booting. You see various lines of technical information flash by on the screen as Linux determines the various components installed on your computer (such as the hard drive, floppy, serial ports, keyboard, or CD-ROM).

4. At the first dialog, scroll through the list of languages, and then press

Enter when the desired language is highlighted.

5. You need to select a keyboard. Again, scroll through the list and press **Enter**.

6. You might be asked whether you want to use a previously saved configuration. OpenLinux enables you to save the installation configuration on a floppy disk. This makes it easier to install OpenLinux on the same model and make of computer. Press **Tab** to toggle between **Yes** and **No**, and then press **Enter**.

7. The next dialog asks about disabling Plug and Play cards, and network configuration. The default is off. Most home computer users should press **Enter**.

8. If you're installing OpenLinux on a computer with a PC card interface (such as a laptop), OpenLinux might ask whether you want PCMCIA support during installation (this can be handy if you have a PCMCIA CD-ROM drive). Select **Yes** or **No**, and then press **Enter**.

9. OpenLinux next shows a dialog listing the various IDE and ATAPI hardware in your computer. Press **Enter** to continue. If you have any installed SCSI hardware, OpenLinux shows a similar dialog next.

10. You then see a dialog asking whether all your hardware has been recognized. At this point, the important thing is that OpenLinux recognizes your CD-ROM and hard drive. Select **No** and press **Enter** to make OpenLinux attempt to further probe your hardware; otherwise, select **Yes** and press **Enter**.

Partitioning the Drive

At this point, you're ready to partition your drive. Simply do the following:

1. OpenLinux asks whether you want to change the partition table of your hard drive for Linux. Select **Yes** and press **Enter**.

2. You see your hard drive(s) listed in the next dialog. Scroll through the list with your cursor keys to highlight the desired disk to partition, and press **Enter**.

3. You're then asked whether you want to proceed and partition your hard drive. Before you select **Yes** and press **Enter**, make absolutely sure you have backed up your existing hard drive. Partitioning your drive is a destructive process. If you're sure you can restore your original data, select **Yes** and press **Enter**.

4. The screen clears, and you find yourself at the command line of the **fdisk** program. Begin partitioning your drive by creating two Linux partitions. The first is your swap partition (used by Linux after you boot to temporarily store parts of your computer's memory). The second is a native Linux partition (where OpenLinux is stored).

5. Press **N** to create a new partition.

6. Press **P** to create a primary partition.

7. The **fdisk** command asks for a partition number. If you are installing OpenLinux so that you can boot Linux and another operating system, chances are that your original operating system already uses partition 1. If this is the case, press **2** and press **Enter**.

8. You then need to enter a number for the first cylinder of the partition. The prompt might look like this:

```
First cylinder (254-525):
```

Tip If you are only going to run OpenLinux on your computer, don't worry—use the entire hard drive for Linux and its partitions. However, if you want to install Linux so that you can boot other operating systems, you first need to repartition your hard drive nondestructively.

Type the first number as follows and press Enter.

```
First cylinder (254-525): 254
```

9. You're then asked to enter a second number; the prompt might look something like this:

```
Last cylinder or +size or +sizeM or +sizeK ([254]-525):
```

You can enter an ending cylinder number for the size of your first Linux partition; alternatively, you can enter a size, such as **+500M**, which tells **fdisk** to create a 500MB partition. You need to create a second partition for Linux, called a swap partition. The size of this partition is usually twice the size of your computer's RAM, so it's easy to determine what you should enter. For example, type **+64M** if you have 32MB of RAM installed in your computer (alternatively, enter **+32M** for 16MB of RAM, **+128M** if you have 64MB, and so on). So assuming you have 32MB of RAM, enter **+64M** as follows and press **Enter**:

```
Last cylinder or +size or +sizeM or +sizeK
➥([254]-525): +64M
```

10. You're now back at the **fdisk** prompt. The next step is to set the new partition to a type of **Linux swap**. To begin, press **T**, and then press **Enter**.

11. You see the **Partition number** prompt. Type the number of the swap partition you created (in this example, **2**), and press **Enter**.

12. You then see a prompt like the following:

```
Hex code (type L to list codes):
```

Enter the number **82** (which represents Linux swap) and press **Enter**. The **fdisk** command reports

```
Changed system type of partition 2 to 82 (Linux swap).
```

13. The next step is to create your Linux native partition. Press **N**, and then press **Enter**.

14. Press **P** and press **Enter**.

15. At the **Partition number** prompt, type the next higher partition number (**3** in this example). You then see the **First cylinder** prompt once again:

```
First cylinder (287-525):
```

16. Note that in this example, **fdisk** has recalculated the number of available cylinders after a 64MB swap partition was created. The first available cylinder is now 287 instead of 254. To create your Linux partition, enter the first number in the prompt as follows and press **Enter**:

```
First cylinder (287-525): 287
```

17. You again see the **Last cylinder** prompt. Type the ending cylinder number (**525** in this example) and press **Enter**.

18. You return to the **fdisk** prompt. Press **T** and then **Enter** to set the partition type.

19. At the **Partition number** prompt, type **3** (which corresponds to the partition created) and press **Enter**.

20. At the **Hex code** prompt, type **83** (which tells **fdisk** to create a native Linux partition) and press **Enter**.

21. To see a list of the partitions, press **P**. The **fdisk** command lists the current partition table.

22. To save and write your changes, press **W** and then **Enter**.

23. OpenLinux reports that the partition table has been modified and that you must restart your computer. Press **Enter** to continue.

24. You see the **Hard Disk Selection** dialog. Select **No further hard disk changes** and press **Enter**.

25. In the **Reboot the system** dialog, select the **Yes** button and press **Enter**. Your system is rebooted.

Continuing the Installation

After your system has rebooted, you can continue the installation:

1. Proceed through the OpenLinux installation dialogs (steps 1–10 in the section titled "Starting the Installation").

2. When you are asked whether you want to change the partition table of your hard drive, select **No** and press **Enter**.

3. In the Configure Swap Space dialog, the swap space partition you created with **fdisk** should be highlighted. Press **Enter** to continue. OpenLinux initializes the swap partition.

4. You're then asked for the installation source. Make sure that **CD-ROM** is selected and press **Enter**.

5. OpenLinux lists the different types of CD-ROM drives; your CD-ROM drive type should be highlighted automatically. For your records, write down the CD-ROM device used (such as **/dev/hdb**). Press **Enter**.

6. OpenLinux informs you that your CD-ROM drive has been recognized. Press **Enter**.

7. Make sure your Linux native partition is highlighted in the **Create Root Partition** dialog. For your records, make note of the device used for the partition (such as **/dev/hda3**) and press **Enter**.

8. In the Format Partition dialog, make sure the **Yes** button is highlighted and press **Enter**. This prepares your native Linux partition for software installation.

9. OpenLinux first asks whether you want to check for defective sectors. This is optional, and probably a good idea, but it takes a few minutes. Select **Yes** or **No** and press **Enter**.

10. You see OpenLinux run the **mke2fs** command on your root partition. Kick back and relax for a moment—the hard work is already finished.

11. Select the installation type you want and press **Enter**.

Tip

The minimal system installation without X11 installs Linux, but you won't have a graphical interface. If you have the disk space, at least choose the minimal system with X11.

The small standard system includes X11, but, according to Caldera, it doesn't include a complete set of programming, utility, and Internet commands.

A good installation, highlighted by default, is the standard system; but if you have the room, instead highlight **Install all packages** and press **Enter**. This saves you time, because you won't need to later install additional software. However, you should know that StarOffice is not installed when you install OpenLinux. You need at least another 150MB of hard drive space, along with the X Window System (X11), in order to install and use StarOffice.

Note This installation can take from several minutes to more than a half hour, depending on the speed of your computer's CD-ROM and how much software you've selected for installation.

Note The first part of the name is the host computer's name, the second part is the domain name, and the third part is the type of domain. Computers using assigned addresses on the Internet must use a registered name. However, you can assign any name you like here if you're using the computer at home.

Note If you choose Yes in step 2, you need to supply the device name of the card. If OpenLinux does not detect a network card, you're returned to the **Hostname Entry** dialog.

You can add and configure a network card after installing OpenLinux. However, configuring network cards is beyond the scope of this book.

12. You need to select an appropriate X-Server for your computer's graphics card. Most (but not all) Linux users should select the XFree86-SVGA server. Select a server by highlighting it and pressing the spacebar. Press **Enter** to continue.

13. You're ready to install the OpenLinux software from your CD-ROM. Press **Enter** to install. A progress dialog appears, showing the percentage of installation performed.

Configuring Your System

After the software installs, OpenLinux uses the **rpm** command to configure the installed software. This takes several minutes. After this is completed, you have to fill in information about your system:

1. The **Hostname Entry** dialog asks for the hostname of your computer. Enter a name you like, such as **hitachi.mydomain.mytypeofdomain**, select **OK** and press **Enter**.

2. If you have a network card, select **Yes** and press **Enter**. Otherwise, choose **No**.

3. Highlight the local time and press **Enter**.

4. Highlight your time zone and press **Enter**.

5. Scroll through the list of mice and press **Enter**.

6. To configure your printer, scroll through the list of printers, select your printer type, and then press **Enter**.

7. Enter a root operator password. Passwords are case-sensitive, generally consist of eight letters, and contain a mix of numeric and alphabetic characters (for example, **fR3wilLz**). Type the password, press **Enter**, and then reenter the password and press **Enter** a second time.

8. In the **Create First Account** dialog, press **Enter**.

9. Erase the field in the **User Login Name** dialog, type a username, and press **Enter**.

10. In the **Enter User ID** dialog, press **Enter**.

11. In the **Select a Group** dialog, press **Enter**.

12. As you see, OpenLinux automagically creates a directory with your username under the **/home** directory. For example, the home directory of user **fsmith** is **/home/fsmith**. Press **Enter**.

13. Use your cursor to highlight the GNU **bash** entry and press **Enter**. This becomes your default shell.

14. Enter your first and last name and press **Enter**.

15. Type the password you want to use to access your account, and then press **Enter**. Repeat this step to confirm your password. Remember, Linux passwords are case-sensitive!

16. OpenLinux presents a Boot Setup Analysis screen. If you're installing OpenLinux as a second operating system, OpenLinux reports that a DOS boot loader was found in your hard drive's first partition. Press **Enter** to continue.

17. From the Linux loader **Boot Manager Installation** dialog, you can install LILO into the Master Boot Record (MBR of your DOS partition, the Linux root partition, or a floppy disk. (You also have the choice to not install LILO.) Scroll through the list of LILO installation choices, highlight the one that works for you, and then press **Enter**.

18. In the **Defaults for LILO** dialog, scroll through the list of boot images that LILO should load by default. Highlight the Linux kernel image with the word **modular** as part of its name and press **Enter**. When you start or reboot your computer, LILO loads the selected boot image.

19. If you want to type a word other than **linux** at the LILO prompt when your reboot your computer, erase the word **linux** in the **Defaults for LILO** dialog and type the word you want to use. Whether you've entered a new word or left the default of **linux**, press **Enter** to continue.

20. The next dialog asks for boot parameters, which are messages that you can pass to the Linux kernel before LILO loads the kernel. Some users might need to use a boot-prompt message, but most do not. If you're not sure, leave the entry blank and press **Enter**.

21. At the **Select Additional LILO Entries** dialog, scroll through the list of boot images to highlight a desired image (such as a DOS image) and press **Enter**. (If you have no further entries, select **No further entries to add to LILO** and press **Enter**.)

22. You see the LILO configuration file. Scroll through and read it, looking for the boot prompts, such as **linux** or **dos**. Also note that by default, LILO waits 20 seconds before displaying the boot image you've selected.

23. OpenLinux asks whether you want to install LILO as configured. Select **Yes** and press **Enter**.

24. After LILO is installed, OpenLinux sends you a message indicating this. Press **Enter** to continue.

25. You must select software services to be started when you boot Linux. Select or unselect a service by pressing the spacebar when a service is highlighted. After all the services you want started are selected (services that have been selected are indicated by a capital X in parentheses to the left of its number), press **Enter** to continue.

26. Select an X server to use for the X Window System (most users want the SVGA server) and press **Enter**.

27. OpenLinux gives you the choice of configuring X for your computer's graphics card and monitor, or waiting until after you boot Linux. Select **No** (that is, select to wait until after you boot Linux) and press **Enter**.

28. At the **Call XF86Setup** dialog, press **Enter**.

Note You can skip installing a printer at this time, but you need to use the lisa command after booting OpenLinux to install a printer later on.

Warning This is the password for the OpenLinux superuser. Don't forget this password!

Note A username usually consists of the first letter of the person's first name, followed by the person's last name. For example, someone named Fred Smith usually has a username of **fsmith**. However, you can use any name you like.

Note After you log in, you can use other shells or even change your default shell.

Note This is your password, so don't forget it!

Note If you install LILO in the MBR or the Linux root partition, when you start or reboot your computer, LILO loads from your hard drive.

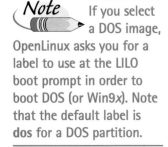

Note If you install on a floppy, you need to use a floppy in order to boot Linux.

Note If you use a commercial boot loader, such as System Commander or Boot Magic, do not install LILO into the MBR of your DOS partition. The MBR is needed by these programs. You must install LILO on the Linux root partition.

Note For more information about the LILO boot prompt, read the Boot-Prompt-HOWTO under the **/usr/doc/HOWTO** directory after you log in to Linux.

Note If you select a DOS image, OpenLinux asks you for a label to use at the LILO boot prompt in order to boot DOS (or Win9x). Note that the default label is **dos** for a DOS partition.

29. If you'd like to save your configuration for later use, remove the install floppy disk (if you used one) and place a blank formatted disk in its bay. Select the **Yes** button, and press **Enter**.

30. At the next dialog, press **Enter** to save the configuration.

31. After OpenLinux saves the configuration, press **Enter**.

Booting Linux

Congratulations! You've finished installing OpenLinux. Now it's time to reboot your computer:

1. Press **Enter**.

2. If you booted with an OpenLinux CD-ROM to do the installation, remove the CD-ROM.

3. Remove your floppy disk and press any key to boot OpenLinux.

4. After a number of messages scroll by, you see a **login** prompt. Type **root** and press **Enter**.

5. Linux asks for your root password. Type it in and press **Enter**.

Testing LILO

If you did not configure X, OpenLinux logs you in and reports the following:

```
The X server is not configured.
Please gather information about your mouse, video card, and
monitor, and run

XF86Setup as root.
```

However, you should first restart your computer and log back in to see whether LILO works correctly. Use the **shutdown** command along with its **-r** (reboot) option, followed by the word **now** or the number **0** like this:

```
shutdown -r now
```

or

```
shutdown -r 0
```

This reboots your computer. You should then see Caldera's splash screen, and the **LILO boot** prompt. To boot Linux, use the label you entered during LILO's installation and press **Enter** to boot Linux:

```
boot: linux
```

Configuring the X Window System

This section shows you how to configure the X Window System for OpenLinux. Although you can use the XF86Setup program to configure X, a simpler program included with XFree86 is the **xf86config** command. This program uses a text-based interface that, unlike XF86Setup, does not have the potential to lock up your display. Do the following:

1. Log in as the root operator and type **xf86config** from the command line. You see the following:

   ```
   This program will create a basic XF86Config file,
   based on menu selections you make.

   The XF86Config file usually resides in /usr/X11R6/
   lib/X11 or /and so on A sample XF86Config file is
   supplied with XFree86; it is configured for a standard
   VGA card and monitor with 640x480 resolution. This
   program will ask for a pathname when it is ready to
   write the file.

   You can either take the sample XF86Config as a base
   and edit it for your configuration, or let this
   program produce a base XF86Config file for your
   configuration and fine-tune it. Refer to /usr/X11R6/
   lib/X11/doc/README.Config for a detailed overview of
   the configuration process.

   For accelerated servers (including accelerated
   drivers in the SVGA server), there are many chipset
   and card-specific options and settings. This program
   does not know about these. On some configurations some
   of these settings must be specified. Refer to the
   server man pages and chipset-specific READMEs.

   Before continuing with this program, make sure you
   know the chipset and amount of video memory on your
   video card. SuperProbe can help with this. It is also
   helpful if you know what server you want to run.

   Press enter to continue, or ctrl-c to abort.
   ```

2. Press **Enter** to continue. Your machine displays the following:

   ```
   First specify a mouse protocol type. Choose one from
   the following list:

   1.   Microsoft compatible (2-button protocol)
   2.   Mouse Systems (3-button protocol)
   3.   Bus Mouse
   4.   PS/2 Mouse
   5.   Logitech Mouse (serial, old type, Logitech
        protocol)
   6.   Logitech MouseMan (Microsoft compatible)
   7.   MM Series
   ```

Note  Essentially, there are only four services that should be started if you use OpenLinux on a home computer. These are Auto Mount daemon, Cron daemon, Print server, and Mail Transfer Agent. You can always start or stop these services after you log in as the root operator by using the **lisa** command. If you're not sure what services to select, press **Enter** to use the default setup.

Note Configuring X after you boot Linux is a good idea, as configuring X has the potential to blank your display. It's best to finish the installation first.

Note To use the **XF86Setup** program to configure X11, you must be logged in as the root operator.

```
8.   MM HitTablet
9.   Microsoft IntelliMouse
```

```
If you have a two-button mouse, it is most likely of
type 1, and if you have a three-button mouse, it can
probably support both protocol 1 and 2. There are two
main varieties of the latter type: mice with a switch
to select the protocol, and mice that default to 1 and
require a button to be held at boot-time to select
protocol 2. Some mice can be convinced to do 2 by
sending a special sequence to the serial port (see the
ClearDTR/ClearRTS options).
```

```
Enter a protocol number:
```

3. Type a number corresponding to your mouse (such as **4** for a PS/2 mouse) and press **Enter**. You see the following:

```
If your mouse has only two buttons, it is recommended
that you enable Emulate3Buttons.
```

```
Please answer the following question with either 'y'
or 'n'. Do you want to enable Emulate3Buttons?
```

4. Press **Y** if you have a two-button mouse. You're then asked for the mouse device name:

```
Now give the full device name that the mouse is
connected to, for example /dev/tty00. Just pressing
enter will use the default, /dev/mouse.
```

```
Mouse device:
```

5. Press **Enter**. You see the following:

```
Beginning with XFree86 3.1.2D, you can use the new
X11R6.1 XKEYBOARD extension to manage the keyboard
layout. If you answer 'n' to the following question,
the server will use the old method, and you have to
adjust your keyboard layout with xmodmap.
```

```
Please answer the following question with either 'y'
or 'n'. Do you want to use XKB?
```

6. Press **Y** and then press **Enter**. You are presented with a list of keymaps:

```
List of preconfigured keymaps:

1   Standard 101-key, US encoding
2   Microsoft Natural, US encoding
```

```
 3  KeyTronic FlexPro, US encoding
 4  Standard 101-key, US encoding with ISO9995-3
    extensions
 5  Standard 101-key, German encoding
 6  Standard 101-key, French encoding
 7  Standard 101-key, Thai encoding
 8  Standard 101-key, Swiss/German encoding
 9  Standard 101-key, Swiss/French encoding
10  None of the above

Enter a number to choose the keymap.
```

7. Type the number that corresponds with your keyboard (such as **1** for a 101-key keyboard with U.S. encoding) and press **Enter**. You must then specify your monitor's horizontal sync range:

```
You must indicate the horizontal sync range of your
monitor. You can either select one of the predefined
ranges below that correspond to industry-standard
monitor types, or give a specific range.

It is VERY IMPORTANT that you do not specify a monitor
type with a horizontal sync range that is beyond the
capabilities of your monitor. If in doubt, choose a
conservative setting.

    hsync in kHz; monitor type with characteristic modes
 1  31.5; Standard VGA, 640x480 @ 60 Hz
 2  31.5 - 35.1; Super VGA, 800x600 @ 56 Hz
 3  31.5, 35.5; 8514 Compatible, 1024x768 @ 87 Hz
    interlaced (no 800x600)
 4  31.5, 35.15, 35.5; Super VGA, 1024x768 @ 87 Hz
    interlaced, 800x600 @ 56 Hz
 5  31.5 - 37.9; Extended Super VGA, 800x600 @ 60 Hz,
    640x480 @ 72 Hz
 6  31.5 - 48.5; Non-Interlaced SVGA, 1024x768 @ 60 Hz,
    800x600 @ 72 Hz
 7  31.5 - 57.0; High Frequency SVGA, 1024x768 @ 70 Hz
 8  31.5 - 64.3; Monitor that can do 1280x1024 @ 60 Hz
 9  31.5 - 79.0; Monitor that can do 1280x1024 @ 74 Hz
10  31.5 - 82.0; Monitor that can do 1280x1024 @ 76 Hz
11  Enter your own horizontal sync range

Enter your choice (1-11):
```

8. Enter the number that corresponds with your monitor's horizontal sync range and press **Enter**. If you'd like to enter your own range, enter **11** and press **Enter**. You see the following:

```
Please enter the horizontal sync range of your monitor,
in the format used in the table of monitor types above.
```

```
You can either specify one or more continuous ranges
(e.g. 15-25, 30-50), or one or more fixed sync
frequencies.

Horizontal sync range:
```

9. Type your own range (such as **31.5-70**) or a single number (such as **31**) and press **Enter**. You need to specify a vertical sync range for your monitor:

```
You must indicate the vertical sync range of your
monitor. You can either select one of the predefined
ranges below that correspond to industry-standard
monitor types, or give a specific range. For interlaced
modes, the number that counts is the high one (e.g. 87
Hz rather than 43 Hz).

   1  50-70
   2  50-90
   3  50-100
   4  40-150
   5  Enter your own vertical sync range

Enter your choice:
```

10. Again, pick a range that corresponds to your monitor. To enter your own range, type **5** and press **Enter**.

11. Enter your monitor's vertical range, such as **50-70**, and press **Enter**. You are then asked for a few description strings:

```
You must now enter a few identification/description
strings, namely an identifier, a vendor name, and a
model name. Just pressing enter will fill in default
names.

The strings are free-form, spaces are allowed.
Enter an identifier for your monitor definition:
Enter the vendor name of your monitor:
Enter the model name of your monitor:
```

12. You can press **Enter** for each item. When you finish, you are asked to configure video card settings:

```
Now we must configure video card specific settings. At
this point you can choose to make a selection out of a
database of video card definitions. Because there can
be variation in Ramdacs and clock generators even
between cards of the same model, it is not sensible to
blindly copy the settings (e.g. a Device section). For
```

this reason, after you make a selection, you will
still be asked about the components of the card, with
the settings from the chosen database entry presented
as a strong hint.

The database entries include information about the
chipset, what server to run, the Ramdac and ClockChip,
and comments that will be included in the Device
section. However, a lot of definitions only hint about
what server to run (based on the chipset the card uses)
and are untested.

If you can't find your card in the database, there's
nothing to worry about. You should only choose a
database entry that is exactly the same model as
your card; choosing one that looks similar is just a
bad idea (e.g. a GemStone Snail 64 may be as different
from a GemStone Snail 64+ in terms of hardware as
can be).

Do you want to look at the card database?

13. Press **Y** and then press **Enter** to see the graphics card database (which
contains definitions for 220 cards):

0	2 the Max MAXColor S3 Trio64V+	S3 Trio64V+
1	928Movie	S3 928
2	AGX (generic)	AGX-014/15/16
3	ALG-5434(E)	CL-GD5434
4	ASUS 3Dexplorer	RIVA128
5	ASUS PCI-AV264CT	ATI-Mach64
6	ASUS PCI-V264CT	ATI-Mach64
7	ASUS Video Magic PCI V864	S3 864
8	ASUS Video Magic PCI VT64	S3 Trio64
9	AT25	Alliance AT3D
10	AT3D	Alliance AT3D
11	ATI 3D Pro Turbo	ATI-Mach64
12	ATI 3D Xpression	ATI-Mach64
13	ATI 3D Xpression+ PC2TV	ATI-Mach64
14	ATI 8514 Ultra (no VGA)	ATI-Mach8
15	ATI All-in-Wonder	ATI-Mach64
16	ATI Graphics Pro Turbo	ATI-Mach64
17	ATI Graphics Pro Turbo 1600	ATI-Mach64

Enter a number to choose the corresponding card
definition. Press enter for the next page, q to
continue configuration.

14. Type the number the matches your graphics card; you can scroll through the database by pressing **Enter**. After you type a selection and press **Enter**, the **xf86config** command then shows your selection:

```
Your selected card definition:

Identifier: Cirrus Logic GD754x (laptop)
Chipset:    CL-GD7541/42/43/48
Server:     XF86_SVGA
Do NOT probe clocks or use any Clocks line.

Press enter to continue, or ctrl-c to abort.
```

15. Press **Enter** to continue. You are instructed to determine which server to run:

```
Now you must determine which server to run. Refer to
the manpages and other documentation. The following
servers are available (they may not all be installed
on your system):

1   The XF86_Mono server. This a monochrome server that
    should work on any VGA-compatible card, in 640x480
    (more on some SVGA chipsets).
2   The XF86_VGA16 server. This is a 16-color VGA
    server that should work on any VGA-compatible card.
3   The XF86_SVGA server. This is a 256 color SVGA
    server that supports a number of SVGA chipsets. On
    some chipsets it is accelerated or supports higher
    color depths.
4   The accelerated servers. These include XF86_S3,
    XF86_Mach32, XF86_Mach8,
    XF86_8514, XF86_P9000, XF86_AGX, XF86_W32, XF86_
    Mach64, XF86_I128 and XF86_S3V.

These four server types correspond to the four
different "Screen" sections in XF86Config (vga2, vga16,
svga, accel).

5   Choose the server from the card definition,
    XF86_SVGA.

Which one of these screen types do you intend to run
by default (1-5)?
```

16. Press **5** and press **Enter**. You see the following:

```
The server to run is selected by changing the symbolic
link 'X'. For example, 'rm /usr/X11R6/bin/X; ln -s
```

```
/usr/X11R6/bin/XF86_SVGA /usr/X11R6/bin/X' selects the
SVGA server.

Please answer the following question with either 'y' or
'n'. Do you want me to set the symbolic link?
```

17. Press **Y** and press **Enter**. You are asked for information about your video card:

```
Now you must give information about your video card.
This will be used for the "Device" section of your
video card in XF86Config.

You must indicate how much video memory you have. It
is probably a good idea to use the same approximate
amount as that detected by the server you intend to
use. If you encounter problems that are due to the
used server not supporting the amount memory you have
(e.g. ATI Mach64 is limited to 1024K with the SVGA
server), specify the maximum amount supported by the
server.

How much video memory do you have on your video card:

    1  256K
    2  512K
    3  1024K
    4  2048K
    5  4096K
    6  Other


Enter your choice:
```

> **Note** The symbolic
> link using X to
> point to your X11 server
> currently works with
> Caldera OpenLinux 1.3, but
> this will change in future
> versions of the XFree86 X11
> distribution. Always read
> the file **RELNOTES** under
> the **/usr/X11R6/lib/X11/doc**
> directory to details about
> changes in configuring
> XFree86.

18. Press a number matching your graphic card's video memory (such as **4** for a 2MB video memory card) and press **Enter**. You are asked for a few description strings:

```
You must now enter a few identification/description
strings, namely an identifier, a vendor name, and a
model name. Just pressing enter will fill in default
names (possibly from a card definition).

Your card definition is Cirrus Logic GD754x (laptop).

The strings are free-form, spaces are allowed.
Enter an identifier for your video card definition:
You can simply press enter here if you have a generic
card, or want to describe your card with one string.
Enter the vendor name of your video card:
Enter the model (board) name of your video card:
```

19. You can press **Enter** for each item. You're then asked to specify a RAM-DAC identifier:

```
The RAMDAC setting only applies to the S3, AGX, W32
servers, and some drivers in the SVGA servers. Some
RAMDAC's are auto-detected by the server. The
detection of a RAMDAC is forced by using a Ramdac
"identifier" line in the Device section. The
identifiers are shown at the right of the following
table of RAMDAC types:

    1   AT&T 20C490 (S3 and AGX servers, ARK driver)
➡                    att20c490
    2   AT&T 20C498/21C498/22C498 (S3, autodetected)
➡                    att20c498
    3   AT&T 20C409/20C499 (S3, autodetected)
➡                    att20c409
    4   AT&T 20C505 (S3)                            att20c505
    5   BrookTree BT481 (AGX)                          bt481
    6   BrookTree BT482 (AGX)                          bt482
    7   BrookTree BT485/9485 (S3)                      bt485
    8   Sierra SC15025 (S3, AGX)                     sc15025
    9   S3 GenDAC (86C708) (autodetected)           s3gendac
   10   S3 SDAC (86C716) (autodetected)              s3_sdac
   11   STG-1700 (S3, autodetected)                  stg1700
   12   STG-1703 (S3, autodetected)                  stg1703


Enter a number to choose the corresponding RAMDAC.
Press enter for the next page, q to quit without
selection of a RAMDAC.
```

20. Press **Q** and press **Enter** if your card does not have a RAMDAC. Otherwise, enter the number that corresponds to your card and press **Enter**. Either way, you need to enter a clockchip setting:

```
A Clockchip line in the Device section forces the
detection of a programmable clock device. With a
clockchip enabled, any required clock can be programmed
without requiring probing of clocks or a Clocks line.
Most cards don't have a programmable clock chip. Choose
from the following list:

    1   Chrontel 8391
        ch8391
    2   ICD2061A and compatibles (ICS9161A, DCS2824)
        icd2061a
```

```
    3   ICS2595
        ics2595
    4   ICS5342 (similar to SDAC, but not completely
        compatible)    ics5342
    5   ICS5341
        ics5341
    6   S3 GenDAC (86C708) and ICS5300 (autodetected)
        s3gendac
    7   S3 SDAC (86C716)
        s3_sdac
    8   STG 1703 (autodetected)
        stg1703
    9   Sierra SC11412
        sc11412
   10   TI 3025 (autodetected)
        ti3025
   11   TI 3026 (autodetected)
        ti3026
   12   IBM RGB 51x/52x (autodetected)
        ibm_rgb5xx


    Just press enter if you don't want a Clockchip setting.
    What Clockchip setting do you want (1-12)?
```

21. Press **Enter** if you don't need a clockchip setting for your card. If you do
    need a setting for your clockchip, type the number that corresponds to
    your card's clockchip, and press **Enter**. You are then asked whether you
    want to probe your clock:

    ```
    For most configurations, a Clocks line is useful since
    it prevents the slow and nasty sounding clock probing
    at server start-up. Probed clocks are displayed at
    server startup, along with other server and hardware
    configuration info. You can save this information in a
    file by running 'X -probeonly 2>output_file'. Be warned
    that clock probing is inherently imprecise; some clocks
    may be slightly too high (varies per run).

    At this point I can run X -probeonly, and try to
    extract the clock information from the output. It is
    recommended that you do this yourself and add a clocks
    line (note that the list of clocks may be split over
    multiple Clocks lines) to your Device section
    afterwards. Be aware that a clocks line is not
    appropriate for drivers that have a fixed set of clocks
    and don't probe by default (e.g. Cirrus). Also, for the
    P9000 server you must simply specify clocks line that
    matches the modes you want to use.  For the S3 server
    with a programmable clock chip you need a 'ClockChip'
    ```

line and no Clocks line.

You must be root to be able to run X -probeonly now.

The card definition says to NOT probe clocks.
Do you want me to run 'X -probeonly' now?

22. Depending on your card, you might be able to probe your card's clocks. Press **Y** or **N** and press **Enter**. You are then asked to check the color-depth modes:

For each depth, a list of modes (resolutions) is defined. The default resolution that the server will start-up with will be the first listed mode that can be supported by the monitor and card. Currently it is set to:

"640x480" "800x600" "1024x768" "1280x1024" for 8bpp
"640x480" "800x600" "1024x768" for 16bpp
"640x480" "800x600" for 24bpp
"640x480" "800x600" for 32bpp

Note that 16, 24 and 32bpp are only supported on a few configurations.
Modes that cannot be supported due to monitor or clock constraints will be automatically skipped by the server.

1 Change the modes for 8pp (256 colors)
2 Change the modes for 16bpp (32K/64K colors)
3 Change the modes for 24bpp (24-bit color, packed pixel)
4 Change the modes for 32bpp (24-bit color)
5 The modes are OK, continue.

Enter your choice:

23. Press **5** and then **Enter**. The XF86_SVGA server (or the server you've selected) automatically checks for valid modes. Press Enter to continue. You see the following:

I am going to write the XF86Config file now. Make sure you don't accidentally overwrite a previously configured one.

Do you want it written to the current directory as 'XF86Config'?

24. Press **Y** to save the file. You see the following:

```
File has been written. Take a look at it before running
'startx'. Note that the XF86Config file must be in one
of the directories searched by the server (e.g.
/usr/X11R6/lib/X11) in order to be used. Within the
server press ctrl, alt and '+' simultaneously to cycle
video resolutions. Pressing ctrl, alt and backspace
simultaneously immediately exits the server (use if the
monitor doesn't sync for a particular mode).

For further configuration, refer to
/usr/X11R6/lib/X11/doc/README.Config.
```

25. Edit the XF86config file using a text editor. If you choose to use pico, type **pico -w XF86Config** at the command line.

26. Scroll through your new **XF86Config** file until you come to the VideoRam setting under the device section. It might look like this:

```
Section "Device"
    Identifier "CLGD7543"
    VendorName "Cirrus Logic"
    BoardName    "7543"
#    VideoRam 1024
    Chipset      "cl7543"
EndSection
```

27. Change the number following the **VideoRam** entry to match your card's video memory and delete the pound sign (**#**) at the beginning of the line.

28. Press **Ctrl+X** to save your file.

29. Copy the **XF86Config** file to the **/etc** directory by typing **cp XF86Config /etc**.

You're finished!

Starting an X11 Session

You can start an X11 session by typing **startx** at the command line. To start an X session using the K Desktop Environment, type **kde** at the command line. To start an X session using more than 256 colors, use **startx** or **kde** like this:

```
startx — -bpp 16
```

or

```
kde — -bpp 16
```

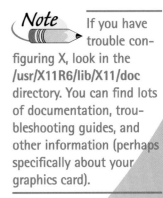

Note If you have trouble configuring X, look in the **/usr/X11R6/lib/X11/doc** directory. You can find lots of documentation, troubleshooting guides, and other information (perhaps specifically about your graphics card).

B

Adding Miscellaneous Hardware

*T*his appendix gives you some pointers on how to configure OpenLinux to support hardware such as an internal sound card, external Iomega Zip drive, or 3Com Palm Computer. You can find support for many different types of hardware and add-on peripherals you can use with OpenLinux. However, finding out how to add hardware or configure Linux for sound can initially be confusing.

The first place to look for technical information is Caldera's Web site. You can find the latest tips, hints, and fixes for configuring OpenLinux to work with your computer. Browse to **http://www.calderasystems.com/support/index.html** for starters. For technical information, try **http://www.calderasystems.com/techquide.html**. You can find information about how to

- ✓ Use a true PostScript printer with OpenLinux
- ✓ Rebuild the Linux kernel
- ✓ Install Linux via your computer's parallel port
- ✓ Configure OpenLinux for sound
- ✓ Set up OpenLinux for dial-in networking
- ✓ Set up OpenLinux to connect to your Internet service provider

Unless you have an off-brand or home-built PC, chances are good that other OpenLinux users have asked the same questions you might ask as a new user. You definitely should read the Usenet newsgroup **alt.os.linux.caldera** to learn new tips, tricks, or traps when using OpenLinux. To participate in discussions about OpenLinux by electronic mail, see Appendix C, "Internet Resources for Linux and OpenLinux," for directions on how to subscribe to the caldera-users digest. ●

Configuring OpenLinux for Sound

*O*penLinux uses loadable code modules to provide sound support for your computer. One of the first things you should do after logging in and configuring the X Window System for your display is to configure OpenLinux to support sound.

Fortunately, most computers today follow common protocols when playing sound. You should be able to easily configure OpenLinux to play sound through your computer's sound card. And if your computer doesn't have a sound card, you can rebuild the Linux kernel to play sound through your computer's speaker (granted, the sound is pretty tinny, but it's better than nothing).

Load Sound Modules

OpenLinux comes with at least 17 loadable code sound modules, found under the **/lib/modules/2.0.xx/sound** directory, where **xx** is the version of your OpenLinux kernel (or the output of the **uname** command with the **-r** option). Before you can begin, you need to find and write down the I/O port address, IRQ, DMA channel numbers, and I/O port addresses for any other sound subsystem for your computer.

Log in as the root operator. At the command line of your console or an X11 terminal window, use the **insmod** command to load the sound kernel modules. This procedure should work for most computers with SoundBlaster or equivalent cards. Type the following (the example works with a Compaq Presario 1240 laptop), replacing the **io**, **irq**, **-dma**, and **mpu io** values with those of your computer:

```
insmod sound
insmod uart401
insmod sb io=0x220 irq=5 dma=1,0 mpu_io=0x330
```

Test Sound

Use the **play** command to test your sound card, like this

```
play /usr/share/sounds/dingdong.au
```

If you've installed StarOffice4.0, try this

```
play $HOME/Office40/gallery/sound/kongas.wav
```

If your sound configuration doesn't work the first time, or if you enter an incorrect setting, you must, unfortunately, reboot Linux to restore system memory and try again. If the sound works, great! You can find numerous sound utilities for OpenLinux on this book's CD-ROM. Some handy utilities include **kmix** for KDE and **xmixer** to control the balance and source of your system's sound.

Quick Recording

Here's a short recording script you can use to record sound with a built-in or attached microphone. The script works by using the **dd** command to save and convert a specified amount of data (in seconds) to your hard drive. Type this script into a file using your favorite text editor:

```
echo -ne "recording "
echo -ne $1
echo -ne " seconds of sound to "
echo $2.au
/bin/dd bs=8k count=$1 </dev/audio >$2.au
```

Save the file with a name, such as **recordit**, and use the **chmod** command to make the script executable like this:

```
chmod +x recordit
```

First, use **kmix** or **xmixer** to set your microphone's input level. To record a sound, type *recordit*, followed by a number in seconds, and then press **Enter**, like this

```
recordit 5 myfirstsound
```

The script responds with

```
recording 5 seconds of sound to myfirstsound.au
5+0 records in
5+0 records out
```

Play the sound by sending it to your audio device like this

```
cat myfirstsound.au >/dev/audio
```

An Easier Way

Of course, there's an even easier way to configure OpenLinux for sound. Browse to **http://www.opensound.com/linux.html**. You can find links to detailed technical procedures for manual sound configuration, or you can use the commercial version of the Open Sound System for Linux, which supports more than 200 sound cards (and which saves you a lot of time and effort).

For a small amount of information about playing sound through your computer's speaker, read the Sound-HOWTO, found under the **/usr/doc/HOWTO** directory. To download the latest release of the PC Speaker software (pcsndrv-1.0.tgz), browse to **http://sunsite.unc.edu/pub/Linux/kernel/patches/console**.

Adding a Parallel-Port Zip Drive

OpenLinux provides out-of-the-box support if you have a parallel-port version of the Iomega Zip drive (**http://www.iomega.com**). The Zip drive is a removable hard drive with a disk storage capacity of about 100MB, and attaches to your computer's parallel printer port. The default OpenLinux kernel (**/boot/vmlinuz-2.0.XX-modular**) provides the three necessary support mechanisms for the Zip drive:

✓ SCSI support either compiled in or available as loadable modules

✓ Parallel-printer support is a loadable module (you must be able to unload the **lp** module before a Zip disk can be mounted)

✓ The **ppa** module is available under the **/lib/modules** directory

Mount a Zip Disk

To install the **ppa** module and mount a Zip disk, first make sure your Zip drive is properly connected to your computer and turned on. Log in as the root operator, and create a mount point for your Zip disk with the **mkdir** command like this

```
mkdir /mnt/zip
```

Insert a Zip disk into the drive. Use the **rmmod** command to make sure the **lp.o**, or parallel printer module, is unloaded, like this

```
rmmod lp
```

Use the **insmod** command to load the **ppa** module like this

```
insmod ppa
```

To make sure that the kernel supports long filenames for the vfat filesystem, use the **insmod** command to load the vfat module like this

```
insmod vfat
```

Then mount the Zip disk by using the **mount** command to specify the filesystem type, the Zip device, and the mount point, like this

```
mount -t vfat /dev/sda4 /mnt/zip
```

Format and Mount a Linux Zip Disk

You can format and mount a Zip disk in Linux's native format (although afterwards you won't be able to use it with that "other operating system"). Create a mount point with the **mkdir** command like this:

```
mkdir /mnt/zipext2
```

Insert a Zip disk into its drive. Make sure the **ppa** module is loaded. Then use the **mke2fs** command to format the disk like this:

```
mke2fs /dev/sda4
```

Mount the new Linux Zip disk with the **mount** command like this:

```
mount -t ext2 /dev/sda4 /mnt/zipext2
```

Printing and the Zip Drive

You cannot print and use a parallel-port Zip drive at the same time. A workaround, however, is to use **insmod** and **rmmod** to load and unload the proper modules.

You can use a shell script called **dozip** to alternate between your printer and Zip drive:

```
# dozip - alternate between Zip disk and printing
#
# assumes Linux ext2 Zip disks are mounted at /mnt/zipext2
# assumes vfat Zip disks are mounted at /mnt/zip
# assumes vfat module is loaded
#
# usage:
# dozip h        show help
# dozip lp       unmount Zip, load printer module
# dozip ext2     unload printer, mount Linux Zip disk
# dozip vfat     unload printer, mount vfat Zip disk
#
#!/bin/bash
option=$1


if [ $option  = "h" ]
then /bin/echo "usage: dozip [h]¦[lp]¦[vfat]¦[ext2]"
fi


if [ $option = "lp" ]
then
# we want to print, so unmount any Zip disk
# and load the printer module
    /bin/echo "unmounting Zip disk"
    /bin/umount /mnt/zip >/dev/null 2>&1
    /bin/umount /mnt/zipext2 >/dev/null 2>&1
    /bin/echo "unloading ppa driver"
    /sbin/rmmod ppa >/dev/null 2>&1
    /bin/echo "loading line-printer driver"
    /sbin/insmod lp
    /bin/echo "done"
fi


if [ $option = "vfat" ]
```

Note Squeezing More Space Out of Your Zip Disk

You can get an extra 5MB of storage on your native Linux Zip disks by using the **-m** option of **mke2fs** with a value of zero (0). By default, **mke2fs** reserves 5% of a volume or partition's size for use by the root operator (space for a **/root** directory). To fully format your Zip disk, use the **mke2fs** command like this

```
mke2fs -m0 /dev/sda4
```

```
then
# we want to use a vfat Zip disk, so
# unload lp and mount at the vfat directory
    /bin/echo "unloading line-printer driver"
    /sbin/rmmod lp >/dev/null 2>&1
    /bin/echo "loading ppa driver"
    /sbin/insmod ppa >/dev/null 2>%1
    /sbin/insmod vfat >/dev/null 2>&1
    /bin/echo "mounting vfat Zip disk"
# make the directory (useful only once),
# then mount the vfat Zip disk
    /bin/mkdir /mnt/zip >/dev/null 2>%1
    /bin/mount -t vfat /dev/sda4 /mnt/zip
    /bin/echo "done"

if [ $option = "ext2" ]
then
# we want to use a Zip in Linux native ext2,
# so unload lp and mount at the ext2 directory
    /bin/echo "unloading line-printer driver"
    /sbin/rmmod lp >/dev/null 2>&1
    /bin/echo "loading ppa driver"
    /sbin/insmod ppa >/dev/null 2>&1
    /bin/echo "mounting Linux Zip disk"
# make the directory (useful only once),
# then mount the ext2 Zip disk
    /bin/mkdir /mnt/zipext2 >/dev/null 2>%1
    /bin/mount -t ext2 /dev/sda4 /mnt/zipext2
fi
```

Enter the script into a file called **dozip**, use **chmod +x dozip** to make the script executable, and copy it to the **/usr/local/bin** directory.

Password-Protecting Zip Disks

Although you can mount a Zip disk as read-only to protect its contents from being deleted (see the **mount** man page), you can use the **ziptool** command to further protect each Zip disk with a password. To use the password feature of Zip disks, browse to **http://sunsite.unc.edu/pub/Linux/utils/disk-management/**. Download the file **ziptool-1.2.tar.gz** and decompress it with the **tar** command like this

```
tar xvzf zip*gz
```

tar creates a **ziptool-1.2** directory. Change directory to this new directory and make and install **ziptool** like this:

```
cd zip*2 ; make install
```

To protect your Zip disk and assign a password, put a Zip disk in its drive and use **ziptool** like this:

```
ziptool -rp /dev/sda
```

The command asks for a password (you can enter up to 32 characters). After you press **Enter**, **ziptool** password-protects and ejects your Zip disk from its drive. Don't forget the password!

Setting Up OpenLinux for the Palm Computer

The 3Com Palm computers have taken the handheld computer industry by storm. There are now more than one million Palm computer owners. If you have a Palm Pilot, Palm Pilot Professional, or Palm III computer, you'll be happy to know that OpenLinux comes with nearly two dozen support programs you can use with Linux.

The handiest of these programs is **pilot-xfer**, which can back up, restore, install, and list the contents of your Palm. To use **pilot-xfer**, first log in as the root operator. Create a symbolic link with the **ln** command to the serial port used to connect your Palm computer's cable like this:

```
ln -s /dev/ttySX /dev/pilot
```

Where **X** represents the number 0, 1, 2, or 3 of the **ttyS** device. For example, if your Palm connects to COM1, **/dev/pilot** should point to **/dev/ttyS0**. Next, to ensure the fastest transmission rate, create the **PILOTRATE** environment variable with the value of the fastest baud rate supported by your serial port. For example, to use 57600 baud, use the **bash** shell's **export** command like this:

```
PILOTRATE="57600"; export PILOTRATE
```

Connect your Palm's cradle cable to your computer's serial port and place your Palm in its cradle.

Back Up Your Palm

Use the **mkdir** command to create a backup directory, such as **ppro**, for the contents of your Palm. To back up your Palm, use **pilot-xfer's -b** command, followed by name of the directory, like this:

```
pilot-xfer -b ppro
```

To start the backup, press the **HotSync** button on your Palm's cradle.

Install a File

Use **pilot-xfer's -i**, or install, option, followed by the name of a Palm PRC or PDB file to install a program or database. For example, to install the file **teezee.prc**, use **pilot-xfer** like this

```
pilot-xfer -i teezee.prc
```

To start the install, press the **HotSync** button on your Palm's cradle.

Note Use KDE? Try the Kpilot App!

If you use KDE and a Palm computer, you definitely should try the Kpilot application. Navigate to **http://www.slac.com/ pilone/kpilot_home/ mainpage.html**. You need to download and install the application, but you get a first-class interface for using your Palm with OpenLinux and KDE.

Internet Resources for Linux and OpenLinux

*W*ant to know how to install a printer? Having trouble getting your PPP connection started? Need to install a new version of OpenLinux? Curious about the best laptop to use? This appendix contains some pointers to helpful Internet resources and can help answer questions you have about Linux. This section is divided into three parts:

- ✓ Usenet newsgroup resources—A partial list of newsgroups about Linux. Note that some ISPs do not provide all Usenet newsgroups (more than 40,000 at the time of this writing) on their news servers.

- ✓ World Wide Web Internet sites—A sampling of choice Linux sites for software or documentation.

- ✓ Mailing lists—Directions and a description of Caldera's OpenLinux electronic mail service. ●

Usenet Resources

*T*his is a list of current Linux Usenet newsgroups. Note that the list does not include international newsgroups in other languages, such as French, German, Italian, or Spanish. Here's a handy tip: If your ISP does not carry the following newsgroups, browse to **http://www.dejanews.com** (and then call your ISP and ask for the Linux newsgroups!).

- ✓ **alt.linux**—Alternative views, discussions of Linux.
- ✓ **alt.linux.slakware**—Alternative views, discussions of the Slackware distribution of Linux.
- ✓ **comp.os.linux.advocacy**—Rants, raves, taunts, and flame wars between Linux's Defenders of the Faith and the minions of the Dark Side.
- ✓ **comp.os.linux.alpha**—Discussions of Linux on the Digital Equipment Corporation's Alpha CPU.
- ✓ **comp.os.linux.announce**—Commercial, user group, and software release announcements.
- ✓ **comp.os.linux.answers**—The definitive source of new or updated Linux HOWTOs, FAQs, and other Linux documents.
- ✓ **comp.os.linux.development.apps**—Discussions concerning porting software programs and using compilers or other languages for Linux.
- ✓ **comp.os.linux.development.system**—Linux kernel and other programming information, such as modules or device drivers.
- ✓ **comp.os.linux.hardware**—Questions, answers, and debates concerning using different hardware with Linux.
- ✓ **comp.os.linux.m68k**—News and development information about Linux on Motorola 68x000-series CPUs.
- ✓ **comp.os.linux.misc**—Miscellaneous questions, answers, and debates about hardware and software for Linux.
- ✓ **comp.os.linux.networking**—Discussions about topics such as communications and networking administration and configuration.
- ✓ **comp.os.linux.portable**—Discussions on using Linux on laptop computers.
- ✓ **comp.os.linux.powerpc**—News and development information about Linux on the PowerPC series of CPUs.

- ✓ **comp.os.linux.setup**—Questions and answers about how to install, set up, configure, or maintain Linux.
- ✓ **comp.os.linux.x**—Discussions about installing, configuring, and using the X Window System and X11 clients with Linux.
- ✓ **linux.appletalk**—Discussions about using Apple Computer's LocalTalk protocol and Linux.
- ✓ **linux.debian.announce**—Announcements about the Debian Linux distribution.
- ✓ **linux.debian.user**—Discussions about the Debian Linux distribution.
- ✓ **linux.dev.***—More than 60 newsgroups discussing program development for different Linux distributions, software, and hardware.
- ✓ **linux.redhat.misc**—Discussions about Red Hat Software, Inc's Linux distribution.

WWW Resources

There are too many Linux World Wide Web sites to list a comprehensive selection, but here are a few that should help you get started:

- ✓ **http://sunsite.unc.edu/LDP**   You can find most of the answers you need through the Linux Documentation Project (LDP).
- ✓ **http://sunsite.unc.edu/LDP/hmirrors.html**   Lists other computers (or mirrors) with the LDP contents.
- ✓ **http://www.calderasystems.com/index.html**   Visit this site if you're looking for answers to questions, technical errata, or news about OpenLinux. This site features Caldera's OpenLinux distribution, which includes the StarOffice suite of applications, DR-DOS, the ADABAS-D relational database, and various Netscape clients and servers.
- ✓ **http://www.calderasystems.com/support/techquide.html**   Visit this site for technical errata about OpenLinux.
- ✓ **http://sunsite.unc.edu/LDP/products.html**   Browse this site for pointers to sites featuring commercial Linux distributions, X software or preconfigured desktop and laptop computers with Linux preinstalled.

Of course, there are any number of sites devoted to Linux-related software, trivia, and other errata:

- ✓ **http://counter.li.org**   Navigate to this site and register as a Linux user if you want to see an estimate on the number of people who use Linux around the world. The latest estimates are six million users worldwide.
- ✓ **http://pobox.com/~newt/**   Looking for a certain Linux logo? This site has a link to three pages of logos for Linux.
- ✓ **http://visar.csustan.edu:8000/giveaway.html**   Have extra copies of old Linux distributions on CD-ROM you'd like to give away or donate? Navigate to this site for more information.

- ✓ **http://www.cdrom.com**   Walnut Creek's Web site is a great starting place to get other free Unix distributions, such as BSD or Slackware Linux.
- ✓ **http://www.cs.utexas.edu/users/kharker/linux-laptop**   This site is the definitive Web site for Linux laptop users, featuring many different links and documentation to solve problems and provide solutions to making Linux and X11 work correctly.
- ✓ **http://www.cviog.uga.edu/LinuxBleed.html**   Want the very latest Linux kernel? Navigate to this site to learn about up-to-the-minute changes.
- ✓ **http://www.debian.org**   This is the definitive site for downloading the Debian Linux distribution.
- ✓ **http://www.emry.net/webwatcher**   Want to know whether your favorite Linux Web site has been updated or new software uploaded? Use this site to watch for daily changes.
- ✓ **http://www.infomagic.com**   A long-time distributor of Linux, Infomagic offers many different sets of software collections available by FTP or on CD-ROM.
- ✓ **http://www.kernel.org**   This site not only offers the oldest and newest kernels, but also more than 20GB of software for Linux.
- ✓ **http://www.mcp.com**   This site is the place to start looking for Linux books published by Sams, Que, and New Riders.
- ✓ **http://www.rahul.net/kenton/index.shtml**   Ken Lee's X and Motif Web site with more than 700 links to different X Window System Web pages (Ken is the maintainer of the Motif FAQ).
- ✓ **http://www.ssc.com/lj**   Home of the Linux Journal, a four-color, 70-page-plus monthly magazine all about Linux.
- ✓ **http://www.xfree86.org**   The great folks of the XFree86 Project, Inc. provide free distributions of the X Window System not only for Linux, but for operating systems on other computers.

Mailing Lists

Mailing lists are an alternative way to participate in discussions about OpenLinux. Most mailing lists work by pumping out email messages to all list subscribers each time a subscriber sends in a message to the list's mail server. Some mailing lists offer daily digests, which are usually a large, single message containing each day's message traffic, and which can be more convenient than having your mailbox continually flooded with individual messages. There are numerous Linux mailing lists. Browse to **http://sunsite.unc.edu/LDP/intro.html** for a list of pointers to Linux mail list sites.

To participate in discussions about OpenLinux using email and to exchange information with other OpenLinux users, send a message to majordomo@rim.caldera.com with the following line in the body of the message:

```
subscribe caldera-users youremailaddress@yourisp.com
```

You'll get an electronic mail message asking you to confirm your subscription. Reply to the message according to its directions.

For more information about this service, send a message to majordomo@rim.caldera.com with the following line in the body of the message:

```
help
```

You'll receive a reply with lots of details about using Caldera's mailing lists.

For the digest version of Caldera's OpenLinux list, send a message to majordomo@rim.caldera.com with the following line in the body of the message:

```
subscribe caldera-users-digest youremailaddress@yourisp.com
```

Glossary

Symbols

Octothorpe, or pound sign. Used in OpenLinux configuration files as a comment character.

$HOME   Environment variable that points to your login directory.

$PATH   The shell environment variable that contains a set of directories to be searched for Linux commands.

.1   Files with this extension contain manual page entries. The actual extension can be any value between **1** and **9** and can have an alphabetic suffix (**.3x**, **.7**, and so on).

:-)   A smiley. There are thousands of variants. Used to express a smile in email messages or Usenet posts.

.ag   Applixware graphics file.

.as   Applixware spreadsheet file.

.aw   Applixware word processing file.

.bmp   Bitmap graphics file.

.c   C source file.

.C   C++ source file.

.cc   C++ source file.

.conf   Configuration file.

.cxx   C++ source file.

.db   Database file.

.dvi   Device-independent TeX output.

.gif   GIF graphics file.

.gz   File compressed using the GNU **gzip** utility.

.h   C or C++ header file.

.html   HTML document.

.jpg   JPEG graphics file.

.m   Objective C source file.

.o   Compiled object file.

.p   Pascal language source file.

.pbm   Portable bitmap graphics file.

.pdf   Adobe Acrobat file.

.ps   PostScript file

.tar   tar, or tape archive file.

.tgz   Gzipped tar file.

.tif   TIFF graphics file.

.txt   Text document.

.Z   File compressed using the **compress** command.

/   Root directory.

/dev   Device directory.

/dev/null   The place to send output that you are not interested in seeing; also the place to get input from when you have none (but the program or command requires something). This is also known as the *bit bucket* (where old bits go to die).

/dev/printer   Socket for local print requests.

/etc/cshrc   The systemwide resource file for the C shell.

/etc/group   This file contains information about groups, the users they contain, and passwords required for access by other users. The password might actually be in another file, the shadow group file, to protect it from attacks.

/etc/inittab   The file that contains a list of active terminal ports for which Linux issues the login prompt. This also contains a list of background processes for UNIX to initialize. Some versions of UNIX use other files, such as **/etc/tty**.

/etc/motd   Message of the day file; usually contains information the system administrator feels is important for you to know. This file is displayed when the user signs on the system.

/etc/passwd   Contains user information and password. The password might actually be in another file, the shadow password file, to protect it from attacks.

/etc/profile   The file containing shell environment characteristics common to all users of the Bourne and Korn shells.

/usr/local   Locally developed public files directory.

/var/spool   Various spool directories (such as for printers).

A

alphabetic characters   The letters A through Z and a through z.

alphanumeric characters   The letters A through Z and a through z; the numbers 0 through 9.

ar   Archive utility.

ASCII   American Standard Code for Information Interchange. Used to represent characters in memory for most computers.

AT&T UNIX   Original version of UNIX developed at AT&T Bell Labs, later known as UNIX Systems Laboratories. Many current versions of UNIX are descendants; even BSD UNIX was derived from early AT&T UNIX.

awk   Programming language developed by A.V. Aho, P.J. Weinberger, and Brian W. Kernighan. The language is built on C syntax, includes the regular expression search facilities of grep, and adds in the advanced string and array handling features that are missing from the C language. nawk, gawk, and POSIX awk are versions of this language.

B

background   Processes usually running at a lower priority and with their input disconnected from the interactive session. Any input and output are usually directed to a file or other process.

background process   An autonomous process that runs under Linux without requiring user interaction.

backup   The process of storing the Linux system, applications, and data files on removable media for future retrieval.

bash   Stands for *GNU Bourne Again SHell* and is based on the Bourne shell, sh, the original command interpreter.

biff   Background mail notification utility.

bison   GNU parser generator (yacc replacement).

boot or boot up   The process of starting the operating system .

Bourne shell   The original standard user interface to Linux (known as the Bourne Again Shell) that supported limited programming capability.

BSD   Berkeley Software Distribution.

BSD UNIX   Version of UNIX developed by Berkeley Software Distribution and written at the University of California, Berkeley.

bug   An undocumented program feature.

C

C   Programming language developed by Brian W. Kernighan and Dennis M. Ritchie. The C language is highly portable and available on many platforms including mainframes, PCs, and, of course, Linux systems.

C shell   A user interface for UNIX written by Bill Joy at Berkeley. It features C programming-like syntax. A compatible shell, called tcsh, is included with OpenLinux.

CAD   Computer-aided design.

cat   Concatenate files command.

CD-ROM   Compact Disk-Read Only Memory. Computer-readable data stored on the same physical form as a musical CD. Large capacity, inexpensive, slower than a hard disk, and limited to reading. There are versions that are writable (CD-R, CD Recordable) and other formats that can be written to once or many times.

CGI Common Gateway Interface. A means of transmitting data between Web pages and programs or scripts executing on the server. Those programs can then process the data and send the results back to the user's browser through dynamically creating HTML.

command-line arguments See *command-line parameters*.

command-line editing Linux shells support the capability to recall a previously entered command, modify it, and then execute the new version. The command history can remain between sessions (the commands you did yesterday can be available for you when you log in today). Some shells support a command-line editing mode that uses a subset of the vi, emacs, or gmacs editor commands for command recall and modification.

command-line history See *command-line editing*.

command-line parameters Used to specify parameters to pass to the execute program or procedure. Also known as *command-line arguments*.

comment characters The pound sign (#) is used as a comment character in Linux configuration files and shell scripts, much like the REM statement in the BASIC programming language, and means "ignore this line." Other characters, such as the exclamation point (!), can also be used by different programs as comment characters.

configuration files Collections of information used to initialize and set up the environment for specific commands and programs. Shell configuration files set up the user's environment.

configuration files, shell For Bourne shell: /etc/profile and $HOME/.profile. For Korn and pdksh shells: /etc/profile, $HOME/.profile, and ENV= file. For C and tcsh shells: /etc/.login, /etc/cshrc, $HOME/.login, $HOME/.cshrc, and $HOME/.logout. Older versions might not support the first two files listed. For bash: /etc/profile/,

$HOME/.bash_profile, $HOME/.bash_login, $HOME/.profile, $HOME/.bashrc, and ~/.bash_logout.

control characters Any nonprintable characters. The characters are used to control devices, separate records, and eject pages on printers.

control keys These are keys that cause some function to be performed instead of displaying a character. These functions have names. For example, the end-of-file key tells Linux that there is no more input; it is usually **Ctrl+D**.

CPU Central Processing Unit. The primary "brain" of the computer—the calculation engine and logic controller.

daemon A system-related background process that often runs with the permissions of root and services requests from other processes.

database server A system designated to run database software (typically a relational database such as Oracle, SQL Server, Sybase, or others). Other systems connect to this one to get the data (client applications).

device file File used to implement access to a physical device. This provides a consistent approach to access of storage media under Linux; data files and devices (such as tapes and communication facilities) are implemented as files, such as those found under the **/dev** directory.

directory A means of organizing and collecting files together. The directory itself is a file that consists of a list of files contained within it. The root (/) directory is the top level and every other directory is contained in it (directly or indirectly). A directory might contain other directories, known as *subdirectories*.

directory navigation The process of moving through directories is known as navigation. Your current directory is known as the current working directory. Your login directory is known as the default or home directory. Using the **cd** command, you can move up and down through the tree structure of directories.

DNS   Domain Name Server or Service. Used to convert between the name of a machine on the Internet (**name.domain.com**) to the numeric address (**123.45.111.123**).

DOS   Disk Operating System. Operating system that is based on the use of disks for the storage of commands.

dpi   Dots per inch.

E

ed   A common tool used for line-oriented text editing.

elm   Interactive mail program.

emacs   A freely available editor now part of the GNU software distribution. Originally written by Richard M. Stallman at MIT in the late 1970s, it is available for many platforms. It is extremely extensible and has its own programming language; the name stands for *editing with macros*.

email   Messages sent through an electronic medium instead of through the local postal service. There are many proprietary email systems that are designed to handle mail within a LAN environment; most of these are also able to send over the Internet. Most Internet (open) email systems make use of MIME to handle attached data (which can be binary).

Ethernet   A networking method where the systems are connected to a single shared bus and all traffic is available to every machine. The data packets contain an identifier of the recipient, and that is the only machine that should process that packet.

expression   A constant, variable, or operands and operators combined. Used to set a value, perform a calculation, or set the pattern for a comparison (regular expressions).

F

FIFO   First In, First Out.

file   Collection of bytes stored on a device (typically a disk or tape). Can be source code, executable binaries or scripts, or data.

file compression   The process of applying mathematical formulas to data, typically resulting in a form of the data that occupies less space.

filename   The name used to identify a collection of data (a file). When not preceded by a pathname, it is assumed to be in the current directory.

filename generation   The process of the shell interpreting metacharacters (wildcards) to produce a list of matching files. This is referred to as *filename expansion* or *globbing*.

filesystem   A collection of disk storage that is connected (mounted) to the directory structure at some point (sometimes at the root). Filesystems are stored in a disk partition and are sometimes referred to as being the disk partition.

finger   User information lookup program.

firewall   A system used to provide a controlled entry point to the internal network from the outside (usually the Internet). This is used to prevent outside or unauthorized systems from accessing systems on your internal network.

flags   See *options*.

foreground   Programs running while connected to the interactive session.

FSF   Free Software Foundation, which distributes GNU software.

FTP   File Transfer Protocol or File Transfer Program. A system-independent means of transferring files between systems connected via TCP/IP. Ensures that the file is transferred correctly, even if there are errors during transmission. Can usually handle character set conversions (ASCII/EBCDIC) and record terminator resolution (linefeed for Linux, carriage return and linefeed for MS/PC-DOS).

G

gateway   A combination of hardware, software, and network connections that provides a link between one architecture and another. Typically, a gateway is used to connect a LAN or Linux server with a mainframe (that uses SNA for networking, resulting in the name SNA gateway). A gateway can also be the connection between the internal and external network (often referred to as a fire-wall). See also *firewall*.

GB   Gigabyte. Usually thought of as one billion characters, but actually 1024[ts]100,000 characters.

GID   Group ID number.

globbing   See *filename generation*.

GNU   GNU stands for *GNUs Not UNIX* and is the name of free useful software packages commonly found in UNIX environments that are being distributed by the GNU project at MIT, largely through the efforts of Richard Stallman. The circular acronym name ("GNU" containing the acronym GNU as one of the words it stands for) is a joke on Stallman's part.

GPL   GNU General Public License.

grep   A common tool used to search a file for a pattern. egrep and fgrep are newer versions. egrep enables the use of extended (hence the *e* prefix) regular expressions; fgrep uses limited expressions for a faster (hence the *f* prefix) searches.

GUI   Graphical user interface.

H–I

here document   The << redirection operator, known as here document, enables keyboard input (stdin) for the program to be included in the script.

HTML   Hypertext Markup Language. Describes World Wide Web pages. It is the document language that is used to define the pages available on the Internet through the use of tags. A browser interprets the HTML to display the desired information.

I-Phone   Internet phone. This is a method of transmitting speech long distances over the Internet in near real-time. Participants avoid paying long distance telephone charges. They still pay for the call to their ISP and the ISP's service charges.

imake   C preprocessor interface to **make** utility, usually used when building programs for the X Window System.

IMHO   In my humble opinion. An expression used in email or a Usenet post.

Internet   A collection of different networks that provide the capability to move data between them. It is built on the TCP/IP communications protocol.

IRC   Internet relay chat. A server-based application that enables groups of people to communicate simultaneously through text-based conversations. IRC is similar to citizens band radio or the chat rooms on some bulletin boards. Some chats can be private (between invited people only) or public (where anyone can join in). IRC now also supports sound files as well as text; it can also be useful for file exchange.

ISP   Internet service provider. The people who connect you to the Internet.

ISV   Independent software vendor. Generic name for software vendors other than your hardware vendor.

K

K&R   Kernighan and Ritchie. See *C*.

kernel   The core of the operating system that handles tasks such as memory allocation, device input and output, process allocation, security, and user access. Linux is the kernel, and OpenLinux is Caldera's distribution of Linux and associated programs.

Korn shell   A user interface for UNIX with extensive scripting (programming) support. Written by David G. Korn. The shell features command-line editing and also accepts scripts written for the Bourne shell. A Linux version, called pdksh, is included with OpenLinux.

L

LAN   Local area network. A collection of networking hardware, software, desktop computers, servers, and hosts all connected together within a defined local area. A LAN could be an entire college campus.

LISP   List Processing Language.

login   The process with which a user gains access to a Linux system. This can also refer to the user ID that is typed at the login prompt.

LOL   Laughing out loud. An expression used in response to an email message or Usenet post.

lp   Line printer.

lpc   Line printer control program.

lpd   Line printer daemon.

lpq   Printer spool queue examination program.

lprm   Printer spool queue job removal program.

LPRng   Enhanced version of lpr printing system.

ls   List directory(s) command.

M

man page   Online reference tool under Linux that contains the documentation for the system—the actual pages from the printed manuals. It is stored in a searchable form for improved capability to locate information.

manual page   See *man page*.

MB   Megabyte. Usually thought of as one million characters, but actually 1024[ts]1000 characters.

metacharacter   A printing character that has special meaning to the shell or another command. It is converted into something else by the shell or command; the asterisk (*)is converted by the shell to a list of all files in the current directory.

MIME   Multipurpose Internet Mail Extensions. A set of protocols or methods of attaching binary data (executable programs, images, sound files, and so on) or additional text to email messages.

motd   Message of the day.

mtu   Maximum transmission unit.

N

Netnews   This is a loosely controlled collection of discussion groups, or Usenet news.

NFS   Network File System. Means of connecting disks that are mounted to a remote system to the local system as if they were physically connected.

NIS   Network Information Service. A service that provides information necessary to all machines on a network, such as NFS support for hosts and clients, password verification, and so on.

NNTP   Netnews Transport Protocol. Used to transmit Netnews or Usenet messages over top of TCP/IP. See *Netnews*.

numeric characters   The numbers 0 through 9.

O–P

options   Program- or command-specific indicators that control behavior of that program. Sometimes called *flags*. The **-a** option to the **ls** command shows the files that begin with . (such as **.profile**, **.kshrc**, and so on). Without it, these files would not be shown, no matter what wildcards were used. These are used on the command line. See also *parameters*.

parameters   Data passed to a command or program through the command line. These can be options (see *options*) that control the command or arguments that the command works on. Some have special meanings based on their position on the command line.

parent process   Process that controls another, often referred to as the child process or subprocess. See *process*.

parent process identifier   Shown in the heading of the **ps** command as PPID. The process identifier of the parent process. See also *parent process*.

parent shell   Shell (typically the login shell) that controls another, often referred to as the child shell or subshell. See *shell*.

password   The secure code that is used in combination with a user ID to gain access to a Linux system.

pathname   The means used to represent the location of a file in the directory structure. If you do not specify a pathname, it defaults to the current directory.

Perl   Programming language developed by Larry Wall. (Perl stands for *Practical Extraction and Report Language* or *Pathologically Eclectic Rubbish Language*; both are equally valid). The language provides all the capabilities of awk and sed, plus many of the features of the shells and C.

permissions When applied to files, they are the attributes that control access to a file. There are three levels of access: User (the file creator), Group (people belonging to a related group as determined by the system administrator), and Other (everyone else). The permissions are usually **r** for read, **w** for write, and **x** for execute. The execute permissions flag is also used to control who can search a directory.

pine Interactive mail program.

pipe A method of sending the output of one program (redirecting) to become the input of another. The pipe character (|) tells the shell to perform the redirection.

POSIX Portable Operating System Interface, UNIX. POSIX is the name for a family of open system standards based on UNIX. The name has been credited to Richard Stallman. The POSIX Shell and Utilities standard developed by IEEE Working Group 1003.2 (POSIX.2) concentrates on the command interpreter interface and utility programs.

PostScript Adobe Systems, Inc. printer language.

PPP Point-to-Point Protocol. Internet protocol over serial link (modem).

pppd Point-to-Point-Protocol daemon.

printcap Printer capability database, found under the **/etc** directory.

process A discrete running program under Linux. The user's interactive session is a process. A process can invoke (run) and control another program that is then referred to as a subprocess. Ultimately, everything a user does is a subprocess of the operating system.

process identifier Shown in the heading of the ps command as PID. The unique number assigned to every process running in the system.

pwd Print working directory command.

Q–R

quota General description of a system-imposed limitation on a user or process. It can apply to disk space, memory usage, CPU usage, maximum number of open files, and many other resources.

RCS Revision Control System.

redirection The process of directing a data flow from the default. Input can be redirected to get data from a file or the output of another program. Normal output can be sent to another program or a file. Errors can be sent to another program or a file.

regular expression A way of specifying and matching strings for shells (filename wildcarding), grep (file searches), sed, and awk.

root The user that owns the operating system and controls the computer. The processes of the operating system run as though a user, root, signed on and started them. Root users are all powerful and can do anything they want. For this reason, they are often referred to as *superusers*. Root is also the very top of the directory tree structure.

ROTFL Rolling on the floor, laughing. An expression used in response to an email message or Usenet post.

RPM Red Hat Package Manager.

RTFM Read the Fine Manual. Kind advice to read the program manual before asking a documented question. Usually in response to a Usenet post.

S

script A program written for a UNIX utility including shells, awk, Perl, sed, and others. See also *shell scripts*.

SCSI Small Computer System Interface.

sed A common tool used for stream text editing, having ed-like syntax.

SGID Set group ID.

shell The part of Linux that handles user input and invokes other programs to run commands. Includes a programming language. See also *Bourne shell, C shell, Korn shell, tcsh,* and *bash*.

shell environment The shell program (Bourne, Korn, C, tcsh, or bash), invocation options, and preset variables that define the characteristics, features, and functionality of the Linux command-line and program execution interface.

shell or command prompt   The single character or set of characters that the Linux shell displays for which a user can enter a command or set of commands.

shell scripts   A program written using a shell programming language such as those supported by Bourne, Korn, or C shells.

SLIP   Serial Line Internet Protocol. Internet over a serial line (modem). The protocol frames and controls the transmission of TCP/IP packets of the line.

special characters   Any of the punctuation characters or printable characters that are not alphanumeric. Includes the space, comma, period, and many others.

special keys   See *control keys.*

stderr   The normal error output for a program that is sent to the screen by default. Can be redirected to a file.

stdin   The normal input for a program, taken from the keyboard by default. Can be redirected to get input from a file or the output of another program.

stdout   The normal output for a program that is sent to the screen by default. Can be redirected to a file or to the input of another program.

sticky bit   One of the status flags on a file that tells Linux to load a copy of the file into the page file the first time it is executed. This is done for programs that are commonly used so the bytes are available quickly. When the sticky bit is used on frequently used directories, it is cached in memory.

subdirectory   See *directory.*

subnet   A portion of a network that shares a common IP address component. Used for security and performance reasons.

subprocess   Process running under the control of another, often referred to as the parent process. See *process.*

subshell   Shell running under the control of another, often referred to as the parent shell (typically the login shell). See *shell.*

SUID   Set user ID.

superuser   Usually the root operator.

symbolic link   Directory entry that provides an alias to another file that can be in another filesystem. Multiple entries appear in the directory for one physical file without replication of the contents. Implemented through link files created by the **ln** command.

sysadmin   Burnt-out root operator (system administrator).

system administrator   The person who takes care of the operating system and user administrative issues on Linux systems.

T

---

tar   Tape archiving utility.

TCP   Transmission Control Protocol.

TCP/IP   Transport Control Protocol/Internet Protocol. The pair of protocols and also generic name for suite of tools and protocols that forms the basis for the Internet.

tcsh   A C shell-like user interface featuring command-line editing.

telnet   Remote login program.

Telnet   Protocol for interactive (character user interface) terminal access to remote systems. The terminal emulator that uses the Telnet protocol is often known as telnet or tnvt100.

termcap   Terminal capability database.

terminal   A hardware device, normally containing a cathode ray tube (screen) and keyboard for human interaction with a computer system.

text processing languages   A way of developing documents in text editors with embedded commands that handle formatting. The file is fed through a processor that executes the embedded commands, producing a formatted document. These include roff, nroff, troff, RUNOFF, TeX, LaTeX, and even the mainframe SCRIPT.

tin   Interactive news reader.

top   A common tool used to display information about the top processes on the system.

U–W

UID   User ID number.

URL   Uniform Resource Locator. A World Wide Web address, such as **http://www.caldera.com**. The method of specifying the protocol, format, login (usually omitted), and location of materials on the Internet.

Usenet   See *Netnews*.

UUCP   UNIX-to-UNIX copy program. Used to build an early, informal network for the transmission of files, email, and Netnews.

virtual memory   Memory that exists but that you cannot see, such as the swap partition for Linux. Secondary storage (disk) is used to allow the operating system to enable programs to use more memory than is physically available.

WAN   Wide Area Network.

Web   See *WWW*.

whitespace   Blanks, spaces, and tabs that are normally interpreted to delineate commands and filenames unless quoted.

wildcard   Means of specifying filename(s) whereby the operating system determines some of the characters. Multiple files might match and are available to the tool.

W9x   Abbreviated label for two versions of a soon-to-be-defunct commercial computer operating system.

WWW   World Wide Web. A collection of servers and services on the Internet that run software and communicate using a common protocol (HTTP). Instead of the users' having to remember the location of these resources, links are provided from one Web page to another through the use of URLs.

WYSIWYG   What You See Is What You Get.

X–Y

X   See *X Window System*.

X11   See *X Window System*.

X Window System   A windowing and graphics system developed by MIT, to be used in client/server environments.

X Windows   The wrong term for the X Window System. See *X Window System*.

XFree86   A collection of programs for a networking graphical interface, the X Window System, on x86 computers.

yacc   Yet another compiler compiler.

GNU General Public License

Version 2, June 1991

Copyright © 1989, 1991 Free Software Foundation, Inc.

675 Mass Ave, Cambridge, MA 02139, USA

Everyone is permitted to copy and distribute verbatim copies of this license document, but changing it is not allowed.

Preamble

*T*he licenses for most software are designed to take away your freedom to share and change it. By contrast, the GNU General Public License is intended to guarantee your freedom to share and change free software—to make sure the software is free for all its users. This General Public License applies to most of the Free Software Foundation's software and to any other program whose authors commit to using it. (Some other Free Software Foundation software is covered by the GNU Library General Public License instead.) You can apply it to your programs, too.

When we speak of free software, we are referring to freedom, not price. Our General Public Licenses are designed to make sure that you have the freedom to distribute copies of free software (and charge for this service if you wish), that you receive source code or can get it if you want it, that you can change the software or use pieces of it in new free programs; and that you know you can do these things.

To protect your rights, we need to make restrictions that forbid anyone to deny you these rights or to ask you to surrender the rights. These restrictions translate to certain responsibilities for you if you distribute copies of the software, or if you modify it.

For example, if you distribute copies of such a program, whether gratis or for a fee, you must give the recipients all the rights that you have. You must make sure that they, too, receive or can get the source code. And you must show them these terms so they know their rights.

We protect your rights with two steps: (1) copyright the software, and (2) offer you this license which gives you legal permission to copy, distribute and/or modify the software.

Also, for each author's protection and ours, we want to make certain that everyone understands that there is no warranty for this free software. If the software is modified by someone else and passed on, we want its recipients to know that what they have is not the original, so that any problems introduced by others will not reflect on the original authors' reputations.

Finally, any free program is threatened constantly by software patents. We wish to avoid the danger that redistributors of a free program will individually obtain patent licenses, in effect making the program proprietary. To prevent this, we have made it clear that any patent must be licensed for everyone's free use or not licensed at all.

The precise terms and conditions for copying, distribution and modification follow.

GNU General Public License
Terms and Conditions for Copying, Distribution and Modification

0. This License applies to any program or other work which contains a notice placed by the copyright holder saying it may be distributed under the terms of this General Public License. The "Program", below, refers to any such program or work, and a "work based on the Program" means either the Program or any derivative work under copyright law: that is to say, a work containing the Program or a portion of it, either verbatim or with modifications and/or translated into another language. (Hereinafter, translation is included without limitation in the term "modification".) Each licensee is addressed as "you".

Activities other than copying, distribution and modification are not covered by this License; they are outside its scope. The act of running the Program is not restricted, and the output from the Program is covered only if its contents constitute a work based on the Program (independent of having been made by running the Program). Whether that is true depends on what the Program does.

1. You may copy and distribute verbatim copies of the Program's source code as you receive it, in any medium, provided that you conspicuously and appropriately publish on each copy an appropriate copyright notice and disclaimer of warranty; keep intact all the notices that refer to this License and to the absence of any warranty; and give any other recipients of the Program a copy of this License along with the Program.

   You may charge a fee for the physical act of transferring a copy, and you may at your option offer warranty protection in exchange for a fee.

2. You may modify your copy or copies of the Program or any portion of it, thus forming a work based on the Program, and copy and distribute such modifications or work under the terms of Section 1 above, provided that you also meet all of these conditions:

   a) You must cause the modified files to carry prominent notices stating that you changed the files and the date of any change.

   b) You must cause any work that you distribute or publish, that in whole or in part contains or is derived from the Program or any part thereof, to be licensed as a whole at no charge to all third parties under the terms of this License.

   c) If the modified program normally reads commands interactively when run, you must cause it, when started running for such interactive use in the most ordinary way, to print or display

an announcement including an appropriate copyright notice and a notice that there is no warranty (or else, saying that you provide a warranty) and that users may redistribute the program under these conditions, and telling the user how to view a copy of this License. (Exception: if the Program itself is interactive but does not normally print such an announcement, your work based on the Program is not required to print an announcement.)

These requirements apply to the modified work as a whole. If identifiable sections of that work are not derived from the Program, and can be reasonably considered independent and separate works in themselves, then this License, and its terms, do not apply to those sections when you distribute them as separate works. But when you distribute the same sections as part of a whole which is a work based on the Program, the distribution of the whole must be on the terms of this License, whose permissions for other licensees extend to the entire whole, and thus to each and every part regardless of who wrote it.

Thus, it is not the intent of this section to claim rights or contest your rights to work written entirely by you; rather, the intent is to exercise the right to control the distribution of derivative or collective works based on the Program.

In addition, mere aggregation of another work not based on the Program with the Program (or with a work based on the Program) on a volume of a storage or distribution medium does not bring the other work under the scope of this License.

3. You may copy and distribute the Program (or a work based on it, under Section 2) in object code or executable form under the terms of Sections 1 and 2 above provided that you also do one of the following:

a) Accompany it with the complete corresponding machine-readable source code, which must be distributed under the terms of Sections 1 and 2 above on a medium customarily used for software interchange; or,

b) Accompany it with a written offer, valid for at least three years, to give any third party, for a charge no more than your cost of physically performing source distribution, a complete machine-readable copy of the corresponding source code, to be distributed under the terms of Sections 1 and 2 above on a medium customarily used for software interchange; or,

c) Accompany it with the information you received as to the offer to distribute corresponding source code. (This alternative is allowed only for non-commercial distribution and only if you received the program in object code or executable form with such an offer, in accord with Subsection b above.)

The source code for a work means the preferred form of the work for making modifications to it. For an executable work, complete source code means all the source code for all modules it contains, plus any associated interface definition files, plus the scripts used to control compilation and installation of the executable. However, as a special exception, the source code distributed need not include anything that is normally distributed (in either source or binary form) with the major components (compiler, kernel, and so on) of the operating system on which the executable runs, unless that component itself accompanies the executable.

If distribution of executable or object code is made by offering access to copy from a designated place, then offering equivalent access to copy the source code from the same place counts as distribution of the source code, even though third parties are not compelled to copy the source along with the object code.

You may not copy, modify, sublicense, or distribute the Program except as expressly provided under this License. Any attempt otherwise to copy, modify, sublicense or distribute the Program is void, and will automatically terminate your rights under this License. However, parties who have received copies, or rights, from you under this License will not have their licenses terminated so long as such parties remain in full compliance.

5. You are not required to accept this License, since you have not signed it. However, nothing else grants you permission to modify or distribute the Program or its derivative works. These actions are prohibited by law if you do not accept this License. Therefore, by modifying or distributing the Program (or any work based on the Program), you indicate your acceptance of this License to do so, and all its terms and conditions for copying, distributing or modifying the Program or works based on it.

6. Each time you redistribute the Program (or any work based on the Program), the recipient automatically receives a license from the original licensor to copy, distribute or modify the Program subject to these terms and conditions. You may not impose any further restrictions on the recipients' exercise of the rights granted herein. You are not responsible for enforcing compliance by third parties to this License.

7. If, as a consequence of a court judgment or allegation of patent infringement or for any other reason (not limited to patent issues), conditions are imposed on you (whether by court order, agreement or otherwise) that contradict the conditions of this License, they do not excuse you from the conditions of this License. If you cannot distribute so as to satisfy simultaneously your obligations under this License and any other pertinent obligations, then as a consequence you may

not distribute the Program at all. For example, if a patent license would not permit royalty-free redistribution of the Program by all those who receive copies directly or indirectly through you, then the only way you could satisfy both it and this License would be to refrain entirely from distribution of the Program.

If any portion of this section is held invalid or unenforceable under any particular circumstance, the balance of the section is intended to apply and the section as a whole is intended to apply in other circumstances.

It is not the purpose of this section to induce you to infringe any patents or other property right claims or to contest validity of any such claims; this section has the sole purpose of protecting the integrity of the free software distribution system, which is implemented by public license practices. Many people have made generous contributions to the wide range of software distributed through that system in reliance on consistent application of that system; it is up to the author/donor to decide if he or she is willing to distribute software through any other system and a licensee cannot impose that choice.

This section is intended to make thoroughly clear what is believed to be a consequence of the rest of this License.

8. If the distribution and/or use of the Program is restricted in certain countries either by patents or by copyrighted interfaces, the original copyright holder who places the Program under this License may add an explicit geographical distribution limitation excluding those countries, so that distribution is permitted only in or among countries not thus excluded. In such case, this License incorporates the limitation as if written in the body of this License.

9. The Free Software Foundation may publish revised and/or new versions of the General Public License from time to time. Such new versions will be similar in spirit to the present version, but may differ in detail to address new problems or concerns.

Each version is given a distinguishing version number. If the Program specifies a version number of this License which applies to it and "any later version", you have the option of following the terms and conditions either of that version or of any later version published by the Free Software Foundation. If the Program does not specify a version number of this License, you may choose any version ever published by the Free Software Foundation.

10. If you wish to incorporate parts of the Program into other free programs whose distribution conditions are different, write to the author to ask for permission. For software which is copyrighted by the Free Software Foundation, write to the Free Software Foundation; we sometimes make exceptions for this. Our decision will be guided by the two goals of preserving the free status of all derivatives of our free software and of promoting the sharing and reuse of software generally.

NO WARRANTY

11. BECAUSE THE PROGRAM IS LICENSED FREE OF CHARGE, THERE IS NO WARRANTY FOR THE PROGRAM, TO THE EXTENT PERMITTED BY APPLICABLE LAW. EXCEPT WHEN OTHERWISE STATED IN WRITING THE COPYRIGHT HOLDERS AND/OR OTHER PARTIES PROVIDE THE PROGRAM "AS IS" WITHOUT WARRANTY OF ANY KIND, EITHER EXPRESSED OR IMPLIED, INCLUDING, BUT NOT LIMITED TO, THE IMPLIED WARRANTIES OF MERCHANTABILITY AND FITNESS FOR A PARTICULAR PURPOSE. THE ENTIRE RISK AS TO THE QUALITY AND PERFORMANCE OF THE PROGRAM IS WITH YOU. SHOULD THE PROGRAM PROVE DEFECTIVE, YOU ASSUME THE COST OF ALL NECESSARY SERVICING, REPAIR OR CORRECTION.

12. IN NO EVENT UNLESS REQUIRED BY APPLIC-

ABLE LAW OR AGREED TO IN WRITING WILL
ANY COPYRIGHT HOLDER, OR ANY OTHER
PARTY WHO MAY MODIFY AND/OR REDIS-
TRIBUTE THE PROGRAM AS PERMITTED
ABOVE, BE LIABLE TO YOU FOR DAMAGES,
INCLUDING ANY GENERAL, SPECIAL, INCI-
DENTAL OR CONSEQUENTIAL DAMAGES
ARISING OUT OF THE USE OR INABILITY TO
USE THE PROGRAM (INCLUDING BUT NOT
LIMITED TO LOSS OF DATA OR DATA BEING
RENDERED INACCURATE OR LOSSES SUS-
TAINED BY YOU OR THIRD PARTIES OR A
FAILURE OF THE PROGRAM TO OPERATE
WITH ANY OTHER PROGRAMS), EVEN IF
SUCH HOLDER OR OTHER PARTY HAS BEEN
ADVISED OF THE POSSIBILITY OF SUCH
DAMAGES.

End of Terms and Conditions

Linux and the GNU system

The GNU project started 12 years ago with the goal of developing a complete free Unix-like operating system. "Free" refers to freedom, not price; it means you are free to run, copy, distribute, study, change, and improve the software.

A Unix-like system consists of many different programs. We found some components already available as free software—for example, X Windows and TeX. We obtained other components by helping to convince their developers to make them free—for example, the Berkeley network utilities. Other components we wrote specifically for GNU—for example, GNU Emacs, the GNU C compiler, the GNU C library, Bash, and Ghostscript. The components in this last category are "GNU software". The GNU system consists of all three categories together.

The GNU project is not just about developing and distributing free software. The heart of the GNU project is an idea: that software should be free, and that the users' freedom is worth defending. For if people have freedom but do not value it, they will not keep it for long. In order to make freedom last, we have to teach people to value it.

The GNU project's method is that free software and the idea of users' freedom support each other. We develop GNU software, and as people encounter GNU programs or the GNU system and start to use them, they also think about the GNU idea. The software shows that the idea can work in practice. People who come to agree with the idea are likely to write additional free software. Thus, the software embodies the idea, spreads the idea, and grows from the idea.

This method was working well—until someone combined the Linux kernel with the GNU system (which still lacked a kernel), and called the combination a "Linux system."

The Linux kernel is a free Unix-compatible kernel written by Linus Torvalds. It was not written specifically for the GNU project, but the Linux kernel and the GNU system work together well. In fact, adding Linux to the GNU system brought the system to completion: it made a free Unix-compatible operating system available for use.

But ironically, the practice of calling it a "Linux system" undermines our method of communicating the GNU idea. At first impression, a "Linux system" sounds like something completely distinct from the "GNU system." And that is what most users think it is.

Most introductions to the "Linux system" acknowledge the role played by the GNU software components. But they don't say that the system as a whole is more or less the same GNU system that the GNU project has been compiling for a decade. They don't say that the idea of a free Unix-like system originates from the GNU project. So most users don't know these things.

This leads many of those users to identify themselves as a separate community of "Linux users", distinct from the GNU user community. They use all of the GNU software; in fact, they use almost all of the GNU system; but they don't think of themselves as GNU users, and they may not think about the GNU idea.

It leads to other problems as well—even hampering cooperation on software maintenance. Normally when users change a GNU program to make it work better on a particular system, they send the change to the maintainer of that program; then they work with the maintainer, explaining the change, arguing for it and sometimes rewriting it, to get it installed.

But people who think of themselves as "Linux users" are more likely to release a forked "Linux-only" version of the GNU program, and consider the job done. We want each and every GNU program to work "out of the box" on Linux-based systems; but if the users do not help, that goal becomes much harder to achieve.

So how should the GNU project respond? What should we do now to spread the idea that freedom for computer users is important?

We should continue to talk about the freedom to share and change software—and to teach other users to value these freedoms. If we enjoy having a free operating system, it makes sense for us to think about preserving those freedoms for the long term. If we enjoy having a variety of free software, it makes sense for to think about encouraging others to write additional free software, instead of additional proprietary software.

We should not accept the splitting of the community in two. Instead we should spread the word that "Linux systems" are variant GNU systems—that users of these systems are GNU users, and that they ought to consider the GNU philosophy which brought these systems into existence.

This article is one way of doing that. Another way is to use the terms "Linux-based GNU system" (or "GNU/Linux system" or "Lignux" for short) to refer to the combination of the Linux kernel and the GNU system.

Copyright 1996 Richard Stallman

(Verbatim copying and redistribution is permitted without royalty as long as this notice is preserved.)

The Linux kernel is Copyright [cw] 1991, 1992, 1993, 1994 Linus Torvalds (others hold copyrights on some of the drivers, file systems, and other parts of the kernel) and is licensed under the terms of the GNU General Public License.

The FreeBSD Copyright

All of the documentation and software included in the 4.4BSD and 4.4BSD-Lite Releases is copyrighted by The Regents of the University of California.

Copyright 1979, 1980, 1983, 1986, 1988, 1989, 1991, 1992, 1993, 1994 The Regents of the University of California. All rights reserved.

Redistribution and use in source and binary forms, with or without modification, are permitted provided that the following conditions are met:

1. Redistributions of source code must retain the above copyright notice, this list of conditions and the following disclaimer.

2. Redistributions in binary form must reproduce the above copyright notice, this list of conditions and the following disclaimer in the documentation and/or other materials provided with the distribution.

3. All advertising materials mentioning features or use of this software must display the following acknowledgement:

   This product includes software developed by the University of California, Berkeley and its contributors.

4. Neither the name of the University nor the names of its contributors may be used to endorse or promote products derived from this software without specific prior written permission.

THIS SOFTWARE IS PROVIDED BY THE REGENTS AND CONTRIBUTORS "AS IS" AND ANY EXPRESS OR IMPLIED WARRANTIES, INCLUDING, BUT NOT LIMITED TO, THE IMPLIED WARRANTIES OF MERCHANTABILITY AND FITNESS FOR A PARTICULAR PURPOSE ARE DISCLAIMED. IN NO EVENT SHALL THE REGENTS OR CONTRIBUTORS BE LIABLE FOR ANY DIRECT, INDIRECT, INCIDENTAL, SPECIAL, EXEMPLARY, OR CONSEQUENTIAL DAMAGES (INCLUDING, BUT NOT LIMITED TO, PROCUREMENT OF SUBSTITUTE GOODS OR SERVICES; LOSS OF USE, DATA, OR PROFITS; OR BUSINESS INTERRUPTION) HOWEVER CAUSED AND ON ANY THEORY OF LIABILITY, WHETHER IN CONTRACT, STRICT LIABILITY, OR TORT (INCLUDING NEGLIGENCE OR OTHERWISE) ARISING IN ANY WAY OUT OF THE USE OF THIS SOFTWARE, EVEN IF ADVISED OF THE POSSIBILITY OF SUCH DAMAGE.

The Institute of Electrical and Electronics Engineers and the American National Standards Committee X3, on Information Processing Systems have given us permission to reprint portions of their documentation.

In the following statement, the phrase "this text" refers to portions of the system documentation.

Portions of this text are reprinted and reproduced in electronic form in the second BSD Networking Software Release, from IEEE Std 1003.1-1988, IEEE Standard Portable Operating System Interface for Computer Environments (POSIX), copyright C 1988 by the Institute of Electrical and Electronics Engineers, Inc. In the event of any discrepancy between these versions and the original IEEE Standard, the original IEEE Standard is the referee document.

In the following statement, the phrase "This material" refers to portions of the system documentation.

This material is reproduced with permission from American National Standards Committee X3, on Information Processing Systems. Computer and Business Equipment Manufacturers Association (CBEMA), 311 First St., NW, Suite 500, Washington, DC 20001-2178. The developmental work of Programming Language C was completed by the X3J11 Technical Committee.

The views and conclusions contained in the software and documentation are those of the authors and should not be interpreted as representing official policies, either expressed or implied, of the Regents of the University of California.

www@FreeBSD.ORG

$Date: 1997/07/01 03:52:05 $

Index

Symbols

(pound) sign, 269

$PATH environment variable, 269

:) (smiley), 269

/ (forward slash) character (root directory), 68, 269

| (pipe) character, 275

3-D View command (Format menu), 151

3-D View dialog, 151

4Front Technologies Web site, 236

A

About xv button, 171

abuse (X11 game), 223

accessing
   directories (dosemu), 227
   templates (StarOffice), 130

Acrobat. *See* **Adobe Acrobat**

Active Movie AVI (Audio Video Interleave) files, 211

Add Player dialog (frisk), 219

adding
   applications (KPanel), 32
   menus (KPanel), 32
   tasks
     KArm (KDE), 198
     routine, 199
   templates (StarOffice), 131
   users 42-43, 227

Address Book command (Edit menu), 140

Address Book dialog, 140

address books (StarOffice), 140

addressing letters
   AutoPilot (StarOffice), 133
   Mail Merge, 141

adduser command, 43

Adjust Time command, 200

Adobe Acrobat
   decompressing, 64
   downloading, 64
   exiting, 65
   installing, 64
   starting, 65

Afterstep window manager, 12-13

.ag filename extension, 269

alphanumeric characters, 270

alt.linux (newsgroup), 264

alt.linux.slakware (newsgroup), 264

alt.os.linux.caldera (Linux newsgroup), 255

Amaya, reading HTML files, 62

American Standard Code for Information Interchange. *See* ASCII

animation. *See also* **TV, watching; video**
   gnuplot, starting, 210

F

J-K

L

M

Q-R

UNIX-to-UNIX copy (UUCP), 277

updating Web sites cache, 101

URLs (Uniform Resource Locators), 277

Usenet. *See* newsgroups

User Configurator dialog, 43

User ID number (UID), 277

User Login Name dialog, 240

usercfg commands, 42

usernames, configuring, 240

users
adding, 42-43, 227
configuring, 42
deleting, 43
managing (LISA), 43

user_guide.pdf (StarOffice), 133

/usr/doc/HOWTO directory (help), 207

/usr/doc/LPRng directory (printing help documentation), 185

/usr/info directory, 55

/usr/lib/dosemu/doc (dosemu documentation), 227-229

/usr/man directory, 55

/usr/X11R6/bin directory, 56

/usr/X11R6/lib/X11 directory, 15

/usr/X11R6/lib/X11/doc directory, 244

/usr/X11R6/lib/X11/fonts, 17

/usr/X11R6/man directory, 55

utilities
ar, 270
LISA, 76
color printing, 163
configuring printers, 183
managing software, 48

managing system services, 52
managing users, 43
printing, 187

Utilities|kpackage command (Application Starter menu), 44

Utilities|Terminal command (Application Starter menu), 120

Utilities|Terminal command (Starter menu), 84

UUCP (UNIX-to-UNIX copy program), 277

V

/var/spool/fax (fax queue), 107

/var/spool/lpd (printer spool), 182

variables, environment ($PATH), 269

video. *See also* **animation; TV, watching**
configuring color depth, 211
gnuplot (animation), 210
Illustrated Audio files, 210
MPEG1 animation
creating, 211
mpeg_play command, 210
xmpeg client, 211
xanim, 211

video cards
configuring, 246-252
X11 compatibility, 236, 244

View menu commands
Chart Data, 157, 165
Master View|Draw, 165
Master View|Outline, 164

viewing, 16
calendars (plan client), 200
colors (cmap client), 17

cursors (xfd client), 23
date (emacs), 115
fax queue, 107
faxes, 107
files
kpackage, 44
properties, 71
folders
glint, 46
kpackage, 44
fonts
xfd client, 16
xlsfonts client, 17
graphics
GIMP, 174
kpaint, 176
kview (KDE), 173
StarOffice, 126
xloadimage client, 172
xv client, 20
xwud command (X Window undump), 172
HTML help, 13
KPanel clock, 31
manuals
indexes, 56
pages, 57
software
glint, 46
LISA, 49
kpackage, 44
subjects, notes (KJots), 195
time (emacs), 115

virtual memory, 277

Visual Directory (ImageMagick), 179

W

W9x, 277

WANs (Wide Area Networks), 277

watching TV. *See* **TV, watching**

X

A Guide to the Linux Directories

- ✓ **bin**   Programs that don't require special software support

- ✓ **boot**   Where the Linux kernel lives

- ✓ **dev**   Devices, such as your hard drive, CD-ROM, or serial or printer ports

- ✓ **etc**   System configuration files

- ✓ **home**   The directory for users' home directories

- ✓ **lib**   Basic software libraries

- ✓ **mnt**   Where other file systems, such as floppy or CD-ROMs, are mounted

- ✓ **opt**   Where programs, such as Netscape, Applixware, or KDE are installed

- ✓ **proc**   A current snapshot of devices used by Linux

- ✓ **root**   The superuser's or root operator's home directory

- ✓ **sbin**   Programs usually run only by the root operator

- ✓ **tmp**   Temporary storage area (usually used by running programs)

- ✓ **usr**   A large directory of programs, libraries, and the X Window System

- ✓ **var**   Program and process-specific directories (for mail, printing, etc.)

HOW *to* USE
Linux®
Visually in Full Color

The Complete Step-by-

How to Use presents you with a str
approach to learning the world's ho
The steps and graphics guide you th
need to perform in Linux—the first
effectively challenge Microsoft® Wi

- Install and use Linux to run y
  computer.
- Connect to the Internet, send email, send and receive
  faxes, word process, and get started with StarOffice.
- Capture and create graphics, play music, watch TV,
  and play games.

*E*asy-to-follow
directions using
visual icons

*F*ind helpful advice
for quicker results

Drag & Drop

Click

Keyboard Entry

*P*ictures lead you easily through each task

Bill
Linu
Unle
othe
Unle

Teach Yourself
...ed Hat™ Linux
...tributor to
...nd Slackware

Category: Operating Systems

Covers: Linux

User Level: Beginning–Intermediate

$24.99 USA / $35.95 CAN / £22.95 Net UK

ISBN 0-672-31545-9

SAMS

www.samspublishing.com

FREE Personal Bookshelf MACMILLAN ONLINE

Register this book and receive a
free subscription to Macmillan
Online's Personal Bookshelf

register.samspublishing.com

7 52063 31545 3

9 780672 315459

92499